On Independence Creek

On Independence Creek

THE STORY OF A TEXAS RANCH

CHARLENA CHANDLER

TEXAS TECH UNIVERSITY PRESS

This book is typeset in Monotype Dante. The paper used in this book meets the minimum requirements of ANSI / NISO Z39.48-1992 (R1997). ∞

Some of the material in this book first appeared in personal columns written by the author for the *San Angelo Standard-Times.*

Library of Congress Cataloging-in-Publication Data

Chandler, Charlena, 1938–
On Independence Creek : the story of a Texas ranch /
Charlena Chandler.
p. cm.
ISBN 0-89672-524-3 (cloth : alk. paper)
1. Natural history—Texas—Independence Creek Preserve.
2. Independence Creek Preserve (Tex.)—History.
3. Chandler family. I. Title.
QH105.T4C48 2004
508.764'922—dc22
2003022980

Printed in the United States of America

04 05 06 07 08 09 10 11 12 / 9 8 7 6 5 4 3 2

Texas Tech University Press
Box 41037
Lubbock, Texas 79409-1037 USA
800.832.4042
ttup@ttu.edu
www.ttup.ttu.edu

For all the Chandlers and Stavleys,
past, present, and future.

CONTENTS

PREFACE

In *The Adventures of Huckleberry Finn,* Mark Twain wrote, "If I'd 'a' knowed what a trouble it was to make a book I wouldn't 'a' tackled it, and ain't a-going to no more." After attempting to tell the story of the ranch and my family back several generations, I now know how much "trouble" writing a book is. In addition to putting together years of memories, I have attempted to compile the many magazine and newspaper articles, and book excerpts, as well as scientific research that directly concern the ranch or contain information pertinent to the area.

So much personal history has been lost through the years, and memory is not always totally reliable. Although this story represents, in all good faith, what I've been told, what I remember, and what I have researched, I cannot vouch that it is totally accurate. But one of the privileges of writing a memoir, I'm told, is selective memory, and I have exercised that privilege freely.

That said, I plead guilty to the Lake Wobegon syndrome. While I do not claim "all the women are strong, all the men good-looking, and all the children are above average" in the part of West Texas I write about, the adjective "wonderful" happens to fit just about everyone and everything I've included in this tale.

I could not have put the story together without my mother, Mildred Stavley Chandler, whose sharp memory and collection of newspaper clippings, letters, and family photographs were invaluable.

I was also more fortunate than most amateur family historians, as I was aided immensely in my quest by many vital pieces of information found in *Terrell County, Texas: Its Past, Its People*. I will always be indebted to Alice Evans Downie and all who helped produce that wonderful history.

I appreciate the support of family members, especially my sister JoBeth, who is a part of this story, and my children Anne and Jeff, and Joe and Nan, and my nieces Jana and Joell.

I am grateful to Verne Huser, author of *Rivers of Texas* and river man extraordinaire, for advice, encouragement, and a push in the right direction. I am indebted to Stephanie Radway Lane, a former stellar student and present professional freelance editor, who offered support and interest in so many ways.

Thanks to Jeff Phillips, TMBR/Sharp, and Paul Simmons, Quality Logging, both of Midland, for their support and appreciation of the ranch. I am indebted to James Scudday, Sul Ross University, whose nomination of the ranch as a natural landmark appears in the appendixes, for his devotion to his profession and to the ranch.

Thanks to Rod Dearth, San Angelo Nature Center Director, for sharing research; to Jimmy Pond, Supervisory Hydrologic Technician for the U.S. Geological Survey, for scientific expertise; to Greg Larson, Region 7 Biologist for the Texas Natural Resource Conservation Commission, for his interest in Independence Creek; to Ross Dawkins of Angelo State University for his ongoing bird-banding project at the ranch; to Cindy Lippincott of the American Birding Association for her assistance with maps; and to Michael Forstner of Southwest Texas State University for his study of animal life on the creek.

On the writing end of it, I appreciate Paul Patterson, writer, cowboy, and teacher, for inspiration; Jack Cowan of the *San Angelo Standard-Times* who, with his acceptance of those *My Turn* columns, unknowingly prompted my first steps in putting this all together, and, of course, the staff of Texas Tech University Press for their patience and assistance.

To those mentioned and so many more, my gratitude is immense. Without the relatives and friends, the campers and hunters and fishermen, the golfers and birders, the rock hounds and geologists, the biologists and zoologists, the writers and photographers, the loafers and dreamers, there would be no story to tell. I regret that I could not include each of them individually.

On Independence Creek

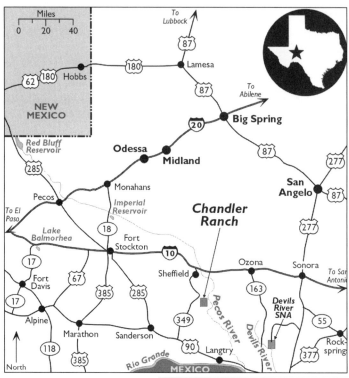

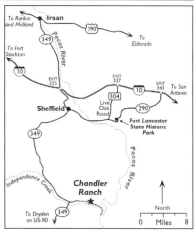

Maps by Cindy Lippincott from Mark Lockwood et al., *A Birders Guide to the Rio Grande Valley* (Colorado Springs, Colo.: American Birding Association, 1999).

INTRODUCTION

Retrieving the past is as slippery as a drive down a muddy dirt road in reverse. That's what I'm doing here, trying to stay in the ruts while carefully inching backward. Memory sometimes gets mixed up with night dreams and daydreams, whispers and illusions, some as fleeting as fireflies that meander through the creek willows, others as vivid as the sudden, violent thunderstorms that shake the world on sun-drenched summer afternoons.

What do I remember first about the ranch? Perhaps sleeping on the porch at Grandad's. It's as good a place as any to begin.

THE OPPRESSIVE HEAT of the endless day in August fades slowly, and the first gentle breeze dances up from the river, carrying the faint heavy scent of the deep Pecos River that runs a stone's throw away, and the promise of dreams.

Three little girls lie on their cots on the east side of the screened-in porch of the small house under the rustling sycamore leaves. They are hanging on the edge of sleep, fighting it, their energy winding down, mesmerized by the beauty of the celestial panorama above them. They know the breezes will come, and they also know that before dawn erases the splendor of the night, they will be reaching for the patchwork quilts at the foot of the beds. But for the moment the cool breeze is welcome in the hot West Texas night.

This routine is as familiar as the sounds on the massive radio by their grandfather's tarp-covered cot at the other end of the porch, booming out the nasal sounds of his beloved *Grand Ole Opry* or *Louisiana Hayride* with enough kilowatt power for the Dunlaps, our nearest neighbors upriver, to surely hear.

Did the sleepy children follow the words of the plaintive tunes of the

Light Crust Doughboys or the Carter Family? Would they remember the lyrics of "Wildwood Flower, "Will the Circle Be Unbroken," or "I'm Thinking Tonight of My Blue Eyes"? Those sentiments expressed the heart of a generation long gone, but meant nothing to the children.

The Mexican border lies some fifty miles south, as the crow flies, and the girls wonder if radio waves cross the border and if the inhabitants on the other side of the Rio Grande have radios. Would they understand these magical sounds? Or would the lyrics suddenly be translated into Spanish as they crossed the border?

After Minnie Pearl's last "How-deee" and the final goodnights from the country music stars, the adults listen intently to the news of the war, a world away in places like Japan and Germany. Finally, the radio snaps off and a million night sounds fill the air. Locusts sing cheerfully, and the frogs add their hoarse croaks to the night music of the Pecos. In the yard surrounding the white frame house, small animals scurry for water, and the farm animals sleep, except for an occasional moan from the milk cows in their pens.

An orange ball of a moon sits low over the hills. If you were to climb to the top of the bluff just over the river, you could surely touch it.

Senses are filled with the scent of the river, the sweetly blooming bee brush, the sharp smell of Ben Gay ointment (part of Grandad's nightly ritual). Inside the house, a cuckoo clock sounds the hour. Outside, a hound dog bays. The stars spin. Sleep comes quickly.

As the porch sleepers dream, ghostly images hover in the rugged, lonely landscape known as the Trans-Pecos. Far away, on top of the rimrock, young native warriors pause on the Comanche War Trail, sharp eyes turned south, surveying the valley as they follow the "Mexican moon." Behind them, tracking their footprints in the dusty earth, stalwart army officers and their Seminole scouts move along in rhythm to a muffled drumbeat heard only to them. A lone cowboy, employed by one of the giant cattle companies, pushing his thirsty herd to water, stops, tips back his sweat-stained hat, scans the scene of the Pecos Valley below him and rides slowly on. Hard on the heels of these ghosts, the early settlers, the first messengers of manifest destiny in this lonely land, appear on the transparent scene unfolding in the moonlight.

But these are only dreams, and I'm backing down that muddy road.

I WAS ONE of the little girls in the bucolic setting just described. The other two were my younger sister, JoBeth, and Granddad's foster daughter, Virginia (Jenny), my dearest childhood friend, who was older than I by three months.

It seems I can sit on the same old porch even now and bring back some of the sights and sounds and smells of those long-ago nights. Staying at the ranch with my grandfather, Charles (always known as Charlie) Chandler and his second wife, Ima Lou, marked my childhood memories so vividly that nothing since those years has ever seemed so real.

Today the house remains, not far from the banks of the Pecos, but details have changed. We have electricity now, indoor plumbing, a telephone, and a satellite dish to bring us entertainment unheard of and not even dreamed about when Grandad rode into the area during the turn of the twentieth century.

As the story goes, some forty to fifty years before the first dreamy summer night just described, Grandad set off from London, Texas, to search for a job. He and his brother Bill left home to venture out west to New Mexico, where they took a job on the Black River breaking a string of small but extremely wild horses.

They sooner or later ended up back in Texas, in Fort Stockton, where they found work with the Western Union Beef Company, an immense, well-organized business with headquarters in the Kampmann Building in San Antonio. The company had bases in Sheffield, Fort Stockton, Uvalde, Del Rio, and Ozona, with thousands of head of cattle bearing the 7D brand ranging up and down the Trans-Pecos. Grandad and Uncle Bill were two cowhands among hundreds employed by Western Union, a company so large that the owners never knew exactly how many cattle they owned. The number must have been astronomical, however, because the company filled huge railroad and government contracts each year and sent herds of thousands on trail drives annually.

There is no way to know exactly what kind of labor the two young Chandler brothers performed, but it's for sure they were riders, along with so many of their generation who sat their saddles lightly and confidently on the range and trail. Nor do we know their wages or even the number of the days they stayed on herding cattle in this unfenced, largely uninhabited country. But eventually a message reached them from their father, Hamp Chandler, telling them to come home. Charlie was wanted back in Junction as a witness in a court trial, so they left the Fort Stockton area by horseback and reversed their journey homeward.

Western Union went out of business in 1897, which may have had something to do with their decision. The company had been profitable, but the days of the open range were drawing to a close. When J. T. McElroy of Pecos bought the company, 30,000 head of cattle, scattered over 400 sections (square miles) of rangeland, had to be accounted for. It took two years to complete the roundup, and it is possible, and most likely probable, that Charlie and Bill took part in this closing chapter of a vanishing way of life.

The brothers took a different route home, riding along the banks of Independence Creek on their return journey. The creek, dry from Fort Stockton until about seven miles before its junction with the Pecos River, and its abundant springs must have made quite an impression on Grandad. It surely was the turning point in his life and ultimately of ours. Many years later and just a month before his death, Charlie, now an elderly cowman, looked back on those days and said, "I stood there that day, where Independence Creek runs into the Pecos River, and said to myself that this looked like mighty fine country. Of course, I had to get back to Junction pronto and couldn't look the country over as I would have liked. But I declared I would come back and ride those hills out."

I like to think of him, stopping his dun horse to water, looking at the sweet promised land around him, and thinking, "This is where I belong."

He returned shortly thereafter, sometime during 1900, and began to work on ranches in the area and to buy land, bit by bit. If these hills could talk, they would tell the story of Charlie Chandler.

One generation passes away, and another generation comes, but the earth abideth forever, according to Ecclesiastes, the preacher Ecclesiastes. The beauty of the land was made by God and given to man, from the primitive native dwellers to the present owners, to inhabit and to care for a little while. That's what we are trying to do today, even though we now have only a remnant of the original ranch. Generations change, but the land remains.

This was the beginning for us, but the land itself was formed thousands of centuries ago. A shallow sea covered the region, filling the famous Permian Basin. When the water receded, the imprints of shells and mussels were left in the limestone rocks that formed the hills and valleys of the Independence and Pecos country, proof of the marine life that once existed here. The "pictures" left behind describe a body of water that inundated the land and then formed it.

When the water receded, some thousands of years ago, it deposited sediments up to 1,500 feet deep. The climate of the Trans-Pecos then was wet and cool, and grass was abundant. Large animals such as mammoths, horses, and bison grazed the land. But as the climate slowly became warmer and dryer, summer heat, rather than a lack of good grazing lands, often drove large mammals miles northward.

Perhaps seven to ten thousand years ago the establishment of desert succulents such as cacti, sotol, and yucca set the stage for the first human beings to settle in or near the area. As the warming trend continued, ocotillo, sacahuiste, lechuguilla, catclaw, and mesquite and cedar trees also flourished.

The origin of the first human beings in this region remains clouded. The earliest Americans were Mongoloid peoples sharing the same basic physical characteristics such as skin color, hair color, and body type. Anthropologists generally agree that the first immigrants from Asia arrived through the most plausible route, a land bridge across the Bering Straits between Siberia and Alaska. The people who left their mark on the Independence Creek valley were members of the Comanche, Mescalero Apache, Pawnee, Kickapoo, Kiowa, and Shawnee tribes, who traversed the area as they traveled into Mexico. Hunters and gatherers, they were attracted to the valley by the same magnet that still pulls the human race universally, water. The river and the creek supplied a constant source of fresh water and produced a lush environment in an otherwise arid region.

These long-ago natives hunted deer, antelope, coyotes, foxes, gophers, wolves, prairie dogs, rodents, bobcats, and beavers along the banks. Bears and panthers evidently roamed farther south and occasionally made their way into the valley. Reptiles, birds of various species, and fish were plentiful, as were turtles. The ancient nomads did not go hungry.

The stomach contents of an Indian burial on the lower Pecos, south of the ranch, provided scientists evidence of an astonishing diet. The deceased's last meals included bat, snake, birds, fish, bone, mice fur, gopher, prickly pear cactus, and grasshopper parts. The people who frequented our region of the Trans-Pecos, the area that became Terrell County and where Grandad settled, most likely enjoyed the same types of food.

Some 2,500 years ago, according to botanists, there was a short-term shift to cooler and wetter conditions again. Large mammals could have roamed south once more during this brief period.

Perhaps the earliest white man to enter the region was Cabeza de Vaca of Spain, who passed this way around 1530, long after the mini–ice age. The next record of Spaniards in the area was some fifty years later, when the Spanish viceroy sent Fray Augustin Rodriguez into Texas to locate sites for the establishment of Catholic missions.

Another early Spanish explorer in the region was Juan Dominguez de Mendoza, who led an expedition from Mexico City into the lower Pecos area in 1684–85 and reported large numbers of bison seeking water in the Pecos valley. Records indicate that he passed through the area of present-day Fort Stockton on January 12, 1684, and his path can definitely be traced from there to Independence Creek based on his complete descriptions of the country. His well-documented journals graphically describe the terrain and the people of the area. Mendoza's aim was spiritual as well as secular. While intent upon trading with the natives, the priests who accompanied him were also eager to convert the natives to Christianity.

The early explorers were treated with friendship. The tribes of the land willingly cooperated with the Spaniards and easily accepted the Christian faith. Catholic rituals appealed to their sense of mysticism, although many historians doubt the veracity of their conversions. But in the early 1600s, this friendship turned to hatred as the Spaniards began to use the Indians as slaves and rule their lives. After 1694, all of the Spaniards, regardless of their intentions, were endangered and the influence of the priests began to wane. For many years thereafter, this land was mostly deserted by the Spanish and left to the Comanches and Apaches, who were warring with each other and also with any Spaniards or Mexicans along the Rio Grande.

The early 1800s saw the commencement of the movement called the Comanche War Trail. Young Indian braves from various tribes farther north in the areas of the Red, Arkansas, and Brazos Rivers began to ride south during the fall of each year to spend the winter plundering, taking captives, and stealing cattle and horses in Mexico. Then during the spring they returned home victorious. One of their trails took them along the Pecos River to Horsehead Crossing, thence to Tunas Springs, Independence, or Myers to the Rio Grande by way of Lozier Canyon. A possible route involved the Independence Creek valley; it went from the site of the present city of Big Spring by way of Grierson Spring, Live Oak Creek, Independence Spring, and Myers Spring.

The raids involved large numbers of young warriors who were expert horsemen, and who O. W. Williams of Alpine, Texas, described in a brochure privately printed between 1914 and 1919 titled *Baja el Sol*:

> The Comanche War Trail became a moving picture show, where parties of these barbaric warriors, in troops of half dozen to a hundred or more Comanches, Kiowas, Plains Apaches, Utahs from the Rocky Mountains, outlaws from other tribes, and even renegades from Mexico, all were hurrying to the Carnival over the Rio Grande . . . to scourge the fertile valley of the Concho River, up to the very walls of Chihuahua or . . . to carry fire and lance into the confines of Durango . . . or to the mines and to the farming valleys, but most of them sought the haciendas where they might find horses and cattle, the great source of savage wealth.

These raids were made with regularity on this route during September, and the season came to be known as the Mexican Moon to the young warriors who made up this picture show. This same lunar spectacle was feared by the Mexicans, who called it the Comanche Moon, and who watched the heavens with foreboding, knowing that the war party was headed south.

A government survey in 1854 noted the presence of Indians at Independence Creek. In the report, which was made to the Secretary of the Interior, William H. Emory reported:

> Our efforts to travel in a southwesterly direction having proved unsuccessful on leaving King's Springs we changed our route to a southeasterly one, and arrived at Independence Creek. Along this distance of forty miles the coun-

try is of much the same character as that first passed over. Whilst the train remained on the creek, a small party made examination in advance. This is a beautiful stream, running boldly among the hills, and is fed by unnumberable springs burst out from its banks. It is a rich treat for the eye in that arid county. Besides a copious supply of fresh, clear water, there is more timber than is ordinarily found upon streams draining these high plains; mezquite [sic] trees grow in large numbers for miles around, and the valley furnishes luxuriant grazing for animals. This place is much frequented by Indians; an oasis in the desert country.

The last of the Indians were either removed by military force or left the area of their own will around 1875, not so many years before Grandad and Uncle Bill came riding down the creek bed from Fort Stockton. The U.S. Army and Texas Rangers had come upon the scene in 1872–73 in northern West Texas and were responsible for driving most of the Indian populations to reservations.

Lt. John L. Bullis of the 25th Infantry was given the command of the "Black Watch Troops," the Seminole Indian Scouts, from March 1873 until June 1881. The Seminoles, some of whom were of African descent, had been removed from Florida to the West in the early 1800s. The scouts, numbering somewhere between fifty and a hundred, were courageous, aggressive, and particularly effective in trailing skills. They were paired perfectly with Lt. Bullis, who possessed the same traits. A natural leader, Bullis was described as "perhaps the most experienced Indian fighter in the United States Army." Typically fearless against all odds, he led his Seminoles by example, sharing their hardships and living conditions, at times even eating the flesh of rattlesnakes.

This thirty-three-year-old Civil War veteran, who ended his army career as a general, spent eight years leading the Seminole Scouts, and during this assignment in the Trans-Pecos he gained a heroic reputation. Part of this time was spent in what is now Terrell County, where reportedly he "had taken up land watered by springs all over the county, Richland, Geddes, Myers, Independence, and Cedar Springs." The term "taken up" implies ownership; we know that Bullis acquired large amounts of property in Terrell County, including land later acquired by Grandad along the creek, and established an outpost at Myers Springs, the site of primitive paintings on rock shelter walls.

The early settlers of Terrell and surrounding counties no doubt felt a great debt of gratitude to Bullis and his compatriots for protecting their ranches from the Indians.

However, the various Trans-Pecos tribes were doomed from the beginning. They faced a foe that was better informed, more united, and, more than anything, better armed. The Indians' defeat was inevitable because of diseases carried to them by their enemy (smallpox, cholera, measles), the destruction of the buffalo, their smaller numbers, and the superior technology of the invaders, including not only firearms but also railroads, the telegraph, and barbed wire.

The epitaphs for these people were never written, their eulogies never spoken. Do their unhappy spirits linger today along the banks of the Pecos and Independence and in the lonely rock shelters of the hills they once inhabited, crying with grief that we will never understand?

But reasonable people do not believe in bad karma. Maybe.

Evidence of early Native American life has been found in great abundance on the land Grandad acquired. The people who came before we did left behind scrapers, grinders, arrowheads, flint knives, burned rock mounds, and grind holes in our valley. Many grinding holes can be seen on flat rock surfaces. Manos, or round stones worn smooth with much pounding and rubbing in these holes and flat rock, have also been found. Pottery, textiles, and other artifacts from burial sites have been discovered south of us closer to the Rio Grande. (The rock art on the walls of caves on the lower Trans-Pecos has not been observed in the area of Independence, although pictographs have been found at Myers Spring.)

One of the most interesting artifacts found on the ranch itself, a foot-long piece of porous limestone in the shape of an animal, either carved or chiseled, was found by my son Joe as he was clearing mesquite brush for a fence line on the side of a rocky hill in July 1997. It resembles some type of male animal of the bovine group, with four short broken legs and testes. However, since there were no cattle in the early days, it is probably the image of a buffalo and was used as a fetish, an animal figurine held as sacred by the early Indians. Fetishes were used ceremonially to bring good fortune, either in hunting or in war, and their legs, ears, or tails were intentionally broken by their makers after their use to deny the magic to others. A "through hole" in the head allowed the user to wear the charm in most cases, although this particular artifact would have been too large for this function. Though its identity is verifiable, the actual use of this artifact is a mystery. We'll never know the story behind it, or how many years it lay partially buried on the hill above Grandad's house on the river.

Through the years, so many wonderful pieces of the past have been carried away by well-meaning explorers and amateur archeologists. Both Grandad and Dad were very generous with their bounty of the land. "Sure, go ahead and hunt for arrowheads" was a comment I heard both of them make many times. "Take whatever you want."

Native Americans had left the area only about twenty-five years before Grandad started to ranch in the area. Including Bullis, others owned the land before Grandad came along, but none of them for as long as he did, more than half a century when he died. The parts of the ranch still owned by Chandler descendants, children of Clarence and Joe, reached the centennial mark after the year 2000. Other sections of the ranch are now owned by the Rode family of Fredericksburg, the Corgill family of Midland, and the Nature Conservancy of Texas.

In the early 1880s, two years before the completion of the Southern Pacific Railroad lines, John Camp of the Seven K Ranch and Daniel G. Franks, foreman for the Pecos Land and Cattle Company, settled in or near Dryden, a small community just a few miles from the Mexican border in the southern part of Terrell County. (Two other Southern Pacific stations in the area were named for the English writers Emerson and Longfellow, but Dryden does not share that poetic distinction; it was the surname of one of the railroad engineers.) The headquarters for the cattle company became the largest shipping center on the Mexican border, and all the Trans-Pecos and Mexican ranchers south of the Rio Grande drove their huge herds into the small village to be shipped.

In 1886, W. W. Simonds, the manager of the Pecos Land and Cattle Company, used a section of school land to build a big frame building that housed a post office, various storerooms, and living quarters for Capt. Simonds and for the Franks family before their move into one of two adobe houses. Various other buildings began to spring up at this time, including the railroad station and lodging for employees of the Southern Pacific. Oddly enough, there was never a saloon in Dryden, but those in need of a drink could ride on to Sanderson, only twenty miles away, to the Cottage Bar. However, there was social life for all. Big barbecues, complete with barrels of pink lemonade and dancing for all ages, were held, with word of mouth bringing everyone for miles around, especially the lonely riders eager for any kind of companionship.

Simonds and the owners of the Pecos Company, which applied its Swinging H brand to vast numbers of cattle, were from Cambridge and Attleboro in Massachusetts. The owners had a financial motive, of course, as explained by John M. Doak, another prominent stockman of the area, who became Franks's son-in-law in 1889. Doak, coauthor of *Life on the Range and on the Trail,* wrote, "One might well wonder why these people from the northeastern part of the United States were away out here in the western part of Texas. But some people all over the United States had visions of what the new country might offer and so there were numerous land or cattle companies scattered over various parts of this western country. As might be expected, some of these moneyed interests were successful; others tired of it in a few years and then folded up and left the country."

There was no lack of ambition or foresight here, as the Pecos Land and Cattle Company owned 106 sections of land extending from Dryden northward to two miles north of King Springs and also leased land from Bullis. The operation thrived until the fencing of the open range brought an end to this long-gone but still celebrated way of life.

A large portion of the land in the Dryden area was also owned by D. Hart of Val Verde County, who controlled nearly all of the land from the Rio Grande to Independence Creek. In 1907 Hart owned over 1,000 sections of land and was one of the state's largest sheep ranchers. Hart also leased land along the creek that Grandad later bought from three New Jersey owners, and he was once sued by the state of Texas for $48,000 for fencing land that did not belong to him, also in the vicinity of the creek. Known as the Cedar Fence, it ran from Independence to the Rio Grande. The state won the lawsuit, and the fence came down.

Both the construction and the removal must have been an awe-inspiring project, considering this length of fence. Not a remnant of it stands today, but Roy Bedicek describes this type of structure in *Adventures with a Texas Naturalist:*

> Fences of cedar also survive, antedating in some cases the fences of stone. The lot and yard fences around homesteads are of cedar, hand-hewed and set upright so close together that a cottontail rabbit must hunt for a hole and then pinch himself a little to get through. This cutting, hewing, fitting, driving, and binding palings to form a vermin proof fence, while not involving the backbreaking labor of stone fencing, was still an enormous undertaking. . . . Many of the pales were fashioned from mountain cedar which lasts like bone.

Obviously, the wire fence had not yet descended upon West Texas, as barbed wire did not enter the picture until 1878. Supreme Court Justice William O. Douglas wrote in *Farewell to Texas: A Vanishing Wilderness,* "It caused a disappearance of the open, free range and converted the range country into big pasture country." With fencing, the rotation of livestock became possible, with some pastures left unused while others were being grazed. Doak describes the first outside fences in which a six-inch ditch, wherever there was dirt, was dug and barbed wire, or "hog-wire," was buried to prevent coyotes from crawling under. "Where there was rock, the ditch was not necessary. We used good cedar posts and put them thirty feet apart for fence panels. Then we put three barbed wires on top of the mesh fence, making a finished fence five feet high. . . . A fence of this kind was not only supposed to be coyote-proof, but it was a good strong fence which horses would not be apt to run into; and if they did, could not easily knock down."

These fences allowed ranches to be divided into pastures and traps, which separated livestock, and converted to sheep grazing. Doak tells of his feelings, which probably echoed those of his contemporaries at that time. He had a strong dislike for sheep, as most cowmen had, but thought this country was better suited for sheep than cattle. He put away his prejudice against sheep when he realized the industry was growing and he didn't want to go "broke" with cattle.

Another of the immense ranch companies in the vicinity of the Chandler Ranch before the general use of fencing was the Independence Cattle Company. This big outfit came into the area in the early eighties and registered its brand, the T-5, in Fort Stockton in 1884. The owners of the company were the Hoosier brothers, jewelers from St. Louis, Missouri. Several foremen actually operated the ranch; among them were Fletcher Harness, Lee Heard, John Light, and D. L. (Doc) Anderson. Light was well known in the cattle business and drove many of his herds up the trail to market. During his tenure, the Hoosier Brothers sold most of their livestock, at which time Anderson bought the rest and ran them on the T-5 for several years. He then moved to Sanderson, where he was elected sheriff.

Grandad began to buy land in the lower creek valley at the turn of the century. He had already begun purchasing land before 1909, when a large part of the T-5 was bought by A. M. Hicks, and Grandad bought land from him also. I've heard (better to use this phrase as I'm still backing down a muddy road here) that negotiations to buy more fell through because of a disagreement concerning water troughs for livestock, but the two families enjoyed amicable relations both before and afterwards.

Hicks's son, Lindsey, who was our neighbor up the creek on the property that was almost part of the Chandler Ranch, built a ranch house and a structure called the springhouse over the free-flowing Caroline Springs, commonly called Carolina Springs, where the old T-5 was headquartered. Lindsey and his wife, Margaret, had two children, Lin, now deceased, and Sarah. They lived at the ranch until they moved to Ozona to send the children to school but continued ownership of the land until oilman Bill Roden of Midland bought it in the early 1960s. This beautiful place is now called the Oasis Ranch, rather than the Hicks Ranch, although a few of us who have been around awhile still use the old name sometimes. It was sold to the Nature Conservancy of Texas in November 2000 and subsequently to Robert McCurdy of Austin, who entered into a lifetime lease arrangement with the Conservancy.

The Carolina Springs are also referred to as the T-5 Springs in Gunnar Brune's *Springs of Texas*. "About 25 kilometers south-southeast of Sheffield are the T-5 Springs on the Oasis Ranch. They break forth at the foot of a hill at an elevation of 610 meters four kilometers east of highway 1217 (now

349). University of Texas studies have enumerated twenty-seven species of fish that live in the spring waters." These springs pump out an amazing 5,000 gallons of water a minute. They are a major source of water for Independence Creek, as is Vanderbeek Springs, located five kilometers west of T-5 Springs. There are many smaller springs and sweeps along the course of the creek that were not significant enough to include in Brune's report. Some of them break out just a few miles upstream from the Oasis Ranch, on land owned by Jack and Peggy Buchanan of Houston. This ranch, founded near the turn of the century by Mr. Buchanan's parents, of Dryden, contains the first source of flowing water in the creek. Independence Creek is an enormously important watershed in the Trans-Pecos. Pouring 27 million gallons a day of fresh water into the Pecos River, it is the single largest freshwater contributor to the Pecos in Texas.

As to how the springs and the creek were named Independence, the two stories that have been told most are these: (1) The Hoosier brothers were originally from Independence, Missouri, and named the company and the creek for their hometown, and (2) The first white settlers in the area discovered the springs and creek on July 4, year unknown, and christened them Independence in honor of the holiday. There is no evidence to prove or disprove either story. However, neither strikes me as likely since Emory referred to the name in 1854, some years before the advent of the Hoosiers. And it is doubtful that there were white settlers in the area before 1854. In *Springs of Texas,* Brune writes that slaves were working on the creek when the Emancipation Proclamation was issued in 1865. Although widely accepted, this theory is also unlikely because of Emory's report some ten years earlier.

There is a fourth possible origin, more acceptable than the others, I believe. When Captain Meriwether Lewis and Captain William Clark made their well-known exploratory expedition in 1804, their purpose was to find the most convenient way by inland water to the Pacific and to discover the courses and sources of the Missouri River. Their journey took them through what was known as the Western Wilderness, and the point that ties them to this story is what occurred on July 4, 1804, on the west bank of the Kansas River. William E. Connelley, in *A Standard History of Kansas and Kansans,* "Lewis and Clark," writes: "After a strenuous day the expedition came to camp on the 4th of July on the north bank of a stream which was then and there named Independence Creek, in honor of the day. The stream still retains the name. The town of Doniphan, Atchison County, stands on or near this camping place. The day was celebrated by firing an evening gun and dealing to each man an additional gill of whiskey, the first celebration recorded to the credit of Kansas." Numerous creeks in the western United States are named Independence, so there is no reason to totally negate the theory that perhaps an early visitor to the area from Kansas or Missouri simply liked the name chosen by Lewis and Clark.

One other piece of history concerning the creek area is worth noting here. On March 25, 1859, Secretary of War John B. Floyd directed Major General David E. Twiggs, commanding the Texas Military Department at San Antonio, to have a complete and thorough reconnaissance made of the country between the Pecos River and the Rio Grande. The purpose of the project was to discover a more convenient route for supplying the military posts in the area, in addition to determining the practicability of using the camel as a beast of burden and means of transportation. The idea had originated with Jefferson Davis, then Secretary of War, who believed that camels' stamina and ability to survive for long periods would make them valuable for military purposes.

Early in May, Lt. William E. Echols, a topographical engineer in the U.S. Army, was detailed to make the reconnaissance. He left San Antonio with an escort commanded by Lt. Edward L. Hartz. The orders were to make the trip to the Big Bend with 24 camels carrying 350 pounds each. The party reached Camp Hudson, east of the Pecos on May 18, 1859; after five days they set out for Fort Stockton, traveling up the Pecos Valley. On June 15, the detachment was split and Hartz set out with 20 camels for Independence Creek via Tunas Springs, averaging about four miles per hour. They turned south and finally descended into a large canyon running into the creek. Following this canyon, they reached Independence Springs. From there they traveled to the mouth of Independence Creek and then returned to the spring. They left the area, turning west towards Fort Davis, their destination. When water was found 30 miles out of Fort Davis, the camels had traveled 110 miles in less than four days without water and were apparently in good physical condition.

With the coming of the Civil War, the use of camels was abandoned. But the experiment leaves another image in my mind alongside that of buffalo dotting the green pastures of the ranch, that of camels watering out of the creek, a sight never again witnessed. And then these images are crowded out with another image, even more powerful, that of the land I love inhabited by a primitive people who thought the earth belonged to them.

I conclude this introduction with a quote from Leon Pope's archeological report on the area: "Your ranch is a beautiful treasure of history, especially the pre-history of the Indians. Any archeologist, as myself, sees your ranch from a view few seem to appreciate." I have something in common with Mr. Pope. Although archeologists have a scientific bent, I suspect they are also dreamers. To be able to look into the past and to envision what was, rather than what is, involves some sensitivity that pure science would exclude.

Chapter One
CHARLIE

Except to paper riders, the Pecos is a lonely and bitter stream. I have that from
men who rode it and who knew that country round, such as
it was, such as it can never be again.
Novelist Larry McMurtry

MY GRANDAD CHANDLER was one of those men who rode the Pecos, who settled his place a hundred years ago and "knew that country round." But that was long before I came along. By that time, Grandad's adventures lay behind him and he was pretty well set in his ways, a man in his sixth decade who had lived long enough to know who he was and where he belonged.

His manner was mild, manifesting no demons. He didn't talk a lot, but when he did he had something to say. I don't recall his ever raising his voice, but we all jumped when he spoke. It was not his size that compelled attention, as he was not quite six feet tall, but his presence. The restless energy that seemed to propel most of his offspring was foreign to his calm and untroubled personality.

In his younger days, Grandad was known to be an occasional drinker and had been quite fond of cigarettes, but those ways were gone by the time I was born, as he had suffered his first heart attack and had been advised to abstain. (He was, however, a fierce snuff dipper in his later years.) From what I gathered, he never pined for his old vices but heeded the advice of his doctor, John Pate of Sanderson, to follow a healthy lifestyle until his death many years later.

During his seventh decade, Jim Carll of the *San Angelo Standard Times* described Grandad this way: "The pioneer ranchman still rides when occasion demands. His blue eyes are sharp, far-seeing. His voice retains the strength of youth. His sturdy figure is block-like in its strength." Carll uses the word "strength" twice in one paragraph to describe Grandad, and, even though he was getting on in years and his health was failing, it's the word I would use if asked to describe him today.

Grandad probably never slept through a sunrise in his life. He called it a day when the sun went down, literally going to bed with the chickens, and arose while the stars still blinked in the night sky. I don't ever remember him sleeping in, an activity as alien to him as eating with chopsticks. Even though it would be too dark for him to go about his morning rounds, there he would be at the kitchen table, sitting in front of the wood cookstove on icy winter mornings, playing solitaire and drinking strong black coffee from a battered old tin cup, impatient to be out and about.

As the weather turned milder, he'd omit the fire, shed his undershirt, and switch from corduroy and wool to khaki. Whatever the fabric, his pants were always tucked into high-topped black boots, as they had been in his cowhand days, and the style rarely varied.

In his younger days on the range, Charlie's attire was probably similar to that of the other cowhands, who wore a good pair of ducking pants, sturdy chaps, the ever-present hat, and high-quality leather boots. (In winter, they wore a pair of checked, woolen "California pants" or "Oregon pants" underneath, along with a ducking jacket.) Those riders were prouder of a good pair of boots and a good saddle than of anything else. And, according to Dryden range rider John Doak, if a cowboy ever showed up wearing a tie, the others would "hurrah" (harass) him.

Like his contemporaries, Grandad chose a plain, almost austere, way of life, compatible with the small white frame house he had built near the abundant springs flowing out of the hills on the north end of the ranch. Nestled in a large yard with a ditch of water from the springs flowing through it, and surrounded by pecan and sycamore trees, grapevines, and various shrubs, the house sat in the valley as neatly as a teacup in its saucer.

There were just four or five small rooms with a porch surrounding three sides of its exterior. The first house on the ranch had been almost primitive in comparison; the new house, built in the early thirties, was a step up but still far from elaborate.

"A house don't make no money" was a common sentiment of many of Grandad's generation, and today there are still West Texas ranches with fine-built pens, barns, and sheds that put the living quarters to shame. There were, of course, large, ornate ranch homes built in other areas of the state, but old photos and sketches of the humble little homes built in the Trans-Pecos take us back to our roots in a hurry.

Always feeling more comfortable outdoors, Grandad slept on a metal cot covered with a tarp on the screened-in porch during the summer months and then moved into the "radio room" for the winter. This was simply a closed-in end of the porch, without an ounce of insulation, barely big enough for a double bed and a large radio. Even in cold weather, his main cover was a canvas tarp. Just as he rose early, he also went to bed early, and as soon as the radio began to blare in the dusky light of evening, we knew it was time to call it a day.

Through the years, Grandad opened his doors to all who knocked. What has become stereotypical Western hospitality was real to him and to all his neighbors. If you'd ridden or driven far, you could count on a meal and a place to sleep. His open door represented a generosity of spirit, a fellowship with other human beings, a helping hand extended in time of need. It reflected the soul of the true old West, now disappearing as a new generation unaccustomed to hardship and less dependent on their fellow human beings takes its place.

Grandad offered his home not only to anyone who showed up but also to two foster daughters, Mary Jo and Jenny. (I use the term "foster" for lack of a better one. While there was no actual legal designation, these children were taken in and cared for by Grandad through some arrangement with their families, who were not able to provide for them.) Mary Jo wrote, years later:

> The Chandler Ranch is a very special place for me. Your grandaddy was very good to me. He taught me so much. He had a jersey milk cow named Tiny and he taught me how to milk and to ride. I've even walked behind a horse

and plow in getting the watermelon patch ready. He bought me a horse to ride to school. (The school was five miles up the creek at the Hicks Ranch.) Oh, how I loved that horse. . . . You will never know how many times I have ridden my horse up to the spring-fed tank or to the creek.

The ranch was also a welcoming place for those who were not exactly hired hands and yet not family. They were the men who came and stayed for a while and then would leave again when their restlessness got the best of them. Two of them were steadier than others, Bill Holcomb of Sanderson and Woody Rutledge of Dryden. These two didn't have much in common except for the way they drifted in and out of our lives and became a part of the ranch.

Bill, sometimes called Uncle Bill, worked for various ranchers in Terrell County, including Alec Mitchell, whose records of Bill's trapping activities appear in the county history book. Bill trapped predatory animals along the Pecos for more than fifty years. He claimed to know every cave, crevice, and canyon along the river from Horsehead Crossing to the mouth of the river, or so he told Marvin Hunter, editor of *Frontier Times*. There wasn't a varmint he didn't know, he said, and he was never doubted. You couldn't look a man like Bill Holcomb in the eye and call him a liar.

As Bill advanced in years, he reluctantly moved into Sanderson, where he delighted in going to movies at the Princess Theater. He would get so carried away with the action in cowboy films that he would yell out warnings and advice to the characters on the screen, prompting a chuckle from his fellow moviegoers.

Woody Rutledge was a tall, gangly fellow who had never learned to read or write. A sometime trapper, when asked how much he had made on his furs, he would take the money from his pocket and thrust it at you, saying, "Here, you count it."

Once, he was caught short of words when telling my mother that he was sure of a good trapping season because he'd seen a lot of sign.

"Sign? What in the world do you mean by that, Woody?"

"Well, you know, Mildred, sign . . . and, uh, what-not." The trapper from Dryden possessed a sense of propriety.

"I'm still not with you, Woody."

"Just sign . . . and one thing and another. That's what it is. One thing and another."

Woody was a congenial soul and had a practical philosophy of life. No matter what he was doing, from sitting in the sun whittling to hitchhiking a ride into Dryden, he'd say, "Beats doing nothing, don't it?" He floated between the ranch and Dryden for years. I don't know what happened to Woody, but both he and Bill were always welcome at Grandad's, where they knew they had a place to stay and plenty to eat.

As a child, I assumed that life was always easy for Charlie, as I never saw him turn a hand or do a "lick of work." Everyone around him labored, thanks to his talent for giving orders in a way that made them seem like favors bestowed. Family members, who always seemed to overflow at the ranch, and employees alike were his willing servants.

Big lady, just step in the kitchen and get me a drink of water.

Step right over there, you girls, and pen those goats before dark.

Big man, that ditch is full of cockleburs. Just step right over there and clean 'em out, will you?

Will someone step out to the trap and separate the cows and calves?. . . won't take but a minute.

We did a lot of stepping. But it beat doing nothing, didn't it?

It had not always been that way. Charlie had paid his dues, and if he could sit back now and enjoy the seeds he had sown in his early years, thanks to hard work, perseverance, good judgment, and frugal living, he deserved every moment of his leisure. In his later years, he enjoyed tending his garden, feeding his livestock, sitting under the shade of a tree whittling away summer afternoons, enjoying the warm stove in the kitchen in winter, driving the ranch roads to just look at his place, and making sure no one slept too late.

His children called him Dad, and I think he was the only person in their lives who had any control over them or whom they held in such esteem. Their mother, their wives, and their children all took a back seat to their father, but none of us resented this, as we felt the same way.

In later years, I learned that he could be a hard and unforgiving man to some, an imperfect person. But I didn't know that when I was young, and the memories I have remain untarnished. He was the dominant figure in my life, the man who loaded his grandchildren into his shiny Chevy and took us to the creek on sultry summer days, who stopped on the way back to let us pick bouquets of bright wildflowers, who drove me to San Angelo and bought me my first formal dress, a creation of pale blue net and shining rhinestones, the most beautiful dress I had ever seen, who took great pleasure in his many-hued roses, who represented stability and strength in the microcosm of life on the ranch that he had founded.

When he died on November 10, 1957, at the age of eighty-one, the extended family unraveled. Without him, the center was gone.

CHARLES ALBERT CHANDLER was born on July 12, 1876, in Comanche County, where his father, Hampton (Hamp) Chandler, had been an early settler. He spent his early boyhood years with his uncle, Rome Chandler, in Kimble County, near London, and Hamp later moved there also.

When asked where the Chandlers were from originally, I have often replied "London," and the comment has usually been, "Well, of course, the name is English."

"London, Texas," I explain.

While our ancestors were likely English, the surname Chandler is derived from the Old French word "chandelier," a maker of candles. Some of the British tradesmen who were our early forefathers branched off into specialized areas such as church candles, while others made and sold candles for ships. Being good merchants, they also began to trade in ropes and other supplies for seagoing vessels. "Chandler" began to be recorded and show usage in England as early as 1273 in the Hundred Rolls, but it is impossible to trace the first use of the name. Most abundant in the counties of Gloucestershire and Hampshire, there were also early Chandlers in Berkshire, Huntingdonshire, Kent, Surrey, Herefordshire, and Sussex. The name shows up in the first census in the United States in 1790, most frequently in Massachusetts, New Hampshire, and South Carolina. Today there are approximately 85,000 adult Americans bearing the surname; it is logical to assume that our common forefathers were among those sturdy merchants who made their way to the New World, but the task of tracing the journey of those men and women remains far beyond my skill as a genealogist.

However, at some point after the Civil War, several Chandler brothers—Hamp, Rome, William, and perhaps another (these names are part of family lore and very possibly inaccurate)—came to Texas from Jackson, Mississippi, after one of them was allegedly involved in a murder. This brother parted from the others after they reached Texas and headed to Mexico to lay low for a while. While accomplishing this feat, he changed his name to Johnson. Today, an entire branch of the family has retained this name.

A first cousin of Charlie's, a son of the fugitive in Mexico, Hackberry Johnson, surely was one of the most unique characters in the family, regardless of surname. As a young man, he had carved out quite a reputation for himself on the rodeo circuit before he suffered a mishap that resulted in the amputation of a leg. He proceeded to fashion his own wooden prosthesis out of a hackberry tree limb, thereby earning his nickname and his fame for being a tough "old booger" and a true cowboy.

He could tell lots of tales, and one of the best was of how Pecos Pete Boone suggested a way for him to excite the crowd on the rodeo show circuit. He would loosen his leg and then start yelling halfway through the ride that he was getting killed. Then he'd let the hackberry leg fly off and the crowd would scream in horror.

Hackberry was described by Rick Smith of the *San Angelo Standard-Times* on February 28, 1992, as a "squinty eyed, one legged, would-be Buffalo Bill, a bewhiskered, bedeviled bedazzler." Smith recounts an interview with Hackberry as the one-time bronc rider showed off his collection of newspaper clippings:

"Here, boy, read this 'un."

Hackberry opened his suit case strongbox, brushed the rat pills off a curled, crumbling clipping from the Denver Post.

"Can't hear you. Read louder!"

I read louder.

Then, after a paragraph: "No," he said, shaking his head, "That ain't right. Why, the first bronc I busted was when I was FIVE years old, by God. That was back in . . . that was back in . . . Hell, I don't remember. It was a LONG time ago."

His breath whistled as he spoke, a sound like wind on the prairie: loud, lonesome, everywhere at once.

"Take this down now. . . . I'm the last one who remembers what it was like, back then. Pecos Bill, Booger Red. All the rest are gone. Nobody else remembers the rodeos, the stories, the songs. Nobody but me. That's why we got to get it right. That's why we got to get it down. Ain't nobody else left. Ain't nobody else."

The white haired "stove-up" old relative was sure enough a reminder of photos of Buffalo Bill, but that may be a subliminal association. After his riding career ended, Hackberry made his living by hauling buffaloes to Texas rodeos. He may have just needed a place to rest his tired body for a few days when he visited the ranch several times in his later years, as it seems he had no permanent home but the road. He came more frequently when Grandad was still with us, but then his visits tapered off, and we lost touch.

Hackberry suffered a heart attack and died in his ninth decade while dancing at a Willie Nelson concert in Austin. His way of passing could not have been more fitting, as he himself would burst into song at the drop of a hat. I hope the last sounds he heard were those of "Milk Cow Blues," one of his favorites.

Charlie's father Hamp married twice. His first wife, my great-grandmother, was Mary Renfro. Hamp fathered twelve children, six with each wife. The birth order is uncertain, but Hamp and Mary's children were Charlie, Bill, Art, Wes, Minnie, and Lillie, four boys and two girls, the identical gender makeup of Grandad's own children. After Mary's death, Hamp married Ellen Crawford, and this marriage produced Rome, Melvin, Lizzie, Annie, Fannie, and Nellie.

Appropriately enough, Charlie's first boyhood job was as a goat herder. Later, in the 1920s, he owned 13,000 head of goats, 3,000 head of Delaine sheep, 300 head of cattle, and several hundred head of horses, but that came long after he herded goats as an eight-year-old for a Baptist preacher named Harrell on Deep Creek in McCulloch County. His wages were $4 a month and four goats, which were then worth about 75 cents a head.

After two years, he moved on and, at the age of ten, started herding sheep in Kimble County for Jess Howard. He tended a flock of 1,300 sheep, for which he earned $7 a month. The range was ten to fifteen miles from the nearest ranch, and it was lonely, tedious work for a grown man, much less a child, but invaluable experience when he began to ranch for himself.

In 1892 Charlie's first real cowboying job came along when he was hired at the age of sixteen by a man named Paxton to help drive a thousand head of horses and cattle from Junction to Cheyenne, Wyoming. "We left the pens on March 1," he recalled, "and when we next saw Junction it was Christmas Day and cold as rip." Grandad says he grew up on that drive; like so many other young riders he was willing to work overtime to prove his worth.

While on this trip during a stop in Marlow, Oklahoma, Grandad saw Quanah Parker and some of his Comanche tribesmen, who had come in off the reservation for the Fourth of July holiday. They had driven a few head of calves into town, which they killed in the sandy street. They then built small fires and roasted the pieces of beef, including the intestines. It was on this same trip that Grandad first put shoes on steers or oxen. They used a pair of work oxen to pull the chuck wagon, and their hooves became so tender that they had to throw them down and tie them before they could be shod.

Along about 1912, Grandad had another harrowing experience in Oklahoma. It was described by J. Marvin Hunter in the *Frontier Times*: "While shipping goats to Kansas City to market, he went along on the train with them. A tornado struck the train about 3 p.m. one afternoon in the vicinity of Hobart, Oklahoma. The storm tore up the tracks and destroyed the town. A freight train was blown off the tracks and only the engine and firebox remained. One of the cars was an emigrant car and contained cows, chickens and household goods belonging to a family moving west."

This car was blown from the rails and turned bottom side up. The crew of the train and Grandad tried to render such aid as they could. Grandad recalled, "The dead and wounded were found lying in ditches full of water and not a house in the town was left standing. People were running everywhere, screaming and crying."

Grandad survived the storm (he called it a cyclone) but forever after suffered a fear of turbulent weather. A storm cellar was built in the yard of his home place, and when the sky looked particularly threatening, all the family would be awakened and herded out to the cellar. We children were more afraid of the musty-smelling cellar and the creatures we imagined living there than of any threatening storm, so we were always relieved when Grandad sounded the all-clear and we could head back to bed.

Grandad was a literate man, but his actual years of education must have been few and scattered. He signed his name in beautiful script and must have been able to read and write at some level, but there are no records of his school days before he became a herder. (His signature was "Chas. Chandler" or "Charles Chandler." I have never learned how he spelled the name by which he was usually called, Charlie or Charley, but I have chosen to use the former because it appears this way several times in my grandmother Chandler's handwriting.)

There are two different accounts on his start as a rancher in Terrell County, after his first ride down Independence Creek. One newspaper article reports that he worked as a ranch foreman for John McKay and eventually started his own flock. This story relates that he purchased two sections of land across the Pecos in Crockett County but later sold them, moved back to Terrell County, and began to lease and later buy land.

The alternate story is that he worked for wages with W. T. Carpenter's old Booger D brand, which was headquartered six miles south of Independence. Carpenter arranged for him to have some range for his own livestock after his second year of employment. It's probable that both reports have some truth to them, as he could have worked for both outfits while trying to get a start of his own.

Grandad began to buy land piece by piece but finally had to quit when there was no land left at a price he could afford. He is quoted in an article in *West Texas Livestock Weekly* as saying, "I bought all the land I could. Some was only 90 cents an acre but, you know, I even had trouble paying for that."

While trying to spread out, he did have one advantage; he was able to maintain a large number of livestock that pastured far beyond his own borders thanks to the open range. Zane Grey mentions this possibility in his version of a rancher's life on the river in *West of the Pecos*: "There was enough unbranded stock along Independence Creek alone to make Pecos and Terrill rich ranchers, and that stream lay between Lambeth Ranch and Camp Lancaster."

Could Grey have envisioned his story in the actual vicinity of the land Grandad settled? Geographically, it sounds as if he must have zeroed on the ranch or somewhere very nearby. If the creek lay between the fictional Lambeth Ranch and Fort Lancaster, and it lay west of the Pecos and north of Comstock (where Pecos Smith and Terrill were married by Judge Roy Bean), the area of the original Chandler land on the river may have been the setting of one of the most widely read Western novels in the country when it was first published.

Of course, the setting could also have been downriver on land owned by the Banners or Goodes or others south of us. Since the author himself never revealed the exact location of his story, this is another cloudy area that contributes to the myths of the region. The beauty of fiction allows us to believe what we choose, no documentation necessary.

It's also surprising that Grey never mentions sheep and goats, referring only to cattle, so he may have done some research on the big cattle companies mentioned earlier. And, let's face it, sheep and goats just don't have the romantic mystique that Western fans demand.

In spite of the title of his novel, there is no proof that Grey was ever in the Trans-Pecos. Did he look at a map to choose a locale? He has all the right names, including the legendary Horsehead Crossing. And the heroine of the novel is named Terrill, perhaps a variation on Terrell, the county's name.

Regardless, Grandad continued in his desire for land, knowing that open range would not last forever. In 1913 he bought 2,614 acres of land for $5,000 from three New Jersey owners. A description of the land notes that the original grantees were the International and Great Northern Railroad Companies for approximately three sections with J. H. Joyner and Mrs. Mary P. Wheelock owning the remainder. The deed notes that the Joyner certificate was Confederate scrip, the Wheelock portion a veteran donation. It also states:

> It is understood that the said surveys are under lease (with other lands) to D. Hart of Val Verde County, Texas, by a lease contract terminating on February 17, 1914, subject to the right of the lessors to terminate it at any time on giving the Lessee written notice mailed to his address at Pumpville,

Texas, six months in advance of the date at which it is desired to terminate it; and this conveyance is made subject to the rights of the said lessee under the said lessee contract. As part of the consideration for this conveyance, the said Charles Chandler binds himself, by acceptance of this deed, to render the said surveys for the taxes for the year 1912 and to pay all taxes lawfully assessed against the same for that year.

Grandad paid $1,000 down at the time to the owner's attorney in Austin and agreed to make four $1,000 payments on January 4 of each year until 1916. The description of this land shows it all to be on the west bank of the Pecos River, thus making up part of the inheritance of Grandad's three older sons: Roy, Clarence, and Herman. The cost works out to almost two dollars per acre. Whatever price he paid for that parcel and the remainder of land he purchased was significantly more than the sum of twelve to fifteen cents in scrip per acre that Bullis had paid years earlier.

Another notable transaction by Bullis in the Pecos County abstracts (Terrell County did not yet exist) reads as follows: "Field notes of a survey of 640 acres of land made for John L. Bullis, assignee, it being the quantity of land to which he is entitled by virtue of land script No. 1798, issued to C. R. Beaty, E. F. Seale and J. M. Farwood, by the Commissioner of the General Land Office, May 18, A.D. 1875. Said survey is situated in Pecos County, on the waters of the Pecos River, a tributary of the Rio Grande River, and is known as Survey No. 321."

Grandad also eventually owned this land, for the original abstract was found in his file of documents. No dollar amount is mentioned in this sale, which was doubtlessly one of many property transactions in the area by Bullis.

One parcel of land that Grandad owned in the Bullis survey featured large sulphur springs. (This land was later inherited by Herman Chandler.) The odor of these springs hit the senses long before they were in sight. Surrounded by white deposits that killed any surrounding vegetation in a large area and lying four meters high on the Pecos River floodplain, the springs flowed from two holes, each two meters in diameter and about one meter deep, and created two large pools of bathtub-temperature water. The chemical makeup of the water was mostly sodium sulfate and chloride, believed to be a healthy combination for both bathing and drinking. At one time, Uncle Herman constructed a bathhouse at the site, but these springs are now completely dry.

After buying additional land from John Camp and Daniel Franks, and leasing other areas, Grandad had accumulated a "pretty decent spread" of ranch land. He also possessed that most precious commodity in West Texas, "live" water from the abundant springs he cherished. It was no small feat for a boy who had started out as a goat herder at the age of eight.

According to a popular story concerning the size of ranches, whenever a reporter asked how many acres (or sections) a certain landowner claimed, the owner would reply, "I don't know. I've never stepped it off." The story makes for a good repeating, but from what I've gathered, most ranchers knew to the acre how much land they owned.

There were, of course, some very large ranches in Terrell County, a county with more land area than some states, but there were smaller places also. County information on a map printed for deer hunters indicates 15,000 acres as an average-size ranch in the area, putting Grandad's place well within that range.

But, ultimately, this is not a story about size. It's a story about home and family and memories and a lot of other things that can't be measured in acres or sections. And the land is just a piece of land in the Trans-Pecos area of Texas cut through the middle by a creek called Independence.

IN 1905 TERRELL COUNTY was organized (it was carved out of Pecos County), and the scattered citizens of that untamed territory elected Joe Bean as sheriff. He in turn named Grandad as his first deputy, a position he held for some twenty-five years.

By 1906, making a living from sheep was risky and still not as profitable as it would become. Lambs were worth a dollar and a half a head and wool sold for only eleven cents a pound. By 1913, the price per head had gone up to two dollars. A big source of financial loss for all ranchers, both then and now, was losses to predators or "varmints," animals regarded as undesirable or troublesome. "A lobo wolf could hamstring a horse, and a panther could kill as many as 20 goats in one night with herders bedded down within alarm clock distance of the bedground," Grandad once told a reporter.

Charlie became a hunter, not for bounty, but for survival, killing panthers, wolves, and bears, both in the Pecos River country and as far south as Mexico. Panthers measured from eight to ten feet long and weighed from 200 to 275 pounds. Brown bears that roamed the country, coming up from Mexico, averaged 300 pounds. During those early years, Charlie killed over 100 panthers, 15 lobo wolves, and several brown bears, according to J. Marvin Hunter. (The panther goes by several names, including cougar, mountain lion, and puma.)

A photo in the *Fort Worth Star-Telegram* shows Charlie, a slender young cowboy, with the hanging carcass of one of these big cats, longer than he was tall. The dogs in the picture are not identified; they could possibly be the legendary Spot, Loud, and Dinah (better known as Diner), his faithful companions. Those were the best hounds in ten counties, I'd heard tell. For a man to have one good hunting dog was a blessing; to have three at the same time was plain Providence.

Although he didn't start out with the intention of farming, the fertile soil and abundant water made an irresistible combination, and Charlie began to farm during the twenties. He constructed an irrigation system that is still used today. According to Solveig Turpin, University of Texas archeologist, it is "most interesting, extensive and well constructed, deserving of a study from a historic perspective."

Charlie was quoted as saying that the soil was rich enough to grow saddles and boots, which may not be quite factual, but it surely did grow just about everything else. With the help of Mexican national workers, he cultivated various grains, watermelons, cantaloupes, sugarcane, and even a few cotton crops, the only cotton ever raised in Terrell County. Hauling the bales to San Angelo by wagon for ginning must not have proven profitable, for it was a short-term experiment. Eventually, Grandad quit supervising the work himself and began to lease the fields to various sharecroppers during the latter years of his life.

As Charlie grew older, tending his garden was one of his few activities (in addition to driving to his sons' places early in the morning to make sure they were up and about). Always a man who loved the soil, he planted every sort of vegetable, including tomatoes, squash, peppers, watermelons, and cantaloupes, and the orchard yielded a bounty of fruit each summer. A lone fig tree stood near the back porch, and several grapevines constituted his small vineyard. The same fields and orchards he tended early on were fertile enough to support later generations, but the crops became alfalfa, oats, wheat, and different grasses. With Grandad's passing, we lost a wealth of knowledge about the land and its fruits, about the weather and the seasons, the time to sow and the time to reap—all the things that life had taught him in this lonely land, the old ways of doing things.

I'd like to say that Grandad sat in the cool of the evening under his favorite shade tree, whittling and telling us stories of the old days, but that's carrying poetic license too far. He may have briefly mentioned some of his past to us but never in enough detail for me to remember his best stories. I'm sad now to think of the many more stories he no doubt had and didn't share, but I'm grateful that some were reported by members of the press, because, as Hackberry said, there ain't no one left to get it right.

Back in the old days, a German trapper lived on the Pecos River somewhere on the ranch near Grandad. Julius Heusinger had several hunting hounds and was a successful trapper of predatory animals. Although well liked by those who knew him, he was something of a loner. As the story goes, he went to Ozona to buy supplies sometime in 1918, leaving his dogs locked in the cabin. When he left Ozona, he reportedly had his supplies and a jug of whisky tied to his saddle.

Ten days later his horse was found in the vicinity of Howard's Draw with the saddle and jug still on its back. Because of his solitary ways, Julius was not missed until the horse was found by area ranchers. His hat was located nearby, but no trace of the man was ever found. The dogs left in the house had died from thirst and starvation. His fate remained a mystery, but the story was passed along, perhaps embellished as the years went on.

Another of Charlie's neighbors, John McKay, the rancher who helped him get his start, met a tragic end also. McKay was a bachelor who ranched a few miles up the Pecos on what became the Dunlap Place. In or around 1913, when Grandad was serving the county as a deputy sheriff, he was told that McKay had been shot by a Mexican hand on the ranch. Accompanied by Louis Friday (possibly Freitag), one of his ranch employees, he proceeded to investigate. He found three Mexican workers sitting around a campfire who reported that the fourth of their group, who worked for McKay, was missing. They refused to answer any questions, so he was forced to arrest and disarm them.

In the house he found McKay's body. He had been beaten to death. In addition, a paint horse and McKay's saddle and pistol were missing. Grandad stayed to guard the others, who proved uncooperative, and sent Friday to get the sheriff in Sanderson. He guarded the men alone until he was finally satisfied that the missing man was really the guilty one. The Sanderson sheriff notified the Texas Rangers, who set up roadblocks, and the murderer was apprehended near Marathon, where he was wounded while trying to escape. He died a few days later. McKay's body was buried on his ranch, and the other three men were released.

I can only imagine Grandad's emotions as he discovered his friend's body. This was a man who had befriended him and helped him survive his early days on the ranch, now brutally murdered, a lone man in a lonely country, who died mourned only by his few neighbors. Perhaps someone said a prayer for John McKay, or perhaps he was laid to rest unblessed. Today, no trace of his grave can be found.

Although it was common for Mexican citizens to cross the Rio Grande and seek work in the area, this type of violent crime was an aberration. The majority of these men were simply looking for employment and hoped to send financial support back to their families. The Mexican laborers we knew were honest and hardworking and generally well treated by their employers. In days gone by, I remember putting together countless bags of food for hungry workers. They were always given food, if not jobs.

McKay's estate was willed to several heirs (he had neither wife nor children) and was valued at approximately $9,000, with the land being appraised at 50 cents per acre. In 1915 A. C. Hoover of Crockett County bought the McKay land for $2 an acre; he sold it in 1919 to Walter Dunlap, also of Crockett County, for $7 an acre. Dunlap and his wife ranched there, just upriver from us, for close to fifty years.

The next owner of the land was Hal Dean Sr. of Midland, who subsequently sold to C. R. Bailey, also of Midland, in 1990. Bailey, the present owner, renamed the property Pecos Bend, although the road leading in to the ranch is still called and officially named Dunlap Road.

McKay was not the only person to rest in an unmarked grave in the area.

In the years that followed, three Mexican nationals, whose families were employed as goat herders, died and were buried on the Chandler Ranch. The first was a man who succumbed after being bitten by a rabid animal, the second a woman who drowned in the pond above the Home Place. Misjudging the depth of the water, she entered the clear water to bathe and could not swim. The last was an infant, bounced from its mother's arms as the wheels of a wagon in which they were riding struck a large stone. Surely there were markers of some kind on their burial sites, even if they were just rocks or crudely fashioned crosses, but these have disappeared with the passage of time.

Grandad lived during some desperate times and coped with drought, predators, floods, and economic depression. During the Great Depression, the Chandler sons worked on neighboring ranches for wages as low as a dollar a day, but this still topped their father's wages as a young man of four dollars a month. Board, usually consisting of frijoles, bread, and molasses, was provided for them on the ranches where they worked. The wife of one rancher also gave the hands a couple of cans of corn each day for over a month at a time until, sick of corn, someone had the courage to request a change of fare.

The Chandler brothers remembered having to slaughter their own livestock during that hard decade as part of a government program to get the economy on its feet again. There was no market for cattle or sheep, except from the government at seventeen dollars per cow and four dollars per head of sheep. There was no market for horses either, and Grandad and his sons eventually had to hunt down and kill the herd of wild ponies roaming the creek pastures, since they took up good grazing areas and destroyed fences.

This killing of the livestock was not to meet the needs of the hungry but to stimulate the economy and create jobs. This task must have been particularly painful for anyone who has worked with or depended upon the well-being of livestock. It went against the grain of every rancher, but there was no alternative. This federal program received a great deal of criticism, but it was eventually accepted as a last resort.

Grandad admired President Roosevelt and the New Deal. He was a partisan Democrat, as were most Texans, especially those with rural roots, at that time. Although I can't say that we were a politically oriented family, it was always understood that the Democratic Party represented the best interests of the workingman and the rancher and farmer, and a straight Democratic platform was best for the nation.

At some point during the Depression years, Grandad bought and leased a spread of land called the K-Bar in Brewster County from a family named Serna, in what is now the Big Bend National Park in the Panther Junction area. This ranch was much larger than the creek property and more complex in both terrain and management. An undated newspaper clipping from the *San Angelo Standard-Times* found in my mother's collection highlights the local importance of this land.

> Owing to unusually good range conditions while most of West Texas is dry, the Big Bend this fall has had the greatest rush of ranchmen seeking grass in many years, Charley Chandler, Dryden ranchman, said here yesterday. Every place that has sheep proof fencing has been in demand. Leasing started at 20 cents an acre per annum and has advanced to a half dollar but no pastures now remain for lease. Most of the leases have been for three to five years. The Whiteheads of Val Verde County are reported to have leased a large part of the Asa Jones Ranch which comprises approximately 300 sections.

In addition to sheep, Grandad ran some 10,000 head of goats on the Serna Place and had to keep them contained with herders, as there were not enough fences to completely hold them in that vast country called the Basin. One of Dad's jobs was to keep the herders supplied with food, so he often rode miles a day loaded with burlap bags, or "tow sacks," filled with staples such as dried beans, sugar, lard, flour, and coffee.

Dad and his brothers spent their high school summer vacations working on the Big Bend land, placing the date in the early thirties. As with many young men of that age who were fond of drinking, Dad and Herman, the brother closest to him in age and temperament, discovered a cheap source of alcohol in the Mexican village of Boquillas, just across the Rio Grande. Dad's friends from Ozona would make the long trip to the Basin, pick Dad up, and head for Boquillas. They would meet at a designated spot and bypass Grandad completely. The young men called the liquor rotgut, but it was probably mescal or tequila. This was not the brothers' only experience with alcohol, as they told of making their own moonshine during Prohibition.

Grandad sold the K-Bar ranch after several years, for $3 an acre, exactly what he had paid for it. Sometime before Mom and Dad married in 1936, Dad, Clarence, and Herman drove the livestock back to the Independence Creek Ranch, which had been leased to M. H. and Nelberta Goode, Terrell County neighbors, during this period. So ended Grandad's ranching in two locations. Interestingly, both ranches he owned obviously had more intrinsic value than he knew at the time. The K-Bar land is now part of the national parks system in Big Bend National Park, and a portion of the original ranch on Independence Creek is included in a conservation easement agreement with the Nature Conservancy of Texas.

Grandad, in his later years, was a school trustee and a Mason. He also retained his position as a deputy sheriff for many years. At his death, he was one of the last of a group of men who had settled and developed the county.

The deprivations, physical hardship, and solitude experienced by Grandad and his fellow ranchers are hard for us to imagine today. Distance and isolation made ranch life far from a bed of roses in that largely uninhabited area. Ozona, Iraan, and Sanderson, the county seat, were the nearest towns. To this day, Terrell County remains the least densely populated county in Texas. These destinations were reached in the early days on horseback or by wagon and team, a round trip of two days at best.

Sheffield, twenty-eight miles from the ranch, and Dryden, some fifty miles away, are so small that you'd best not blink as you drive through. Dryden has only a post office, but it still maintains rural delivery three days a week, so our mailing address at the ranch is Dryden, although Sheffield is closer.

There were no roads at all in the Independence Creek country when Grandad bought his first automobile. He recalled:

> I bought that car—one of the first Model-T Fords—from A. Madison of Del Rio. I didn't know how to drive it, so I paid a man $50 to drive me home. It's only 150 miles to Del Rio by present roads and highways, but we had to travel approximately 180 miles. We came up through Comstock, Ozona, and Sheffield.

We crossed this land, several miles east of Sheffield, on a ferry operated by a man named Locklear. From that point on, we followed the best cow trail on the ranch. That car was hard to start on cold mornings. Getting to town was a problem. First, I'd have to hitch the car to a saddle horse and take out across a pasture until the motor kicked over. Then I'd work out through the hollows to the wagon road leading to Sheffield and Dryden. I fixed flat tires more often than I took a chew of tobacco—and I was Terrell County's champion tobacco chewer. My average speed was 20 miles per hour.

Once when I averaged 25 between the ranch and Dryden a friend told me I was going to kill myself. He said God didn't intend for man to travel that fast.

I'm not sure what God's plans were, but I would like to believe that He intended for Charlie to settle on the Independence Creek and Pecos River and leave an indelible mark on those rugged acres he inhabited for almost sixty years.

Chapter Two
MINERVA

*It was a country good for men and dogs, but hell on women and horses, as the
cliché goes. Could be, but seems to me it was hell on everyone
who chose life on the banks of the Pecos at the turn of the century.*

CHARLIE NEVER SPOKE Minerva's name in my presence. In childhood innocence, I never connected the two or realized that they had been married. To this day, I have never seen a photo of them together, other than the unrecognizable images of them standing in front of their house on the lower ranch, or even heard their names spoken in the same breath. Hearing vague references to "the divorce," I assumed my parents or aunts and uncles were talking about someone else. Not given to discussing his personal life with his grandchildren or anyone else, Grandad was a product of a different time, a time of privacy and reticence.

The event itself had to have been traumatic for all concerned, sending waves of shock and disapproval through the ranching community. Divorce was almost unheard of in Terrell County in 1929, and my grandparents' was possibly the first.

Another woman was certainly in the picture, as Charlie married Ima Lou shortly thereafter. The sequence of events appears obvious now, many years after the fact. Both before and after Ima Lou had been hired as a governess for the Chandler children, Gran was absent from the ranch for long periods of time as she suffered various illnesses and sought medical help for relief of both physical and emotional pain.

Paul Patterson of Crane, part legend himself and a local authority on the Pecos River, believes that loneliness contributed to and was sometimes the major cause of a woman's unhappiness in this land. "In the old days, when the men were off working cattle, a lot of women would be left by themselves for long periods. Some of them would lose touch with reality and lose their minds," he said. Gran did not lose her mind, but it's a miracle to me that she kept it.

Gran's story was fact; Terrill Lambeth's was not. The heroine of Zane Grey's *West of the Pecos* reacted with dismay at her first sight of the river: "Oh, Dad! Take me back! This dreadful Pecos can never be home!" But surely Gran was not so shocked, as she had only traveled up river a short way to meet her destiny and knew what to expect.

I don't know why Gran began to leave the ranch, but it's possible that her illnesses were exacerbated by her need for human companionship and relief from the never-ending physical labor. This may have initiated Charlie's interest in Ima Lou, but that is pure conjecture on my part.

In discussing his childhood, my dad often said, "Mama was always gone." He and his brothers and sisters must have felt the absence of their mother painfully, and their father's remarriage to a woman for whom they felt no affection only added to the trauma of their family life. Today, this family situation would be labeled "dysfunctional," but terms like that weren't used in 1929.

After twenty-six years of marriage, Gran received a cash settlement and relinquished her claim to the property they had acquired during their marriage. Charlie had to sell part of the mineral rights to pay her settlement, and that was done with great resentment on his part.

She, weeping, reportedly attempted to speak to him on the courthouse steps after the trial, but he turned his back on her, and they never saw each other again.

Gran lost everything on that bleak day: her husband, her ranch, her children (even though she was given custody of the younger ones, they all gravitated more and more toward Grandad and the ranch as they grew older), and her social status, as the stigma of divorce and the scandal that it caused were no small things then. Gran never remarried and mourned her loss for the rest of her life. Indeed, the Pecos is a lonely and bitter stream, and in my mind, symbolic of the bitterness of my grandmother Chandler, a woman who had tried to carve out a life on the riverbanks, but was left finally with only failure and a broken heart to show for her struggle. The Carter family could have been singing to my Gran in their song "Wildwood Flower":

He told me he loved me, and promised to love
Through ill and misfortune, all others above.
Another has won him; ah, misery to tell
He left me in silence, no word of farewell.

Asked if she would ever remarry, Gran said, "Never. I was once married to Charlie Chandler."

Turning increasingly to her spiritual faith, she began to write religious poetry. Some of the verses she composed, while demonstrating the style and sentimentality of the day, give her descendants some insight into her grief. This poem, abridged, was found in her collection with "written for Charlie" on it in her handwriting.

INDIAN SUMMER

When Indian Summer is in the air,
And you hear the lonesome coyote whine,
Do you feel life has been unfair,
Do you worship at an empty shrine?

Do you think of the many years
We wandered hand in hand?
Do your eyes grow dim with tears,
Do you feel the clasp of a work-worn hand?

A hand that would hold you
In spite of sin and strife
Just keep holding tight and true,
One who was fighting for your life.

Please keep the faith with Jesus,
While I battle for the right;
Remember I'm still here,
Praying in the night.

Another, titled "Divorced," gives a glimpse of her anguish.

The world is dark and dreary,
The clouds are bleak and gray;
I'm asking thee, dear Father,
To send a better day.

My heart is sad and lonely,
My soul is sick with dread;
My life is not worth living,
Now love is cold and dead.

Gran attended Grandad's funeral services in Sanderson but did not sit with her children, giving that place up to Ima Lou in the small white chapel filled with ranch families who had come to pay respect to one of their own. Years later, upon hearing of the death of the woman who ruined her life, she said, with sad satisfaction, "I outlived them both."

THROUGH THE CLOUDINESS of years, scant details of the wedding ceremony of Minerva Jane O'Bryant and Charles Albert Chandler remain for those who were given life from their union. Justice of the Peace J. R. Bean performed the ceremony and recorded the marriage the next day in the Crockett County Courthouse. The groom was twenty-seven, the bride twenty-two.

Many decades later, Gran recorded her memories of that time:

I will never forget my first sight of the wild and rugged hills bordering the Pecos River. They were high and lofty with the rough crags of a rocky bluff some three hundred feet above the winding river. Its muddy water, when on a rize, was swift and dangerous, having beds of quicksand in several places.

My husband and I were married at the Ozona Hotel, Ozona, Texas, December 6, 1903. The morning of the seventh, we went shopping; we bought a few dishes, some cases of dried fruits, coffee which was in the form of coffee beans which we parched in our nice new skillet till it was brown. We then had to grind it in our coffee mill, which we acquired along with sugar, syrup, onions and free holder beans. We did not buy flour as my husband's friend Johnny McKay was to bring out several hundred pounds. The McKay Place was situated in a thick live oak grove, a one-room picket shack on the banks of the Pecos, hemmed in by thick mesquite brush.

The road from the old T-5 Ranch was a rough cowtrail on down the river. After we had bought a huge lunch, we headed west in a wagon loaded with supplies. My husband had come to the Pecos, I believe he said, four years before he met me. He was of a rambling disposition and decided to come west. He told me he traded a few horses for twenty head of Angora goats and got to the Pecos driving his little bunch of goats and leading a packhorse. Charlie had at last found the land of his dreams.

The land was wild, rough, and unsettled, overrun by panthers, wild cats, coons, foxes, skunks and ringtails, javelinas and musk hogs and quite a few bear and rattlesnakes galore. Last, but not least, big herds of deer, as many as fifteen ran off a little ways and stared at us as we jostled along the rough trails. My husband said when he landed on the Pecos, he felt it was the end of the trail and he was home at last.

He got work from W. T. Carpenter as a cowhand. The Carpenter Ranch is in Terrell County four miles west of the Pecos River. He (Carpenter) ran the Bugger [Booger] D Ranch till he died. My husband ran his little bunch of goats with Johnny McKay's flock.

Mr. Carpenter and my husband were partners in the hog business. These hogs ran wild up and down the Pecos from our ranch on to the Hoover Ranch in Crockett County and the McKay Ranch and Goode Ranch in Terrell County and what I mean they were wild.

We drove on our way that first day till we came to Independence Creek which headed above the T-5 Ranch. It was nearly night so we unloaded our bedroll, skillet and lid and camped for the night under a pecan tree by a big spring. This was the only pecan tree for miles. There was fresh watercress and ferns growing around this spring. It was the most beautiful spot I ever saw. The big live oak trees along the creek were so stately and tall. It was like a dream to me as I gazed about me at the green willows and grass-lined banks of the creek. The water was clear as crystal. We could see pools of catfish and pretty silver bass swimming around. I, like my husband, felt that we were in the land of opportunity and adventure. So we were happy in our love for one another and our surroundings. Our honeymoon started there on the banks of the Independence Creek about one mile from where it ran into the Pecos.

Minerva's description of the land into which her husband had brought her is idyllic, but away from the creek, there's another look to the Trans-Pecos country. Elmer Kelton, western writer and historian, describes the typical terrain in his foreword to Jack Skiles's *Judge Roy Bean Country:*

> It was and is a land which seems larger than life, and the gritty folk who pioneered it also seem larger than life, eking out an elemental, often dangerous existence under conditions which most of us today would find intolerably spartan. It was a land given to furnace heat and perpetual drought, to snakes and centipedes and the stinging vinegaroon, to plants which wore an armor of thorns for self-preservation, and to independent minded people who could be kind-hearted and open-handed, yet could quickly become as prickly as the cacti around them.

The young couple had become acquainted when Gran's parents, Jacob and Mary Kelly O'Bryant, then living in Comstock, had visited the ranch on a fishing trip. During his courtship of Minerva, which apparently lasted a year, Grandad traveled to Comstock and Langtry and during this time established an acquaintance with the colorful Roy Bean, saloon owner and self-made judge of Langtry, who gained fame as "Judge West of the Pecos." Judge Bean died in 1903, but for a short time the two indeed knew each other, as Grandad told me once in a passing comment. He didn't add that the two enjoyed some of Bean's libations together, but that would seem to follow.

Gran's ancestors migrated to the United States from Dublin, Ireland.

The Irish immigrants first settled in Missouri and Arkansas and then moved on to Texas, where they laid the foundation of Old Fort Utopia in the Sabinal River Canyon. (Utopia is located some ninety miles northwest of San Antonio in Uvalde County.) The Kellys and O'Bryants traveled to their new home in wagons drawn by oxen with other families of Irish descent in June of 1852. Other families on the trek were the Thompsons, Anglins, Snows, Wishes, and Nortons. (Kincheloes and Wares entered the area in the same year; the latter, who were already in the canyon when the wagon train from Arkansas arrived, later founded the town of Waresville, the first white settlement in the Canyon de Sabinal. This is of interest because many of Gran's family are buried in the Waresville Cemetery, including her great-grandfather Laban Kelly and his wife Sarah, great-grandfather Wilson O'Bryant and wife Millie, grandfather Elijah O'Bryant and wife Elizabeth, and grandmother Mary Jane O'Bryant.)

Most of the families making up the expedition to Texas were related either by blood or marriage. Their trip was the realization of a dream. They all homesteaded claims of 160 acres of farmland in the Sabinal Canyon.

Gran's grandfather O'Bryant first entered West Texas in a most unusual fashion. As a young man, he drove one of the first stagecoaches to carry mail over the Old Spanish Trail from Camp Bullis to Comanche Springs. He undoubtedly stopped off at Fort Lancaster, just up the river from the site of the future Chandler Ranch. The hill on the east side of the fort was so treacherous that the wheels of the wagons had to be tied to keep the drivers from losing control on the descent. Gran told an amazing story of her grandfather driving down steep Lancaster Hill, just a mile or so from the fort, at breakneck speed with Indian warriors "hot on his trail."

Founded in the 1850s, Fort Lancaster was established as a defense for the westbound mail run and a stop-off for western immigrants, but it had no noteworthy effect on the development of the area. A report in the *San Angelo Standard-Times* by Harry Wood under the headline "Knowledge of Old West Texas Fort Scant, and Most Is Bad" gives a bit of background on the fort. Apparently, the military of the day was not at its best during those wild times: "The post was infamously known for its 'poor recruits' and shenanigans. Less than a year after it was founded, an Army inspector came to the fort. The inspector found the recruits so untrained he was afraid to let them demonstrate rifle firing. . . . 'They could not drill as skirmishers, nor could they drill at the bayonet,' said the inspector. 'I dispensed with target firing for the same reason.'"

Great-grandfather himself returned to his more hospitable home in Uvalde County, most likely with unforgettable memories of his wild rides down Lancaster Hill.

Years later, Gran, who was born on February 25, 1881, in the community of Exile on the Dry Frio River in Real County, wrote a book titled *Pioneers of the Past,* which chronicles the O'Bryants' and Kellys' trip by wagon train to Texas. Although she had little formal education, Gran had beautiful penmanship and a vivid imagination. She was a prolific writer during most of her adult life. In addition to *Pioneers of the Past* and religious poetry, she also wrote song lyrics, which she would sing to us in a high thin voice after the lights were dimmed at night. She also composed a novel, *The Mystery of the Devil's Cup.* I often think of her small form bent industriously over her writing table as I sit in front of my computer screen waiting for inspiration.

Some of her work was printed in local newspapers, but her books were never published. Naylor Publishing Company of San Antonio expressed interest in her family history. Mrs. Joe Naylor, in a letter dated February 22, 1960, wrote: "Our editorial department has given us a favorable report on your manuscript of *Pioneers of the Past,* and they feel that it will make up into a most attractive book. Our editor reports 'A carefully done account of some of the settling of Southwest Texas. The tale is vivid, and obviously true, and the whole manuscript has praiseworthy historical value. Much of what is told here will be lost if this manuscript is not published.'" She then elaborates the various services her company would provide, but concludes: "With these thoughts and ideas for designing, publishing and merchandising your book in mind, we will be happy to send you our detailed publishing agreement. Remember that this will call for an investment on your part, since a book of the type you have written does have a somewhat limited appeal and consequent sale."

Gran was apparently unable to pay part of the expenses, but she never gave up on her book. In her last days, she still spoke of someday getting her work published. Although her dream never saw fruition, it provided her with a reason for living and much conversation with friends and family members.

Most of Gran's brothers and sisters settled in or around Comstock, Texas. In the 1920s, so many O'Bryants lived in the area that the town was often called O'Bryantville. They were employees of the Southern Pacific Railroad, ranchers, trappers, hunters, freighters, and grocers. Many of them are buried in the Comstock Cemetery.

One brother, Isaac, married Annie Laura Felts in 1895 and first settled on a ranch in Real County. They later moved to Comstock and bought a ranch on the Pecos River. Ben O'Bryant owned the O'Bryant Hotel in Comstock, and George O'Bryant was the owner of the meat market, a popular spot in the summer as he kept ice-cold soda water for his customers. Walter O'Bryant carried mail for three years from Juno to Comstock, and Oscar O'Bryant ranched at Langtry and also lived in Comstock. Clara, Gran's only sister, married Fate (Fayette) Bell, and they also settled in the Comstock area.

Gran and Grandad's earliest home was built of pickets, rather than the usual sotol stalks used in some early houses in the county. The thatched roof was supported by walls made of cane stalks gathered at the mouth of the creek. The fireplace was considered a luxury. (The little house, on land within walking distance of the Pecos, was later inherited by the oldest son, Roy.) The simple house was later replaced by a sturdier structure, which was the birthplace of the last three Chandler children.

A woman who made a home and brought up a family in the rugged surroundings of the Pecos had plenty of work to do. Gran cooked outdoors over an open fire at first and then indoors on a cast-iron stove as she helped Grandad perform the labor of the ranch, riding sidesaddle when they worked livestock. With her long black hair flowing free in the harsh wind or bound up in one of Charlie's hats, she could ride "like a wild Indian" and "work like a man." But she also had many strenuous duties around the house. Ashes from the stove were saved for making soap. Laundry was done by hand with a scrubbing board, hung out to dry, and ironed with heavy flatirons. For supplies, trips involving several days' travel had to be made to Del Rio or San Angelo. Fresh meat was never a concern with a plentiful deer population, and the river and creek were full of fish. Strips of beef were salted and peppered and put outdoors in the sun to dry and preserve them for later use.

Illness and death were also worries that Gran had to deal with. Elmer Kelton's description of early settlers on the Pecos as "kind-hearted and open-handed" is borne out by a letter Gran wrote in January 1912 to the mother of a ranch hand who had died on the neighboring McKay Ranch.

Dear Friend,

We will endeavor to answer your appreciated letter. Your letter found us all well with the exception of severe colds. I sincerely hope this reaches you better than when you wrote us. Mrs. Brittain, it is useless for me to try to tell you how very sorry I was for you all in your great trouble for there is no words to express how deeply I felt for you through it all.

Grandma, I know very little but will tell you all I know about your boy. Mr. McDonald came down here one day about 11 o'clock and told me Fernando was at John McKay's sick. And they could not get him to eat anything hardly. He asked me if I had any milk so I fixed up some sweet milk, butter, eggs and, in fact, everything I had on the place that I thought he might eat. Some medicine, too.

So Charlie came in and went up there and I kept looking for him to bring him down all evening. But he never came till after dark and he told me he was weaker than he had ever seen him so I wanted to go set up that night and there wasn't a gentle horse for me to ride and so dark they couldn't find a team.

So Charlie and Louis F. went back. Charlie said he would take me up there the next morning so he died that night. And I never got to go. It hurt. But it couldn't be helped. They told me he died so easy.

Charlie sent McDonald to phone for you and a Dr. when he got up there the first thing that evening. He told Fernando he had sent for you. And maby you could fix things better for him if you were there. And he just said, maby she could and maby she couldn't, that is the only thing he said. He spoke Will's name a time or two, I think. I could not tell you whether he realized he was going to die or not.

Charlie got him to drink some egg nogg. And everything on earth could be done was done, I am sure. So for God's sake don't blame yourself because you could not be there. I feel like he was glad to be released from his troubles. He suffered so long. And God is always so merciful. I have not heard from Will's folks but Charlie seen Will in Sanderson a few weeks ago. And they were all well. Grandma, I hope you every blessing on earth and if you can, come and see us.

Your true friend,

Minerva Chandler

P. S. Little Herman is walking everywhere, fat and fine, full of fun as a little monkey. Tell Mrs. Williams Charlie will answer her letter soon. He was gone when I wrote this.

Fernando Brittain, a bachelor, was more than likely buried on the McKay Ranch as his great niece, Norma Fisher of Tucson, has unsuccessfully searched all area cemeteries for his resting site. He was not related to the Chandlers; the title "Grandma" used in the letter was one of respect. The letter and the feelings expressed give us a picture of some of the hardships of life on the river and a glimpse into Gran's character.

Nothing was easy on the ranch, and Gran wore out early on. A small woman with a delicate frame, it's probable that bearing six children added to the hardships of her early married life. She was gritty, but even grit has its limit.

Three of her children were born on the ranch, including my father, Joe, the youngest of the Chandler brothers, on August 13, 1912. Dad was originally named Wesley Lloyd after a brother of Grandad's, but a family friend at the time was a great supporter of a gubernatorial candidate named Joe Bailey. The friend was also quite taken by the new Chandler son and often remarked, "This is a real Joe Bailey boy." The name stuck and Dad was known for the rest of his life as Joe Bailey.

The birth order of the six children is as follows: Charles Roy in 1905 at Gran's mother's home in Vance; Clarence Allen in 1906 at the Comstock Hotel in Comstock; Iva Lorine in 1908 in Ozona; Herman Byrd in 1910; Joe Bailey in 1912; and Effie Lee, always called "Kat," in 1914. The arrivals of the last three in my grandparents' simple little ranch house were attended by their step-grandmother, Ellen Chandler, Hamp's second wife. "I don't know what I would have done without Ellen," Gran said, when recalling their births.

The children grew up, both before and after the divorce, with a minimum of parental supervision. When I think of the Chandler children on the ranch, I am reminded of a herd of unruly kid goats, roaming the hills free and undisciplined, forever after impatient with rules and restraints.

They began to work and fend for themselves at an early age. Dad told of taking his .22 rifle and some provisions when he was just a little boy and being gone for long periods of time before he was missed. Once, after an absence of several days, the Pecos overflowed its banks after a rain, and someone thought they had spotted one of Dad's boots floating in the rapidly flowing water. His family presumed he had drowned. They gathered at the river crying and calling his name until he miraculously reappeared, safe and sound and wondering what all the fuss was about. They were so happy to see him they tanned his hide to a fare-thee-well and threatened to kill him if he ever wandered away like that again. But he did, and they didn't.

"Little Joe" knew every rock on the Chandler Ranch and those adjoining it, and he learned them as a small, adventurous boy, exploring his rugged surroundings, hardened by the wild environment. A tough little fellow, he was, but life on the river didn't breed weak ones or tolerate whiners.

For Gran, it was another story. After so many years, the fragile wildwood flower began to wilt. The physical brunt of maintaining the household and caring for her growing family drained her strength, but perhaps the hardest burden for Gran to bear was the loneliness. Although visits from neighbors, mostly the Goodes, Banners, and Turks, and also the Chandler and O'Bryant relatives, provided Gran and Grandad with some companionship, neighbors were few and far apart and daily life on the ranch was isolating. Other friends and acquaintances, such as the Hoovers to the east across the river in Crockett County, the Andersons of the T-5 about five miles up Independence, the Dunlaps to the north upriver, and Henry Packenham on the road into Sheffield, were seen less frequently.

Gran's dearest friend was Effie Turk, for whom she named her youngest daughter, Effie Lee. Mrs. Turk recalled, during Gran and Grandad's marriage, being awakened once in the middle of the night by the sound of creaking wagon wheels. Gran had left the ranch alone and driven a wagon some fifteen miles up the creek to the Turk Ranch, on dirt roads and through many gates, without another human being for miles around. This may have been the only time she left or one of many, but the picture of her driving in desperation through the night to find a consoling friend is a haunting one.

After the divorce, Gran lived in both Abilene and Comanche, and then settled in Kerrville, where she owned a small white house surrounded by a white picket fence and shade trees on the Guadalupe River. I doubt that she ever loved any place as much as the house she and Grandad had built on the site that we call the Home Place or the Old Place, several miles upriver from the original Chandler home. On the back of a photo of this house she wrote, "My home on the Pecos 1929." It was torn down and another built in its place after the divorce, leaving no trace of Minerva on the Chandler Ranch.

In Kerrville, Gran had a vegetable garden in her backyard, which she irrigated and tended herself, a chore that gave her great pleasure. Ironically, both she and Charlie loved their gardens in their later years and spent many happy times working in them, he on the banks of the Pecos, she on the banks of the Guadalupe, watching the fruits of their labor ripen, but not together.

A small, dark-haired lady with bright blue eyes, Gran was known for her energy, her love of family, and her devotion to her faith. She was a devout member of the Church of Christ, having been baptized by a traveling evangelist at the age of fourteen near Reagan Wells. Gran also truly loved fishing. She frequently visited us at the ranch, and I can see her now with her cane pole and red coffee can filled with worms, scrambling over the rocks and bluffs of the Pecos, near her old original home, looking for a good deep hole. She usually found one, too, as she had gotten to know the land and river well during the years she called the ranch home.

When she came to visit her children, she would have to be driven directly in front of Grandad and Ima Lou's house, en route from our place to Herman's or Roy's. She never looked in that direction, but kept her eyes on the road ahead.

Oh, he taught me to love him and called me his flow'r
That was blooming to cheer him through life's dreary hour.
Oh, I'm longing to see him through life's dark hour,
He's gone and neglected this pale wildwood flower.

The only legacies I have from Gran are an old wedding photo, the yellowed lace collar of her wedding gown, copies of her writing, a packet of Christmas and birthday cards from her children and grandchildren, and a rather melancholy streak that is said to be an Irish trait, and that manifested itself in many of her family members. She died in Odessa in 1970 at the age of eighty-nine. She is buried next to Charlie, the man she loved, in the Cedar Grove Cemetery in Sanderson. They were united in death, if not in life.

Chapter Three
SAINTS AND SINNERS

"Shall we gather at the River, where bright angel feet have trod. . ."
For whatever purposes, many did gather there at the ranch, for gold stolen
from a train, for spotted-butted horses, and, yes, for the blessings of the gospel.
The quest for the pot of gold at the end of the rainbow often started and
sometimes ended on Independence Creek and the Pecos River.

STORIES OF BURIED TREASURE abound in the West. Here is ours, true or not.

The long, lonely miles of railroad track in Terrell County were the site of several successful robberies and several that were thwarted. One that succeeded, near Dryden, involved the ranch through a relative of one of the *bandidos*, Ben Kilpatrick, who was a friend of Grandad's.

Ben was not the most famous member of this gang of robbers. That dubious honor goes to Black Jack Ketchum. The name has quite a ring to it, evoking images of smoke-filled saloons, gun-slinging men, and daring train robberies. Hollywood couldn't have chosen a better name for a desperado. Black Jack built himself quite a reputation as a bad guy in the 1890s, when he terrorized Southern Pacific stops at Lozier, Pumpville, and Dryden.

A photo from April 26, 1901, in *Terrell County, Texas,* shows Black Jack just before he was hanged in Clayton, New Mexico; he appears as a handsome man of stoic expression. He was captured after shooting and killing the sheriff of Folsom, New Mexico, during the attempted robbery of a passenger train.

Black Jack was a member of a notorious gang of robbers who delighted in train robberies in West Texas. Some of the gang had themselves photographed for posterity in Fort Worth around the turn of the century. One such photo depicts five respectable-looking men in the prime of life posing stiffly, perhaps unaccustomed to their hats, ties, and jackets. They look more like bankers, ranchers, or college professors than train robbers.

The caption under the photo reads "A keen-eyed Wells-Fargo detective, Fred Dodge, glanced at this picture in a Fort Worth gallery in the winter of 1900–1901 and the gang had to scatter. Standing are: Will Carver, who was killed in a holdup at Sonora, Texas, and Harry Longbaugh, alias the Sundance Kid. Seated in the same order are Harvey Logan, alias Kid Curry; Ben Kilpatrick, killed while attempting to rob a train west of Dryden; and George Parker, alias Butch Cassidy. The gang's Texas hideout is said to have been just northeast of Terrell County." The group is not named in the caption, but they have been called the "Hole in the Wall Gang" in some references. (This may or may not be the actual gang or original group to have used this name. Keep in mind that there's a lot of conjecture in this tale.)

The caption would have been more accurate if it had said "in northeast Terrell County" rather than "northeast of Terrell Country," for during those times Grandad had befriended a young man named Boone Kilpatrick, gang member Ben's younger brother, who also ranched in the area south of Sheffield. Seated in the center of the photo, Ben appears as a striking man of some size. It was said that Boone and Ben bore great family resemblance, but since I only remember Boone as an older man, I cannot vouch for that.

Nevertheless, after one of their robberies of the Southern Pacific, the gang headed for the Chandler Ranch, knowing that Ben's brother worked there and would aid them. Unknown to Grandad, the younger brother kept the robbers supplied with food for several weeks. While hiding out in the hills, they made plans and buried a cache of gold and silver coins valued at some $30,000. They also evidently divided the stolen currency, worth thousands of dollars, that had been on its way to the bank in Alpine before the theft.

Perhaps with a sense of foreboding, Ben held a conference with his brother before the gang left and disclosed the hiding place of the coins on a crudely drawn map. It was to be claimed in case none of the gang returned. Sworn to secrecy, Boone promised not to reveal the hiding place, or so the legend goes.

The gang departed.

With the passing of time, the members of the gang went their separate ways. Some evidently continued their wayward path. Among them were Ben Kilpatrick and Ed Welch, who were killed during a train robbery just outside Dryden on March 13, 1912. A railroad employee named David Trousdale killed Welch with an ice maul and then shot Kilpatrick. A gruesome photo of their corpses being held up by onlookers appears in the Terrell County history. Others in the gang were said to have died less sensational deaths; some just disappeared and were not heard of again.

In the course of time, Boone moved to Iraan, still in possession of the map given to him by his brother. As the years passed, Boone waited patiently for some of the original gang to return. When it became evident that he seemed to be the sole possessor of the only clue leading to the lost treasure, he returned to the ranch to begin his search.

I remember Boone visiting the ranch many times during my younger years and, as news of his search spread, other fortune hunters joined him. Technology, forked sticks, and guesswork failed equally. At one point, a metal detector reacted near the mouth of a likely cave. But when the cave was torn open with dynamite, only an old rusty kettle was found.

Sadly, the futile search lasted a lifetime. Perhaps the map was incorrect, or it may have been that time and weather had changed the surrounding landmarks. Or the bandits themselves may have returned and claimed their prize, unknown to Boone. In any case, the cave or shelter that should have contained the treasure was never found.

Just enough evidence emerged to keep interest in it alive, though. Dad found the skeleton of a pack mule of the type used to transport some of the cache and an old wooden saddle bearing the initials BK, perhaps for Boone or Ben Kilpatrick or Black Jack Ketchum? Also found were several gold coins, which had become buried in the dirt by wind and weather over time.

Dad gave the saddle to J. Marvin Hunter, a writer-historian for *Frontier Times,* who later displayed it in his museum in Bandera. Mr. Hunter called the ranch "an ideal retreat" for the robbers. "In the deep canyons and yawning caves were plenty of good hiding places, where a whole army of officers could not dislodge them."

Well into his eighth decade of life, Boone Kilpatrick, a respectable citizen, died a few years after his last search for the hidden treasure. Apparently, his brother had done his job well. To this day, the gold and silver coins may still lie buried in some lonely cave along the Pecos River. While many ranches in the Trans-Pecos land, especially in Pecos and Terrell Counties, could claim this story, only the Chandlers have a link with the brother of one of the gang members. Though even with that, the tale is surely as much legend as fact.

THE CHANDLER BROTHERS themselves were never known to have robbed a train or stolen horses, although they were not above borrowing a few head of sheep or goats from each other come shearing time. Sometimes they were returned, especially if the borrower was caught red-handed.

But all the brothers were horse people. How could they not have been? Their father at one time owned several hundred head, which he broke and sold to neighbors as cow ponies, and their mother was a graceful rider. They grew up surrounded by horses, and saw them as a natural part of life, like the air they breathed.

Strangely, I don't recall hearing that the Chandler daughters, Iva and Kat, had anything to do with horses. They both married young and left the ranch. They could have ridden as children, but I don't have any information pertaining to their experience or lack thereof as cowgirls.

The brother who was especially interested in horses was Herman; it seemed like Herman's name and horses were always mentioned in the same breath. So many of the older generation of horsemen in the area today, and there aren't so many, say, "I didn't know your dad, but I knew Herman." Elmer Kelton, the Western novelist, remembers that he once went to the ranch with his uncles to see Herman about a horse. Kelton's journalism teacher in Crane High School, Paul Patterson, also connected Herman with horses. He remembered him as the "Pecos River Kid" and an "Elmer Kelton type, modest, outgoing, friendly, and a bronc rider of considerable skill and renown." The origin of this nickname is unknown today, but my uncle enshrined it for posterity in stone on the part of the ranch eventually owned by Uncle Roy: "Herman Chandler—The Kid 1933."

Dad and Herman, the youngest of the four brothers on the Pecos, were experienced horsemen at an early age. As youngsters barely able to hang on to the saddle, they did the ranch work of older men but had some fun doing it, too. They rode with abandon and skill, bringing to mind the Comanche horsemen who rode those hills long before the Chandlers came along. Riding was second nature to them, along with their love of horses.

On horseback they often drove stray cattle belonging to the neighboring Crockett County Hoovers back across the Pecos, splashing wildly and shouting "H Double O, Hoover cattle!" referring to the brand on the cows. The cry of "H Double Ooooooo" bounced off the high bluffs and echoed back to the young boys, louder each time, until the cattle crossed the river to the cliffs on the other side.

As young men during the early thirties, Joe and Herman, and possibly Roy and Clarence, helped produce rodeos at the ranch during the summer. They built an arena and staged roping and riding events of every kind, with a company called Butler Bros. supplying the livestock.

One of the most unusual rodeo events in those days was the goat-milking contest. My parents, Joe and Mildred, won this competition at a Dryden rodeo before they were married. The gentleman would rope a goat, and then his lady would run out with a bottle and squirt a drop or two of the goat's milk into it. The couple accomplishing this feat in the least amount of time was named the winner.

"Come on, Joe, rope 'er," the crowd would shout.

He'd ride out, horse snorting, rope swinging. When he had the animal secured, Mom would race into the dusty arena, as quickly as she could scramble in her stylish little outfit.

"Run, Mildred, come on," they shouted.

They were quite a team all right, my mom and dad.

One undated newspaper clipping announces a typical event: "Chandler Brothers annual rodeo will be held July 26 and 27 at the ranch 30 miles from Sheffield. John Lindsay will be the clown. Tom Slaughter will announce the results. This rodeo is held in the deep country."

Crowds of friends and relatives would gather at the ranch to camp out and cook on the creek, visit, and socialize during the summer days. The Stavley side of our family was also represented, according to the *Sanderson Times:* "In the bronc riding there were three entrants with Bill Stavley again winning first money by his clean riding on the Banner bay. Arnold Ellis on 'Big Canyon' and Edwin Smith on 'Buddy' gave good exhibitions." Uncle Bill was my mother's brother, and she was no doubt on the sidelines cheering him on.

One of the delights at these events was the "colored" band hired to play for the dances on the concrete slab built about a half mile up the creek from the Pecos in a beautiful grove of large oak trees. The music didn't stop until the sun came up on dance nights, and the gregarious Chandlers never wanted the party to end.

Those deep-country girls could dance. They'd waltz and foxtrot and two-step the high heels off their dancing pumps and never break a sweat. And when they got tired of the dance floor, some good-looking, sweet-talking cowboy would escort them down to the creek bank for some serious courting. There's no telling how many romances were kindled or hearts broken under a full moon by the waters of Independence. Many of those fast-stepping young ladies were no doubt Baptists or Church of Christ members, or Methodists, but who said it was a sin to smile at a man or hold his hand a bit, anyway?

Now, dancing, that was another story, but it was a long way from the banks of the creek to the steps of the church house when good times were taking place at Chandler's.

I'm sure Dad's love of having people at the ranch was fostered by the ropings and dances during the Depression years. My folks worked hard, but they evidently played hard, too. And when all the ropers, riders, dancers, and party-goers went home, they no doubt took along good memories that would ease their lonely way of life in the rough Trans-Pecos country until the next bit of socializing came along.

Dad's love of horses extended to riding in rodeos (in Texas that's "ro-dee-os," accent on the "ro") in several West Texas locales, including the most famous of all, Pecos. He once also rode a buffalo as a stunt and said there wasn't much to it.

Dad may have been the performer, but Herman was the entrepreneur. He loved to buy and sell horses, and was always pulling a huge rattling trailer behind his big car. Ranchers then didn't have the pickup trucks they do now; they liked long four-door sedans, usually Cadillacs, complete with fins, or big bulky Lincolns that looked like they could have housed a family of four. Uncle Herman always seemed to be heading down the highway to the next horse show or horse sale or roping, or any place that horses could be found.

Uncle Herman had a special interest in Appaloosa horses, the spotted breed (also called spotted-butted) that the Indians favored. One, named Sputnik, was stolen from the ranch and became the object of a long search and many rumored sightings. Herman spent many years and countless dollars searching for Sputnik; the quest became an obsession. That horse, or one resembling it, was finally found in Mexico, but not before gaining the attention and aid of horsemen throughout several states.

Uncle Herman's wife, Aunt Myrtle, was a rider, too, and what I consider a true ranch woman. A daughter of a ranch family herself (her maiden name was Stapp, and her family was from Judge Roy Bean country), she could do anything he could do just as well and maybe better. Many times when he was off on a wild horse chase, she was at the ranch doing the chores, raising the dogies, tending a garden, and keeping the home fires burning.

Ben K. Green, a veterinarian and author of *The Village Horse Doctor,* tells of a strange experience he had with a horse of Herman's. It was his best roping horse. Herman had hauled the horse to several doctors, but none of them had been able to diagnose what was wrong with the animal, which hadn't been able to eat or drink for five days. Dr. Green asked if anybody who examined the horse had ever looked in his mouth. No one had. So, according to Dr. Green's account:

> Chandler got down on the ground and cradled the horse's head up in his lap and held his nose high for me to put my hand and arm down in his mouth and into his throat. I felt the stub end of something and when I touched it, the horse went into a struggle and moaned like he was in great pain. I came back out of his mouth and got a long pair of heavy-duty forceps and went back and got a hold of this strange object. It took all of Chandler's

strength to hold his head when I pulled. When I jerked it out as fast as possible, I had about a five foot length of sotol blade with little sharp daggers that grew out on each side about a half inch apart and were turned pointed down, which caused them to be embedded in the horse's throat about the length of the entire blade.

The horse then drank a couple of tubs of water, and Uncle Herman was told to take him home. No further treatment was necessary. The horse had been trying to survive in a drought by eating desert plants, according to Green.

Two of our cousins, from both ends of the spectrum in age, Clarence's daughter, Mary Ellen (the first Chandler grandchild), and Herman's daughter, Cathy, were truly dedicated horsewomen. They both rode competitively and well, winning many awards for their skill and showmanship. An action photo of Cathy appeared on the cover of the *Texas Appaloosa Bulletin* in September 1964 with the caption: "Cathy Chandler and her Appaloosa gelding Cricket are a real winning combination." As reported in the August issue of the *Bulletin*, "Cathy and Cricket won the stakes at the Alpine AJRA Rodeo, Alpine, Texas, where she placed third with a time of 18.5 running in the mud. At the AJRA in Big Lake, Texas, Cathy placed third in the pole bending with a time of 18 seconds flat, the fastest time of the rodeo but had a 5 second penalty, and won the barrel race with a time of 17.1. Cathy is the daughter of Mr. and Mrs. Herman Chandler, well-known breeders of fine Appaloosa horses."

Uncle Herman, always on the lookout for adventure, ventured south and in the 1950s owned a ranch in Mexico, or "Old Mexico," as most West Texans used to say. He was ranching at the time on the border of the Rio Grande, but to own land in Mexico he had to go into business with a citizen of that country. He found a Mexican partner, and the two proceeded to move some of their sheep and goats across the river on an improvised bridge. But after a few weeks, some drunken *federales* (Mexican border police) showed up at Herman's place and told the family they were under arrest for having brought their Jeep into the country illegally.

In Aunt Myrtle's words: "We had a nice old Mexican vaquero working for us, and he told us not to let them separate us, as they would try to kill us." So they talked the police into following them to the nearest border town, Ciudad Acuña, across the river from Del Rio.

Along with Cathy, who was two at the time, they began the strange procession with the *federales* riding behind them. But they were stopped at an abandoned ranch house along the way, where they were separated by the lawmen. Myrtle recalled:

> I heard a shot and Herman ran around the house with the police after him. I think they were trying to shoot Herman, but were so drunk they missed and shot their own man and blamed Herman for it.
>
> They threw the wounded man into the vehicle and we told them we'd go to the Diego Ranch and call a doctor to meet us along the way. It was getting dark by then and I was opening gates on the run and closing them to slow the police down. We stopped at the Diego Ranch, told them about the shooting and lit out toward Acuña with the Jeep lights off.

The police must have gotten lost trying to follow on the bad dirt roads, she said. "We got across the border safely, but we were sure shook up. We knew the *federales* wanted to blame the shooting on us so they could take our livestock. Later on we found out the wounded policeman wasn't hit bad and survived." With a bad taste in their mouths, they left their livestock in Mexico and gave up on ranching south of the border.

ANOTHER COLORFUL EVENT of a totally different character took place at the ranch for several years beginning in the 1930s when the Church of Christ camp meeting was held on the banks of Independence. It took place at the site of the old goat camp in a large motte of oak trees. (Grandad had employed herders to watch his goat herds; during the day the kid goats were tethered to stakes while their mothers, called "nannies," roamed and grazed.) Many of the area's faithful decided to convene at the ranch, combining duty to the Lord with a good camping trip.

The leader of the group was Brother Dave Black, a friend of Grandad's. Although he and his wife stayed at the house with Grandad and Ima Lou, rather than camping, and although Grandad is listed as an early church member in the official encampment history, I'm not sure how many of the Chandler family actually became church members. Believers they may have been; churchgoers they were not.

"It wusn't that the Chandlers wus *against* religion, as I recall," one old-time friend said. "It's just that they wusn't exactly *for* it either."

However, some of them were fond of saying, "These hills are my church." (This echo of Psalm 121 may have satisfied their churchgoing acquaintances.)

The Church of Christ is a fundamentalist Protestant denomination whose members used to be called Campbellites, a term they didn't care for much. A. C. Greene writes in *A Personal Country* that the confusion arose with Alexander Campbell, who founded a denomination called the Disciples of Christ back in the nineteenth century. This group is now called the Christian Church, but somehow the label "Campbellite" got stuck on the Church of Christ members. Greene said this was a cause for hurt feelings, and the name was not tolerated, even jokingly, in the old days.

The Church of Christ believed then and now in a literal interpretation of Scripture, which includes the cleansing of sins by total immersion. The waters of Independence Creek provided an ideal location for this ritual. To me, the River Jordan could not have been more beautiful, and I would venture to say that those who were baptized in the creek never forgot the beauty of the pristine setting.

The Welch sisters from Sheffield—Aline Hale, Ella Mae Welch, and Johnnye Holmes—shared their memories of the encampment during the early forties. They told stories of camping under the shady oak trees, bringing water from the creek, and cooking over coal oil stoves. Each family cooked individually and then pooled their resources. The sisters had memories of gathering watercress in the creek and wading and swimming in its crystal clear beauty. Tents filled the shady areas, but some chose to sleep outdoors in the cool West Texas breeze.

Some of the families who were most faithful in organizing the encampment and who never missed a summer were the Owenses, Hardgraves, Trotters, Allens, Hales, Holmeses, and Harrells. They were all ranchers from Sheffield, Ft. Stockton, and Sanderson who loved the Lord and saw no conflict in catching a catfish or two from the Pecos when the preaching was done. Since this particular domination sings unaccompanied by musical instruments, all they needed was a song leader. The echo of hymns rolled through the valley.

The following recollection of the encampment, written by Susan Hayre, a great-granddaughter of Terrell County ranch pioneers, was printed in the *Iraan News:*

> Clint and Stella, Laura and Jeff, Ella Mae, Aline, Morine, Hub and John-nye, and the Hardgraves and Allens became call names to an era gone by.
>
> Mrs. Aline Hale of Sheffield said, "I guess it was before 1941 . . . a few years before the camp meeting began as known today that we all met on the Chandler Ranch. Mr. Chandler said we could have the site. . . .
>
> Back in those days, everyone had coal oil stoves. As I recall, Laura Owens was having trouble with hers as it had legs and was trying to stand it up when she found that the parking brake to her car wasn't on. The car started rolling forward and rolled over the tent and the pole went right through the windshield!
>
> Without electricity, the campers improvised while on the creek. "In the beginning we didn't have electricity. I remember everyone would donate their car for a night to use the lights to see by," she said.

One reason given for the end of this pleasant summer activity was the onset of World War II. As young sons in the area were called to duty and tires and gasoline were rationed, the Independence camp meetings were temporarily halted. However, the meetings never returned to Independence. After the war, it was decided that a location nearer Sheffield would be more convenient, and the group relocated to the Holmes Ranch, thanks to the generosity of Hub and Johnnye.

The event endures today and is now called the Church of Christ Pecos River Encampment. The faithful gather every June, no doubt singing some of the same old hymns sung on the banks of Independence. Some of the original founders' children, grandchildren, and even great-grandchildren carry on the tradition.

The first time I recall sitting in a house of worship with all of my immediate family was at Grandad's funeral in the Church of Christ in Sanderson.

Some of his children and grandchildren have remained with that denomination, while others have followed different paths. Ours was a house divided in matters of faith.

Many years later, in the 1980s, Jim Bob Cox, a young man from Iraan and a relative whose mother was a cousin to the Chandlers, worked at the ranch. He lived with his wife, Rita, in an area called Shady Oaks, one of the most scenic places on the creek. She was a devout Catholic girl who presented an ethereal and original vision when she told us, "There are angels in these oak trees."

While I've personally never seen an angel on the ranch, I am not inclined to disbelieve anyone who has. In early times Native Americans believed that springs were sanctified. For them, for the Catholic missionaries intent upon converting the Indians, and for the faithful at the outdoor encampment, perhaps this land has indeed been consecrated.

As the old hymn goes, "Precious memories, unseen angels . . ."

There are moments of hushed quiet in the canyons in the early morning or late evening, when a gentle breeze bestows a sweet balm that wraps everything in peace. At these times man and nature seem to be connected, and the fleeting thought comes that God's in his Heaven and all's right with the world.

These hills are my church.

Chapter Four
THE STAVLEY PLACE

"Son, not everybody thinks that life on a cattle ranch in West Texas is the
second best thing to dying and going to heaven," a lawyer tells John Grady Cole
in Cormac McCarthy's All the Pretty Horses. *The Stavley Place near Dryden*
was a sheep ranch, not a cattle ranch, and whether it was heaven or
not, it helped to make us what we were.

JOE CHANDLER was twenty-four when he took the fateful step of marriage. He was as wild and reckless and happy-go-lucky as any Pecos River cowboy who didn't know where his next dime was coming from could be. His greatest assets were his abilities to ride anything put in front of him and to present a dashing image on the dance floor of any place in West Texas when the music began to flow.

His bride, Mildred Elizabeth Stavley of Sanderson, was only seventeen when they married on the morning of September 16, 1936, an autumn day as bright and clear as a shiny new penny. Dressed in a two-piece outfit of navy blue silk with tiny red bonnets on it, she was, with her dark hair, fetching smile, and petite figure, one of the most striking girls in the county, and Terrell County had a fair share of them, from what I've heard. The young bride had a kind disposition and sunny outlook on life that attracted many friends in the local high school, where she was a senior.

Despite their age difference, Joe and Mildred were well matched in many respects. He was the youngest son in his family, she the youngest daughter in hers. They both came from rural backgrounds, from hard-working, unpretentious people who could be called the salt of the earth.

Their family ranches were located only some forty miles apart, connected by an unpaved road that is now Hwy. 349, so it's surprising they had not met until a year before their marriage.

When they met, the Depression was just ending. Like many brides and grooms of their era, they had few possessions, no financial security, and did not know what tomorrow held in store. "I married Joe because he was the first boy I ever met who wore shoes!" Mildred exclaimed. But this was said for a laugh, surely, as Joe wore mostly boots, day in and day out, and the young men of Sanderson were not shoeless backwoods boys.

My mother and father were married by Dr. John McCall in the parsonage of the Presbyterian Church. Their witnesses were another young couple of approximately the same age, Mary and Weldon Cox. (Weldon, who was known as Coxy, had come from Fort Worth to Sanderson for a job on the railroad.) The occasion marked the beginning of a long and not always smooth union that would last more than fifty years.

The wedding lunch was celebrated at the Southern Pacific depot in a humble establishment called the Beanery because Mildred didn't want to go to the much more elegant Kerr Hotel. A self-conscious bride, she wanted to avoid the attention of the usual lunch crowd that ate at the hotel. Instead, they lunched with the railroad crew. The menu is long since forgotten, but it's doubtful that champagne was served at the Beanery in honor of the occasion.

MILDRED WAS BORN on March 21, 1919, in Juno, Texas, a small dot on the map in Val Verde County.

Her father, Charles F. Stavley, evidently had gone out on his own as a very young man and had sought out several types of employment during his growing-up years. His family was from Moore, Texas. His father, Bryan O'Neil Stavley, was a teacher who spent several years in Mexico teaching English at the university in Mexico City. He was also a stonemason who helped to construct the state capitol in Austin in his later years.

One event in my maternal grandfather's young life that left a horrifying impression on us was the hurricane in Galveston in 1900. He and a friend had taken up residence there to attend college when one of the deadliest storms our country has known slammed in from the Gulf and devastated the city. The rooming house the boys had chosen was one of the few left standing. A collection of photos of the wreckage was later printed in a book he acquired, and JoBeth and I pored over them as children with morbid fascination.

Charles had a variety of jobs after that hurricane and before his marriage. He worked as a railroad machinist in Del Rio before going to Mexico to work for the Mexican National Railroad as a fireman. After returning to Texas, he worked as a bookkeeper for W. R. Prosser at the Prosser Ranch and then as a bartender in Juno for Walter Edwards.

There he met Lena Schraffl, the daughter of Joe and Bertha Schraffl, German immigrants who owned a ranch, a store, the post office, and the livery stable in Juno, a small community between Ozona and Del Rio. He was twenty years older than Lena, but he must have pleased his prospective in-laws for they consented to the marriage. Charles and Lena were married in 1907 at her parents' ranch home. Papa Stavley, as family members called Charles later, then went to work for Wells Fargo at the stage stop on Devil's River.

The following year, the Schraffls sold the ranch to the Cauthorn family and their store, the Juno Mercantile, and other businesses to their son-in-law and daughter. Charles and Lena ran the store for eighteen years. During this time, my grandfather Stavley decided to sell gasoline. He had it freighted to Juno in barrels and poured into one- and five-gallon cans. Using a funnel, he then poured the gas directly into customers' vehicles. Those in the area said it was the highest priced gas in the world.

After the Schraffls left Juno, they went to LaVernia, a farming community near San Antonio heavily populated with other German immigrants. There they purchased property and turned to farming for a living. After my parents were married, they visited the farm in LaVernia where Mildred's grandmother would ask, in her heavily accented English, "Joe, would you like to drink some gut vine? Made from mein gut grapes, by Gott." I'm sure he was quite happy to accept the invitation and later said, "By Gott, it *was* good."

The Schraffls had both come to the United States as children. My great-grandmother Bertha's maiden name was Matke and her family was from Dresden; I do not know great-grandfather Joe's story or where the two met. They were stern disciplinarians of the old school and did not allow their five children to speak English at home. "English for school, German for home," they said. Therefore, my grandmother Lena spoke German fluently and, with the later addition of Spanish, became trilingual.

The other Schraffl children were Lena's brothers Albert, Oscar, and Alec (Alexander) and a sister named Ella, who was later the head housekeeper of the St. Anthony Hotel in San Antonio, the family's home for many years after they sold the farm in LaVernia. None of the brothers ever married; they were called "the boys" all their lives by the rest of the family. Uncle Oscar, who was born blind, was taken care of by the other siblings. He attended the State School for the Blind in Austin and learned to read Braille. When I was a child, I carried on a long correspondence with him, as he typed well and wrote interesting accounts of his days and family life in the small house on East Young Street, just off of South Flores in San Antonio.

Of this family, I probably knew Aunt Ella best as she frequently came out to Sanderson to visit her older sister, Lena. The only red-haired member of the family, she was an industrious person, vivacious, kind-hearted, and warm. Her son, Jim Robson, was the Stavley children's only cousin.

At the beginning of World War II, my great-grandmother Schraffl, by then a widow, was still a citizen of Germany. Because Germans were regarded with suspicion at the time because of fears of espionage, she was threatened with deportation unless she obtained American naturalization papers. Although she was well up in years and spoke only broken English, she did her homework and passed the exam to become an American citizen.

Lena and Charles had seven children. They were Bertha, born in 1908; Charles Howard, born in 1910; Bill, born in 1912; Mae, born in 1914; my mother Mildred, born in 1919; Bryan Ross, born in 1924; and Frank, born in 1926.

With the six sets of aunts and uncles on the Stavley side and five on the Chandler side, I had twenty-two aunts and uncles and eventually twenty-seven cousins. There were so many relatives that I seldom stopped to think from which side of the family tree each one came. JoBeth and I grew up surrounded by extended family. The assorted aunts and uncles represent to me the best and strongest of their Depression-era generation.

Myrtle, Lillie, Effie, Elsie, Mae, Bertha, Iva, Maybelle. They don't make names like that anymore. And they don't make aunts like that anymore either. My aunts worked all summer getting ready for the winter, busy as squirrels stashing away their horde. They cooked and cleaned, scoured and scrubbed, stitched and hemmed, took care of the sick, and buried the dead. Resourceful and frugal, they worked hard, made do or did without, used things up, and rarely threw things out.

And yet I think they enjoyed life more than anyone I've ever known. They loved visiting and gossiping and getting together for meals. It was a simpler time, a harder time, but they took the proverbial lemons of life and made lemonade. I would give anything to sit down on the front porch with them now at the end of the day and share some of that lemonade.

In 1921 Papa Stavley moved his wife and children into Del Rio so that the oldest children could start school, while he stayed in Juno to operate the business. My mother was not old enough for school but remembered learning to speak Spanish as a very young child, as Grandmother always had household help from the Mexican community. Del Rio is located on the international border between Mexico and the United States, and it was a common practice for families in that area to have Mexican nationals employed in their homes. "Mildred, you speak Spanish so well, you must be from Mexico," her high school teachers told her years later.

All the Stavleys spoke Spanish as a result of their early upbringing (Aunt Bertha was especially fluent). Two sons, Howard and Ross, later worked in Mexico under a program to eradicate hoof-and-mouth disease and put their language skills to good use.

"Ustedes hablan espanol?"

"Sí, como no?"

Of course we do.

After the sale of the Juno store in 1926, Papa Stavley bought a ranch of "average" acreage on Big Canyon in Terrell County out of Dryden. (Remember, average in Terrell County was 15,000 acres.) He moved his family into Dryden, less than twenty miles from the Mexican border, where they lived during the school year, riding a bus into Sanderson, the county seat, every day. In the summer months they lived at the ranch. Not many people can say they were born in Juno or lived in Dryden, but Mildred and her brothers and sisters can claim this distinction. For those not familiar with West Texas, both of these communities seemed like the ends of the earth, with Dryden being a bit closer to the drop-off than Juno.

Dryden was no longer the vibrant little center of cattle shipping that it had once been. Life had calmed down by the time the Stavleys settled there, and my mother and her brothers and sisters lived a tranquil existence in comparison to the turbulent times of the past.

After moving his family into this small community, Papa Stavley acquired Box 10 at the post office. Mildred and Joe kept the same number when they leased the Stavley Place years later. Today, with the passage of some seventy-five years, Box 10 in Dryden is still our home address.

The community in the 1920s was a bit livelier than it is today. Several families lived there, mostly the wives and children of ranchers. Younger students attended the small community school but had to ride a bus to Sanderson, the closest high school, when they were older. Today the entire town consists of a post office, two closed stores, and perhaps three or four houses at most. The stores were run mainly for tourists traveling to or from the Big Bend who needed a candy bar or shotgun shells or a postcard to prove to their friends back home that places like Dryden still existed. But the amount of business wasn't enough to sustain them. (Other than Interstate 10, Highway 90 is the most traveled route between El Paso and San Antonio.)

In Dryden, one of Mildred's closest friends was Martha Bassett, who, along with her sister and brother, rode the bus with Mildred. Martha's father, Julian Bassett, owned over 300 sections of land in the area. When he sold the land, he prudently kept the mineral rights, and later was one of the co-owners of the Brown-Bassett field, a major natural gas field in the county, located about halfway between the Stavley Place and the Chandler Ranch. The Browns were also good friends later on, as Herbert Brown and his wife Chich were our neighbors at the Chandler Ranch.

After a number of years in Dryden, the Stavleys moved to Sanderson, twenty miles away so the children would not have to ride the bus anymore and Grandmother Stavley could have the necessities of life a little closer.

The family continued the pattern of going to the ranch on weekends and for most of the summer, just as we did and many ranch families do today.

But these were not vacation trips for there was work to be done. The country was suffering, and cash was hard to come by. My mother and her brothers and sisters took it for granted that when they didn't finish the food on their plates, that same food would reappear for the next meal. "Again?" they'd complain. "Yes, again," was the reply. For Christmas, the children each received an orange as a special treat. When they were sent to town to buy a newspaper for Papa and he gave them a dime, he expected a nickel back.

Yet Mildred took dancing lessons from Miss Fleda Belle Jernigan, and we have several photos of her in costumes that must have represented a financial sacrifice, even though they were no doubt sewn by Grandmother Stavley. Mildred and her brothers and sisters appear stylishly dressed in other photos. But her parents were frugal and did not believe in spending unnecessarily. It could be that the family's financial situation was a bit better by the time Mildred was a teenager since the older children were gone and there were not so many mouths to feed. It's also possible that the youngest daughter was given a bit more; according to some family members, the "baby girl" was "spoiled" by her parents. Papa Stavley called her Middie, the rest of the family said Mit.

When Mildred was fifteen, she attracted the attention of a young man named W. H. "Coon" Chandler, a cousin of Dad's. Coon was never called anything but that, but it never seemed to bother him. One day, Joe went by the Stavley house in search of his cousin and met the girl he was to marry.

Joe and Mildred were becoming a serious couple in 1934 and 1935 and during one of the Chandler brothers' rodeos, Mildred made her first visit to the ranch. Grandad had heard of her tap-dancing abilities and insisted that she perform for him. He cranked up the Victrola, and she put on such a show for him that he called all his friends in and she did an encore, tapping away on the concrete floor of the ranch house porch. She was never shy when it came to dancing, and tap dancing especially was in favor in those years, as attested by its popularity on the silver screen. Possessing a good sense of rhythm and stage presence, Mildred seemed to have the potential for greater things in life, but she decided to marry the rancher's son and accept whatever their journey together would bring.

Dorothy Sullivan, the high school Spanish teacher in Sanderson at the time, relates that Mildred was a very bright student and that she tried to dissuade her from such an early marriage. "I had taken a group of girls hiking in the hills around Sanderson and tried to talk Mildred out of marrying so young. Her reply was, 'But Joe is so good looking!' I couldn't disagree with that."

There were others who tried to talk her out of marrying Joe, and not just because of her age. "Mildred, Joe's no saint," some said. "Why don't you marry a railroad man?" (Several of Mildred's admirers worked for the Southern Pacific.) But it didn't take her long to decide. For her the pros outweighed the cons, and she threw caution to the winds and said yes.

After their marriage, Mildred withdrew from school. Education was not a big priority for girls then, but finding a husband was. In this respect, Mildred was an early success, as were her amiable, easy-going sisters, Bertha and Mae, who both married in their teens.

As newlyweds, my parents moved to the Chandler Ranch, where they spent the first two years of their marriage in a small two-room house located just between the river and the creek. They had neither electricity nor indoor plumbing in the beginning, but as they said, the creek was running just below the house, and they didn't have any reason to stay up late at night. My first home was that humble little house, although I can't remember living there.

With a wedding gift from Papa Stavley of twenty-five yearling ewes, Joe got his start in ranching. When they had been married a year, he gave them another twenty-five head. This was an appropriate gift for a young ranch couple who had both grown up in the sheep business. As a little girl, Mildred had attended Sunday School at the Baptist Church and learned to sing, "We shall come rejoicing, bringing in the *sheep*." (For those unfamiliar with the old Southern gospel hymn, the correct wording reads "sheaves," not sheep. But for Terrell County, Mom's version was quite in tune with the place and the times.)

During this time Dad also ventured into farming, following in Grandad's footsteps. There was a watermelon patch near the little house on the creek, which Uncle Frank Stavley remembered well. He went down to spend a few days with Mom and Dad, and they, apparently thinking there was sufficient food on hand, left him alone while they went to Del Rio. Uncle Frank, however, was a hungry teenager, and the food supply quickly dwindled. So he turned to the watermelon patch. He said he would have a yellow melon for breakfast and a red one for dinner (lunch) and then start over again.

Frank recalled, "Mr. Charlie drove up and said, 'Ima Lou's got some dinner ready, are you hungry?'"

Frank didn't hesitate. "I was never so hungry in my life," he said.

As the youngest in the Stavley family, Frank spent a lot of time with the Chandlers during their first years of marriage. He was likable and outgoing, as were all of the Stavleys' sons.

The Chandler children gathered frequently at Grandad Chandler's house. They all lived nearby on various parts of the ranch, not always in a spirit of brotherly love, and at one time or another all lived in Grandad's house.

Once, on a hot summer afternoon when Mildred was there, Joe's older brother Roy, who occupied himself smoking hand-rolled cigarettes and picking out mournful tunes on a guitar, began to lament, "Nothing ever happens around here, just sunup and sunset." He continued to complain to high heaven about how bored he was, coughing and blinking nervously, until he finally went to take a nap under a shade tree. As he lay napping, Mom snuck up quietly with a bucket of cold spring water and poured it over him.

He came to life pretty quickly. "Where is that damned woman? She's trying to get my goat, and I swear to God I'm going to kill her."

Scared out of her wits at his reaction, Mom hid in a closet until he calmed down and resumed his nap, still mumbling and grumbling. Maybe she didn't get his goat, but she made something happen, all right, as she usually did.

Uncle Roy's first marriage ended in divorce, and his ex-wife took their only child, a son, to California, never to return. He, Roy Chandler Jr., is the second of the Chandler grandchildren, and the cousin I have never known. His mother, Thelma, wanted no part of the family she had married into, obviously. Roy then married Frances Cunningham, who outlived him by many years and stayed on the ranch on the lower Pecos alone until her second marriage.

Clarence and Lillie's children were the Chandler cousins I knew best, a gregarious, handsome bunch of folks that JoBeth and I loved to see arrive at the ranch. They lived there before I came on the scene, but we were not neighbors since they later moved to a part of the ranch down the Pecos that was not easily accessible to us on the creek because of the rough terrain. Uncle Clarence had inherited land that could only be reached by going out to the highway, turning at the Brown-Bassett field, and then driving down a dirt road to the river.

I was born in Sanderson in Grandmother Stavley's house on June 23, 1938. Since there was no hospital available (there still isn't), home births were common and doctors made house calls. My arrival was assisted by Dr. Lester and his wife.

Mildred had gone into town several weeks early to await the event, while Dad stayed at the ranch. When Uncle Bill Stavley drove down to tell him he'd better get into Sanderson, as he was going to be a father, he arrived in town shortly after I did. He had driven in on a flat tire and had on one brown shoe and one black one, his boots apparently forgotten that morning. Just as he arrived, the sun appeared over the eastern hills, and the milkman drove up, right on schedule to make his morning delivery. Dad, the milkman, and the fresh milk for the day arrived at the door together.

"Come on in and see our baby," Dad shouted to him. After admiring the new arrival, the milkman went on his way, delivering the news of the morning to all the households of Sanderson: the Stavleys and Chandlers had a new granddaughter, and mother and baby were doing well.

I was named Charlena after both grandfathers, Charles Stavley and Charles Chandler, and Grandmother Lena. JoBeth followed two years and nine months later on March 6, 1941. The "Jo" came from our dad's name, while the "Beth" came from Mom's middle name, Elizabeth. If Joe was disappointed that he didn't have a son, I never knew it.

Joe leased the Stavley Place from Mildred's parents when I was two years old. It was our home for the next six years, until we returned to the Chandler Ranch once again. The house, located some seven miles off the Dryden highway, was not a grand affair. It may not have shouted hard times, but it surely whispered it. The house didn't have a redeeming feature; it was cold in winter, especially when a blue norther came whistling in, hot enough in summer to "melt the horns off a billy goat," and miserable in between. But it seems that our small family lived there quite happily.

Papa Stavley died in October of 1941. He was a man of strong character and mild disposition who was esteemed by those who knew him.

Grandmother Lena was left a widow in her fifties with two teenage sons, Ross and Frank, still at home. She owned the ranch, from which she derived her livelihood until her death, and the house in Sanderson, but her strong work ethic compelled her to supplement her income with various jobs. She never considered working for a salary beneath her. *"Arbeit mach das Leben süß,"* her parents had told her, and indeed, "Work makes life sweet" was her motto throughout her life. At various times, she waited tables, worked in a variety store, and delivered the *San Angelo Standard-Times* early each morning. After moving to the Brown Ranch to live with Aunt Bertha, she delivered fresh milk, cream, butter, and eggs to Sanderson.

During those years, the two ladies cultivated a vegetable garden, made preserves from their fruit trees, and cooked welcoming dinners each noon as if they were expecting company to drive up at any moment. Their expectations were usually fulfilled. They knew how to put the big pot in the little one, those ladies did.

Aunt Bertha got quite a reaction when she arrived in town alone one day and walked into the doctor's office. "Where's Lena, Bertha?" someone asked.

"Home skinning a goat," she said, not understanding why her reply brought a burst of laughter from those waiting to see the doctor.

Don't all ranch ladies of a certain age stay home and skin goats if the occasion arises? And plant their gardens on Good Friday, splash their Christmas fruitcakes liberally with bourbon, put up or pickle every fruit and vegetable in sight, and click the knitting needles during rare moments of leisure? There was not a minute to be wasted.

Lena's industriousness was a trait she passed on to her children, as all the Stavleys were hard workers. Howard, Bill, and Ross worked for the Southern Pacific Railroad until retirement (Uncle Frank worked for an oil company in Houston), but they were always involved in other endeavors. They cultivated peach and pecan trees, raised livestock, and had diverse interests that made them interesting to be with.

The Stavley Place, located some twenty miles out of Dryden on Big Canyon in some pretty desolate country, is the embodiment of lonesome. I can remember driving out the dusty, rutted ranch road more than I can remember driving in, as my parents found plenty of reasons to seek relief from their solitary days at the ranch.

Life during the first years at the Stavley Place was not always tranquil. One of my first memories involved the night Joe wrecked a car on the Pecos River High Bridge going to Del Rio. Doc Turk, an early-day rancher, recorded the event in his journal on a date of historical importance:

> December 7, 1941: Japan declared war on the United States. Partly cloudy and cool. Today Walton Poague [Poage] will rope Sonny Edwards [at] a match roping in Odessa. I think Sonny will win. They are both good ropers. Looks like it will snow. Joe Chandler was hurt when he turned his new Buick over somewhere between here and Del Rio a few days ago. He is in hospital in Del Rio now. Over the radio from Honolulu came the news of a violent outbreak from Japan on United States citizens and property. It seems now that all chances of a peaceful settlement with this country are at an end and that war cannot be averted now. No one knows the outcome yet. It seems too bad that our country has to be drawn into war.

I remember standing in front of Grandmother's house in Sanderson, crying to go with Dad that night because I wanted so badly to ride in his pretty new car. Although I was insistent, Mom and Grandmother did not budge, and I shed more tears. I was three years old, beyond reasoning.

When notified that he was in the hospital, Mildred, angry with him for the accident and the drinking that had preceded it, at first refused to see him. But my stoic German grandmother made the trip to Del Rio. "He's still my son-in-law," she said.

DURING THE DEPRESSION and war years, hitchhikers were often seen along the area's highways. They looked for work as they roamed, victims of wanderlust and hard times. Dad was prone to giving every one of them he encountered a ride and a meal. Mom got used to his hospitable ways but sometimes worried that they couldn't provide room and board to so many extras. Somehow, they stretched the meals to fill the stomachs of these guests and gave them a bed, sending them on their way after a few days or weeks or even months.

But Mom's patience snapped the day she came back to the ranch from Sanderson and found the family of Okies. Children and adults alike were making themselves at home. A tow-headed, blue-eyed child was peering around every corner, and the female members of the extended family were going through the bedroom closets, as busy as clucking hens.

"Mildred, look who we've got this time. They're from Oklahoma," Dad announced, proud of his latest feat.

Then the missus of the Okie family appeared. "Damnation, Mildred," she said. "That's a right pretty red dress you've got in there." She was probably twice Mom's size.

"Well, damnation, take it—it's yours," my mother replied. And then to my father, "Joe, get them out of here and you get out with them!"

Seems that she cooled down, though, and provided the visitors with a decent meal before Dad loaded them up and took them back to Dryden, richer by one red dress.

In spite of the various visitors who came to the ranch, it was a solitary place. Years later, when we had a phone at the Chandler Ranch, a neighbor ranchwoman down the Pecos used to call Mildred up just to chat: "Mildred, I just get so god-derned lonesome for the sound of a human voice." No doubt that's how my parents felt when they lived at the Stavley Place. When we sat out on the porch at night, we could clearly hear the whistle of the Southern Pacific trains as they passed through Dryden. There is no sound more lonesome than a train whistle to start with, but those long blasts seemed even more poignant as we sat in the empty landscape under the starry canopy of the West Texas sky. We felt like we were the only people on the face of the earth.

But we weren't, of course. Listening to that same sound were our nearest neighbors (still miles away) and my parents' closest friends during those years, Vic and Alma Jewel Littleton and Joe and Dorothy Friend.

Once, when JoBeth was just a baby, the four of us were sitting on the front porch one summer night, enjoying the cool evening breeze. Joe, the proud new father, asked me, "When you're a big girl, what are you going to call baby Sis?"

"JoBeth," I said.

"What are you going to call Mommy when you're a big girl?

"Mother," was my reply.

"And what will you call Daddy?" he asked expectantly.

"An old son-of-a-bitch," I said.

He executed a surprised about-face. "Mildred, did you tell her to say that?"

Doubled over with laughter, she couldn't answer. When he joined in, I began to giggle also. I didn't know why they were so happy, but it was a good moment for the three of us as JoBeth, better known as Baby Sis, continued her nap, and we laughed and laughed. (I don't remember this scene personally at all, but when a child hears a story so many times, it becomes reality.)

My parents had a busy social life. They were always off to a dance or party in Dryden, Sanderson, or Del Rio. The solitude of ranch life made them and others seek companionship and no doubt gave rise to the legendary hospitality of the ranching community.

On one of these occasions, a formal dance in Sanderson, an event occurred that made Dad something of a hero. I have heard variations of the tale from several of his old cronies, but they all pretty much told it like this:

> We were taking a break between sets when somebody dropped a cigarette on the floor. All the ladies had on those filmy sorts of dresses with long skirts, pretty as pictures they were. Well, that burning cigarette ignited the skirt of one of them. She went crazy, she was so scared and bolted from the crowd and ran for the exit.
>
> The rest of us just stood there, frozen, but Joe didn't hesitate, he broke and ran the length of the dance floor, catching the lady just before she went out the door. He tackled her and rolled her in a coat, putting out the flames. We were all pretty damned impressed. Joe always was a quick thinker. He may have been full of piss and vinegar, but he was the kind of fellow who, if

the chips were down and he said follow me, you better believe we all would have done it.

Although entertainment for children at the Stavley Place was nonexistent, JoBeth and I had our own diversions. We always had dolls, and we made up endless scenarios with them and with all the pets we had, the dogs and cats and calves and baby lambs. We played outside the house much more than in it, living in our own little world.

On the hill behind the house stood a creaking windmill, which filled a large concrete tank, The water from the tank in turn filled the water troughs for the livestock, so its purpose was utilitarian rather than recreational. However, Mom and Dad used to swim in the tank on summer days. Since it was too deep for me and JoBeth to reach bottom and we had not yet learned to swim, Dad built a wooden platform, submerged it, and weighted it down with rocks for us to stand on. We found it very entertaining to play and splash on that platform while our parents swam in the refreshing cold water drawn deep from the rock formations below.

In spite of such good times, the move to the Stavley Place proved to be Dad's financial downfall. He could not have chosen worse years to ranch, as a terrible drought, one of the worst in recent history, had descended upon West Texas. In his best years there, Joe (and the bank) owned approximately 3,600 head of sheep and 1,200 head of goats. But when a livestock owner starts to borrow money to buy feed and when the sky is watched in vain for any sign of clouds, year after year, making a living becomes more and more difficult. The long dry spell, which is vividly described in Elmer Kelton's *The Time It Never Rained,* worsened and brought ranchers, hat in hand, to banks all over West Texas. When it finally did rain again, it was too late for Joe to recover from the years of financial drain.

The most severe years of the drought in West Texas were the 1950s, but it started for us in the Trans-Pecos in the 1940s. One dry spell just rolled into another. Sometimes a few sparse clouds would appear and send down scattered drops of moisture, just enough to arouse our hopes but never enough to break the drought.

The land, where grass and weeds should have grown, turned concrete-hard and cracked under our feet. Hope had literally turned to dust, and the carcasses of dead sheep dotted the land.

Ironically, these dead sheep provided a small source of income as Joe picked "dead" wool by hand and sold it to keep his family afloat. He made enough to buy groceries or a tank of gas but not enough to satisfy the banker.

Another blow hit ranchers during this era in the form of screwworm. Any open wound on a sheep was an invitation for *Cochliomyia hominivorax,* a common fly, to lay its eggs, which would hatch into larvae and then worms that would devour the wounded sheep. To help prevent this, after shearing, each nick or cut was daubed with a malodorous purplish-black tarlike liquid called *tecole,* a ritual I sometimes was assigned. But it was impossible to protect an animal from every scratch, either from shearing or wire cuts or encounters with other animals or even mesquite thorns, and thousands of sheep in the Trans-Pecos area died from screwworm.

The swabbing of cuts after shearing was preventive, but we also treated sheep already infected. I often accompanied Dad on his search for "wormies," and it was easy to spot them. If we saw the poor animals with their heads down restlessly stomping their feet, that was a sure signal of their distress. They would be roped and treated and sometimes taken back to the pens, usually to little avail. When the shiny black buzzards, or turkey vultures, that drifted through the cloudless skies began to circle and then swoop to the ground, we knew that we had lost again.

Salvation, in the form of science, came in the 1960s and 1970s when we were no longer ranching. Boxes full of sterile male flies were dropped from planes into the vast expanse of West Texas to mate with native females, and the dreaded screwworm was eradicated. I recall the buzz of the small planes and the tiny boxes floating to earth after we had moved back to Independence and gotten out of ranching.

During this time we also bottle-fed the orphan lambs, called "dogies," whose mothers had succumbed to screwworm or the drought, with milk supplied by the milk cows. We kept the weaker, smaller babies in boxes in the kitchen on cold spring nights, hoping they'd survive to morning. The hungry lambs, and also kid goats, became my pets, and I always was heartbroken when any of those beautiful little animals didn't make it. We were in a constant struggle with death at the Stavley Place.

During those lean days, Dad developed another source of income: trapping and hunting varmints. Raccoon, ringtail, and fox skins could be sold for cash. Mom would drive him up to the Big Canyon Bridge on the highway on winter nights and drop him off. From there he would follow the rugged gorge home, a distance of several miles, hunting half the night with a rifle and headlight. Then he would skin the animals and stretch the hides and take them into town to sell. The skins only brought a small amount, but the extra cash helped to keep food on the table.

The hard times at the Stavley Place included a long period of poor health for my mother. She had several unsuccessful surgeries, and during her lengthy stays at Scott and White Hospital in Temple, JoBeth and I were left with Grandad and Ima Lou and other relatives repeatedly. Mom's extended absences created some anxiety in us that lasted into adolescence. Eventually, Mildred underwent a successful surgery performed by Dr. Curtis Rosser in Dallas and enjoyed good health again. His name was spoken reverently by our parents, as if he had performed a miracle, and perhaps he had.

In a time of no hospitalization insurance, my mother's long illness put the family deeper into debt, but Dad persevered. I can say, unequivocally, that of all the elements of Dad's character that I admired, it was his refusal to quit in the face of adversity that I admired most.

DURING THE WAR YEARS, we went through a period of hoarding sugar from Mexico. We had a hollow wall in the house of the Stavley Place where we stored the contraband. JoBeth and I were cautioned not to tell anyone, as if federal officials were planning a raid on our remote little home. The sugar police never came, so our supply remained safe.

Another vivid wartime memory was a train trip to Del Rio with Ima Lou and my friend Jenny. It was not a pleasure trip; perhaps some bank business or a medical appointment prompted the plan. I was to meet Grandad Chandler, along with Ima Lou and Jenny, at the turnoff to the Stavley Place for the drive into Dryden to get the train. Either we were late or they were early, but we missed the rendezvous. Thinking that I had missed my chance to go on the trip I had been dreaming about, I started to cry.

Then Dad hit the accelerator. We flew down the caliche road, winding through hills, with Mom clutching little JoBeth, and me crying my heart out, pigtails blowing straight back and tears streaming down my dusty cheeks. We arrived in Dryden just in time to catch Ima Lou and Jenny boarding at the water tower, where the train had come to a stop. In the nick of time, I joined them.

Slowly, the engines came to life and slowly we began to roll along, out of Dryden, away from Grandad, Mom, Dad, and JoBeth, all waving good-bye. But now, did I really want to go? I felt a mixture of sadness and exhilaration as the great engine picked up speed, pulling its long black tail behind. Next stop, Del Rio!

There was not an empty seat to be had, as we were on a troop train full of uniformed young men leaving home to serve their country. When we, a woman and two little girls, appeared at the door, seats were suddenly available all over the car, as soldiers and sailors crowded up, relinquishing their places to us. Clad in blue and brown and khaki rather than shining armor, youngsters, really, with bright eyes and fresh cheeks, they remain an image of chivalry.

I remember some of them were singing songs with strange lyrics: "Mares eat oats and does eat oats, and little lambs eat ivy. A kid'll eat ivy, too, wouldn't you?" or so it registered with me. And: "Hutsutralson, ontherillarye, and a brawlabrawlasewet." The words made no sense, but they had a soothing rhythm that matched the humming of the wheels.

When we arrived in Del Rio, we went to claim our room at the Roswell Hotel, the epitome of sophistication and city life to me, only to find the same problem, wartime overcrowding. Somehow, we got a room with one narrow double bed and ended up sleeping crossways on it, with Ima Lou using a chair for her feet to rest on. She snored, which made Jenny and me giggle until morning, it seemed.

Ima Lou completed the purpose of her trip, and then we returned to the train station to reverse our long way across the Pecos River bridge, back through miles of uninhabited land, to the water tank in Dryden.

The only other experience I remember from the time of the war was writing letters to Uncle Ross. Mom's younger brother, the only one of the Stavley or Chandler family to serve in the military, was with Patton in Europe and was awarded the Purple Heart for injuries suffered during battle. During his long convalescence in France, he was the object of much worry and the topic of many conversations.

He returned after the war, a handsome bona fide war hero, and married Pelham Rose Bradford, a beautiful young lady from Pumpville, who had just finished school at San Marcos Baptist Academy. An impressionable ten-year-old the first time I met her, I was dazzled by the sight of my uncle's girlfriend in her stunning black evening gown, as they left for a social event in Sanderson. Not one of the Depression-era aunties, she was in a class and age group by herself. Purr, as she is called, has a delightful laugh and a warm spirit, and is still a cherished beauty to all who know her.

MILDRED AND JOE seemed to go to Mexico at the drop of a hat, to the border town of Ciudad Acuña, then called Villa Acuña (and before that Las Vacas), ostensibly to buy groceries but also to socialize with friends in restaurants and bars. Joe would imbibe, while Mildred was the teetotaling driver. She could enjoy social gatherings more than anyone without a drop to drink.

One family story is that they once left me in the car, when I was a baby less than a year old, in the parking lot of Crosby's Restaurant, a popular meeting place. When Mrs. Crosby heard me crying she went out and "rescued" me. From that time on, she apparently developed quite a fondness for me and helped look after me when my parents frequented her place. She called me "la niña," or little girl. Today, I feel quite at home on the narrow streets of Ciudad Acuña, crowded with vendors and the sounds of the Spanish language and the aroma of highly seasoned Mexican food. Mrs. Crosby's legacy, her restaurant, remains a popular attraction in the little border town.

San Angelo was another favorite destination of my parents. There Mildred and Joe visited Ma Goodwin's Tavern, where they heard Bob Wills and his Texas Playboys perform their favorite, "Rose of San Antone," or the Hanger on the Mertzon highway, where Pop Harrison's Texans played their theme song, "Little Red Wagon." Dad's sister, Aunt Kat, and her husband, Uncle Alvin, were living in San Angelo at the time and often went out with Mom and Dad, while JoBeth and I stayed with Jessie and Araminta (Tootsie), their pretty, popular teenage daughters, whom we greatly admired.

ALTHOUGH OUR YEARS at the Stavley Place were short, they left indelible memories. Living in the small ranch house, we were surrounded by sheep pens and rocky pastures and a clear sky that stretched forever. At the Stavley Place, unlike at the Chandler Ranch, we were ranchers with no other distractions, no other way of life.

All the land was fenced, mostly with barbed wire, so we didn't have herders, as Grandad had when he began ranching. But we still were greatly dependent on others, especially the Mexican workers who helped with the manual labor. We also had to have extra help at different times of the year for tasks such as marking (ear notching), docking, castrating, paint branding, vaccinating, shearing, and shipping lambs.

The arrival of the shearing crews added excitement to everyday ranch life. Headed by the *capitanes,* the crews led a nomadic life, moving from ranch to ranch during shearing season. The early sheep shearers used hand clippers, but the modern-day crews were totally mechanized with six to eight "drops" on each side of their truck. The shearing was done on a specially constructed platform, and the wool was picked up in the center of the floor and deposited into tall woolsacks held upright in specially constructed stands.

JoBeth and I loved the job of standing in the sacks and packing down the wool as tightly as possible; we probably didn't weigh enough to do much good, but it made us feel essential. We also liked to watch the "lead goat," owned by the crew, which was trained to lead the sheep into the pen. The gate would be thrown open, and the lead goat, with a bell around its neck ringing merrily, would strut into the shearing area with the sheep following behind.

The shearers were paid for the number of sheep they sheared and were given a token for each shorn animal. The *capitan* was responsible for all the expenses of the crew, such as equipment, food, and the cook's salary. The cook held an exalted position on the crew, just as in the old chuckwagon days of the cowboys. At mealtime, everyone gathered around to devour the delicious, spicy food prepared by the cooks on an outdoor fire. Many times we sampled the food and wondered why we couldn't cook as well as those men, who had such a way with seasoning. The staples of their menu were meat, usually goat donated by the ranchers, beans, rice, tortillas, and hot chili peppers that seared our tongues and brought tears to our eyes.

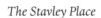

THINKING OF THOSE DAYS at the Stavley Place brings back all the sights, sounds, and smells of a ranch in West Texas: the feel of a sheep pen, the mournful bawling of lambs separated from their mothers, the smell of fresh-sheared wool, the sight of black buzzards circling, the creaking windmills pulling water from the earth, the dry wind whistling around the house at night, the searing hot sun and empty sky, the laughter of two little girls splashing in a stock tank, and the lonely whistles of distant trains.

Chapter Five
HUNTING: DEER TALES

Hunting was a way of life for my family and for most West Texans. I, who have
never put finger to trigger, grew up assuming that everyone owned hunting rifles
and that the quest for the white-tailed buck was a natural
thing, ordained by God.

MOM COULDN'T BELIEVE what was happening.

She and Dad were hunting on the G. K. Mitchell Ranch between Sheffield and Sanderson on a blustery winter day in the fifties. As guests of the Mitchells, they were confident there were no other hunters for miles around. Mom had just started into a canyon. She wore a deerskin jacket that blended into the rugged cedar-choked countryside (no camouflage or orange vests then) and carried a .30-30 rifle. An experienced hunter, she had no premonition of the danger ahead.

Sensing a slight movement on the hill above, she looked up to see a man in a long dark coat slowing swinging a rifle in her direction. She could not see the silhouette of the rifle either to the left of the skylit hunter or the right. Horrified, she realized he was aiming at her.

Not a moment too soon, she hit the ground just as the gun discharged. Snow and mud flew up into her face, indicating that the rifleman must have been aiming at the spot where she stood. The hunter must then have realized that his intended target was not a deer but a human, for he was gone from sight before Mom composed herself enough to look toward the top of the rimrock again.

The full impact of being the hunted rather than the hunter didn't set in until she reached the pickup, and by the time Dad arrived she was in tears. "Someone tried to kill me," she sobbed.

Their hosts assured them there was no one else on the ranch that day, but there was some suspicion that the villain was a ranch hand with "buck fever." Or he could have been a trespasser poaching on private land and shooting at anything that moved. The mystery was never solved.

Mildred never forgot that experience. The story, repeated through the years, became a family standard, but the ending would have been tragic if she had not fallen when she did.

Our family albums are full of photos of successful hunters holding up their trophy horns, yet these pictures represent only a minute fraction of the deer actually slain by the Chandlers. And what tales the hunters told.

Some of my best memories are of driving Grandad, along about sunset on frosty winter evenings, around the ranch to make a "little run," as he called it. He favored Chevrolets and always seemed to have the latest model, so away we'd go in style down those dusty roads along the Pecos, a man now in his seventies, and I in my early teens, in his Chevy coupe. Our conveyance was quite a contrast to the camouflaged, highly equipped, four-wheel-drive vehicles that some hunters use today. They would have laughed to see us. (Or vice versa.) Together, until his eyesight failed, we kept the pantry full.

At Grandad's funeral, as the hearse pulled away from the church, Dad spoke about their greatest bond, their love of hunting. "There goes my hunting partner," he said. And mine, too, I thought.

There are so many stories. "Have you heard the one about Uncle Roy shooting the horse?" someone would say. And yes, we'd heard it, but we wanted to hear it again. Uncle Roy came to visit us on the Stavley Place, ready to hunt. He left on horseback one fine morning to get him a buck worth bragging about, he said. When he hadn't returned by nightfall, we all felt anxious.

Finally, Roy walked in from the Big Canyon pasture, both deerless and horseless. He blinked a few times, with a sly expression and a couple of coughs. "Doggone, I shot that horse," was all he had to say. And sure enough, he had, saddle and all.

Another favorite story is that of Mom killing the buck with the butcher knife. She was alone on the ranch on one of those beautiful clear fall mornings that called for putting on a sweater and pouring a second cup of coffee to enjoy on the porch, when she saw a trophy buck grazing on the abundant fallen acorns just below the pool. Unable to pass up the opportunity to surprise Dad when he returned, she ran for a rifle.

As she aimed, the buck stopped his grazing and looked at her. She fired. But in her haste she just managed to wound him, and the rifle was now empty.

Leaving the wounded, thrashing animal in the grass near the creek, she ran back to the house but couldn't locate another shell. So, with pioneer determination, she grabbed a butcher knife from the kitchen.

I wish I could have witnessed the scene that followed. It's not that simple to stab a buck deer that is armed with a dangerous rack and fighting for his life. He was still powerful enough to put up a struggle against the slight little woman wielding a butcher knife. Deer and woman wrestled, tearing up the turf and scattering blood everywhere. But Mildred prevailed and, when Joe returned, she had another story for the family history book, with the cuts, scrapes, and bruises to prove it. Not to mention one of the biggest bucks killed that season, and the only one slain with a butcher knife.

The shy and lovely white-tailed deer roam at will all over the ranch and throughout most of West Texas, unless a landowner puts up a deer-proof fence to contain them. Otherwise, they can leap any barrier with grace, despite their size. In Texas, the average adult bucks weigh 81–170 pounds.

They are beautiful, swift animals, and run with their heads and tails erect, flashing the white flag for which they are named. The does have no antlers, but the males sport impressive racks, arched forward and averaging six to ten points. These horns are shed each winter and begin to develop again each spring or summer, when they are said to be "in the velvet."

Herbivores, they graze on green plants in the summer season, acorns or corn in the fall, and any vegetation available in the winter. The ranch is deer heaven with its nearly year-round food supply, including a bountiful feast of acorns from the oak trees, wheat or oats in the fields, and plenty of grass along the creek banks.

There are numerous stories of deer, supposedly dead, being transported to the ranch in the trunk of the car or the back of a pickup and then miraculously coming to life when they arrived at the house. Jumping out of the vehicle and heading for the hills, the "dead" deer would leave their observers standing in shock as they watched the white tails bounce away into the distance.

No respecter of automobiles, Dad thought nothing of taking his car out into the countryside, over rocks, brush, hill, and dale, to pick up his latest kill and throw the bleeding carcass into the trunk. There was no such thing as a hunting vehicle to my parents and their contemporaries; they used whatever was available to stalk their quarry or retrieve their bounty.

One of our hunters had this story:

> I shot a big ol' buck—man, he had a set of horns on him—on one of the rimrocks just before sundown. Knowing he was too heavy to get off the hill without a vehicle, a couple of us started back to the house to get my Jeep.
>
> We met Joe on the road, cruising around in his Cadillac. He heard our story and told us to get in and he'd give us a ride. So we got in, figgerin' we were going back to the cabin. Damned if Joe didn't gun that ol' car and head straight up the hill. We were bouncin' around and hanging on for dear life, thinking he'd lost his mind. But. . . he maneuvered around those big rocks and mesquites and cedars and, with a few directions from us, got us to within twenty or thirty yards of that buck. We drug that deer to the car and Joe helped us load him into the trunk, bleeding all over the place.
>
> Well, we got him back to the house all right just about dark and figgered Mildred would jump all over us for messing up her car, but it didn't faze her. Guess she was used to it.

Deer were not the only animals that were hunted at the ranch. One time, JoBeth and her friends Mike Kropp, Don Dishong, and Don's sister, Betty, (now Renfer), all from Odessa, drove to the ranch late at night and decided to go coon hunting without awakening Mom and Dad. As Betty later recalled, they decided a moonlight hunt would be fun, but as Don was inspecting one of the rifles, he shot a hole in the living room floor. Joe, with Mildred close behind, ran into the living room and shouted, "What the hell's going on here?" A bewildered Don replied, "It just went off!"

But Mildred and Joe were good sports about it. Mildred relieved the tension by saying she'd been wanting new carpet anyway and thanked Don for helping her get it. And Joe claimed that Don probably saw a raccoon run under the house and was only trying to defend them.

Once Dad and Uncle Frank drove a pickup truck with high sideboards up onto the side of a hill to pick up a dead buck, but Dad didn't want to take the sideboards down, according to Uncle Frank. "Grab hold and throw," Dad commanded. Each took a set of legs and prepared to swing the carcass into the pickup. Throw they did but not high enough, and the deer splatted against the sideboards. "Higher, damn it," They threw again. And again. Finally, in disgust, they lowered the sideboards, loaded the deer, and bumped down the hilly slope.

Dad had a reputation as a sharpshooter. He brimmed with a self-confidence that bordered on cockiness, but he usually lived up to his reputation. "I'm going hunting," he'd say, and we would ask how many shells he had. "One," he'd reply. "That's all I need."

Or he'd say, "I just killed a good buck." If we asked, "How many times did you shoot?" he'd give the same answer. "One." Finally, we quit asking. Uncle Alvin McGilvray boasted that Dad was the best shot he'd ever seen, and he'd seen a lot of them.

Although Mom didn't hunt as much as Dad, her skill rivaled his. She wrote in December 1969: "Last week we went for the day up to Kat's and Alvin's hunting. We rode up and down those hills (and hung on for our lives) until all my muscles hurt—and some I didn't even know I had! Anyway, I killed a 6-point and a 9-point. Daddy got an 8-point. Season was over yesterday and I'm glad."

All in a day's work.

Another time, she described a "turkey morning": "The sun is just coming up and it looks beautiful. We've had lovely weather, not cold at all, only a little frost every morning. Daddy just came back in the house with two of the biggest wild turkeys I believe I have ever seen. He still has on his pajamas, robe and houseshoes—he is something else!" It became a Thanksgiving ritual for him to announce that we would have wild turkey for our feast, much to our dismay. We'd plead, "No, please, we want a Butterball."

Dad hunted without regard to boundaries or seasons. He was not alone in his lawlessness; most of his contemporaries did the same. He hunted from the highway anytime he saw a good deer that had the bad timing to appear just as Dad drove along. He could field dress an animal in seconds and have it loaded before we could blink an eye. But he didn't kill wantonly or recklessly, and we ate the fruits of his sport, the end result a bountiful spread on the dinner table. Venison sausage and chili and fried backstrap (a tender cut of meat near the backbone) were staples at our winter meals, along with fluffy buttermilk biscuits, mashed potatoes drenched in butter, and cream gravy made with sweet milk. To make the meal complete, we'd add watermelon pickles or pickled peaches brought up from the cold cellar.

Elsie Hoskins of Odessa remembers another illegal incident. She and her husband, Boaz, were visiting when Dad had killed an out-of-season buck. They had not been at the house long when the game warden drove up. As the men talked to the state official in front of the house, Elsie and Mom grabbed the freshly killed deer from the back porch and wrestled it into a bedroom, where they threw it under a bed and pulled the bedspread down to cover the evidence.

"Come on in and have supper with us," Dad said to the game warden. "Mildred's got a good one going."

"Much obliged, Joe. Don't mind if I do," replied the courteous gent. Far too polite to question the chuckles and smiles of the other four adults at the table during the course of the meal, he most likely drove away thinking his hosts sure were happy folks.

One last example of suspect activity that my family took part in was raising fawns on a bottle and keeping them as pets. When a fawn is small, the doe will hide it in the underbrush while she goes off to forage for the day. When we found those babies and adopted them, we knew their mothers really had not abandoned them, but we convinced ourselves that we were saving their lives. We loved our gentle little pets, who followed us like puppies, and put bells around their necks to protect them from hunters during deer season. When they were old enough to survive on their own, we returned them to the wild. Today, the law prohibits this activity and with good reason. Deer raised in captivity are not afraid of humans and have been known to become aggressive; in other cases they never learn to survive on their own in nature.

Many ranchers now depend upon hunting leases to supplement their incomes, as ranching is a risky business today. Who would ever have dreamed that the white-tailed deer would support us? Deer are plentiful in the Trans-Pecos, in fact, too plentiful. Their numbers have to be held to a certain level or they reproduce to the point of overpopulation. Thus the quest for the white-tailed buck can be justified, except to those who do not believe in hunting under any circumstances.

Another animal at the ranch that was popular with hunters in the past is the javelina, whose other name is the collared peccary. These little wild pigs roamed in small herds, and some hunters enjoyed tracking them. Although they are still seen occasionally in this area, it is very unusual to spot a herd. Some say they are fit for human consumption, but I cannot vouch for that.

These interesting little animals traveled in areas they marked as their territories, which normally did not overlap. Living near water supplies and in areas of succulent plants, the javelina eats sotol, mast, lechuguilla, prickly pear, and mesquite beans. Contrary to popular belief, they are not carnivorous and are not threatening to humans, although they could scare anyone with their daggerlike tusks and loud grunts and squeals.

JoBeth and I and Gay Hoskins, Boaz and Elsie's daughter, were roaming the hills one day when we spotted a herd of perhaps a dozen javelinas. I was the eldest of the trio and could not have been more than eight or nine years old at the time, which would have made JoBeth and Gay six or seven. Even though JoBeth and I should have known better, we became frightened and decided to hide. Of course the pigs didn't know we were hiding or care, but as we crouched behind a large rock formation listening to their snorts and watching their black forms run by, Gay began to pray, "Dear God, I'm too young to die. Please get me out of here." Her panic must have been contagious, for all of a sudden the pigs seemed twice as close and twice as large. The three of us ran down that rocky hill in record time, as if a hundred pigs were snapping at our heels.

In addition to fawns, we also had several baby pigs as pets. They were easy enough to catch on the road, but you had to have a vehicle ready for escape from the enraged mother. Mom or Dad would snatch one up and then hold its little jaws together so that it couldn't squeal.

The piglets very quickly became gentle, begging for bottles of warm milk and following us around, delighting everyone with their constant little grunts of contentment. I remember one in particular that was so small Mom carried it in a shirt pocket, where it snuggled down and slept happily. When the pigs grew up, they, like the deer, went back to the wild.

Dad was also an enthusiastic hunter of raccoons and other varmints. I loved to bundle up on cold, brisk winter nights and accompany him. I would hook a finger into one of his belt loops so I could stay close to him and see ahead in the beam of his headlight. Under the oak trees across the creek, we walked as quietly as possible through the leaves and acorns, shining the light up into the branches, until we spotted a set of eyes catching the reflection. Then came the blast of the gun in the quiet winter air, and the sound of the varmint falling through the branches to the ground.

Just as Grandad ventured into Mexico on a bear hunt many years ago, Dad also traveled beyond the United States to hunt. After many trips to Colorado and Arizona on deer and elk hunts, he flew to Saskatchewan, Canada, in 1960 with Jack Tillery of Odessa. (Jack was the owner of the insulation company that helped build the El Paso Natural Gas Plant on the Brown-Bassett Field just over the hill from us. During the construction, he and his wife Marge lived at the ranch.) With Jack piloting his private plane, the two had quite an adventure traveling over miles of scenic wilderness. The mounted horns of a moose from Hudson Bay still adorn the entrance to the clubroom at the ranch.

We have also granted many hunting leases through the years. One of the most interesting groups, who stayed with us for eighteen years, was from El Campo, Garwood, and Nada. These fellows were of German descent, and most were related to each other by blood or marriage. Many were rice farmers, others businessmen. This group had more fun than anyone. They also brought fantastic food to us: soft, sweet kolaches, tart pickles, and the finest sausage, all home-made.

Leonard Staff, one of the organizers of the group, killed his first deer at the ranch. His wife Rose Marie said, "All the guys still get together every once in a while and talk about their trips to the ranch. We thought a lot of your mom and dad. They always made us feel at home. We also spent a lot of summers down there and always enjoyed it." (Many years later, for Dad's funeral, they sent a spray of flowers with a miniature buck deer attached.)

This group epitomized the best of deer hunting. They hunted for sport and enjoyment, yet respected the land, the wildlife, and each other. Their camaraderie around the campfire at the end of the day made everyone look forward to their arrival.

Jack Smith from Odessa remembers a time hunting at the ranch years ago when Dad saved him and his friends from going home deerless. "We drove down to the ranch to negotiate a day hunt. We'd already been to one of the neighboring ranches and had been told the going price was $20 a day. Joe said he could beat that and would guarantee us a deer." But the following day's hunt was not successful. As the group was loading up to go home, Joe told them to wait. He said he'd have them a deer in twenty minutes. The hunter recalled, "I swear he was back in fifteen, dripping wet, with the prettiest little doe we'd ever seen. He'd had to jump in the river and swim after her since he had wounded her. We went back to Odessa and had a feast. That was the best deer meat I've ever eaten."

We've had several groups of lessees from Odessa through the years, and I think the majority of them left with good hunts and good memories. Some of those I remember were Sheets Eye Clinic, Independence Gun Club, Sewell Ford, Ideal Derrick, and Orion-Pacific. There were a few disgruntled hunters, I'm sure, but most returned home satisfied.

We know our ancient ancestors hunted for survival, but hunters today do so for other reasons. Many hunters feel that venison is better than beef, and most know that hunting keeps the herd population down, which does need to be thinned out regularly to balance the distribution of the herd. But beyond these reasons, most hunters enjoy the challenge of tracking an animal in its environment and trying to outsmart it.

However, I can't help but believe that the way we hunted in times gone by put the hunter and the deer on a more even playing field. A sporting chance, you might say. Sitting in a stand and waiting for the animals to approach a deer feeder brimming with corn, the favored method of today, seems pretty well loaded in favor of a man and a high-powered rifle with a telescope that can hone in to the next county. On the other hand, early hunters may have welcomed anything that would have made their quest a bit easier. Let's not romanticize the past too much here.

Bud McDonald, an outdoors columnist for the *San Angelo Standard-*

Times, wrote about hunting on the ranch in an article dated December 7, 1986: "I was situated about 12 feet from the ground, just above the top of a thicket of salt cedars about 50 yards from the river's west bank. A seldom-used wagon track wound through ankle-deep buffalo grass from the river to an old sorghum field about 100 yards distant. . . . In the matter of minutes it took for all this terrain to sink in, a young four-point buck wandered out of the salt cedars into a clearing about 25 yards from my stand." He describes aiming at the deer, then waiting for something bigger to come along. "The decision wrinkled my nose a little, but the thought of the razzing I would have to take back at camp about shooting Bambi was enough to snap the safety back on the Remington." A couple of does later wandered across the clearing, but three hours later, he was still waiting.

McDonald then goes on to describe the ride up the jeep road, an unforgettable experience for anyone intrepid (or foolhardy) enough to attempt it. The road itself was a fairly new addition to the ranch, having been constructed through one of the roughest and steepest cliff and rimrock sections on the surrounding hills. Built when the El Paso Natural Gas Company installed a pipeline through the ranch from the Brown-Bassett Field, the steep road cut through thick sheets of limestone and curved out dangerously at one point along an awesome drop-off. Dad drove the road skillfully and without hesitation. He was always sure of what he was doing; it's just that his riders never were. "I don't know which scared me more, making it to the top or having to face the ride back down," one passenger said.

Hunting methods have changed and so has our observance of propriety and regulations. We're all law-abiding citizens down on the creek now. We observe seasons and quotas and rules, but life is a bit dull in comparison to the lawless days.

The deer still abound, descendants, no doubt, of some of those we took aim at and missed. They hole up in the brush on winter nights, seek the warmth of the sun in the thin dawn light, and fill our hearts with happiness when we encounter them in their habitat. They pause, throw up their heads, and freeze for a moment in reflection. Then they're gone, their white tails bounding away from us, their enemy, their protector.

Chapter Six
ONE-ROOM SCHOOL

I sit, as small and tightly folded as my six-year-old body will allow. If I'm very quiet, no one will see me or the tears gathering in my eyes.

It's my first day of school, and Mom is leaving. Fighting the desire to jump up and run to her and beg to go back to the Stavley Place with her and Dad, I refuse to meet her eyes. But I accept the inevitable. I'm six years old, and six-year-olds in Texas must go to school. There's no escape. I'm the unhappiest first grader in the state, or at least on the ranch.

The others sit in their seats, as quiet as I am. Are they fighting back tears also, or am I the only one who wants to disappear?

Ima Lou stands, waiting to commence our edification, the first day of seven years in a one-room school. In a cloud of heavy Tabu cologne, Mom approaches my desk. Her embrace is not returned. "We'll come for you this weekend."

I am now a boarder. Not only must I go to school, but I have to live with the teacher. There's no escape. My education has begun.

STAYING WITH GRANDAD and Ima Lou on their ranch so I could go to school was not an unhappy interlude. But I missed my parents constantly and lived in anticipation of their return. This feeling was not new, however, as JoBeth and I had already spent a great deal of time with Grandad and "Moo" as a result of Mom's chronic health problems.

We were cared for physically, as far as being fed and clothed, and that was all that was expected. In retrospect, it seems that Jenny, Grandad's foster daughter and our best friend, and JoBeth and I were little maids as well as boarders, which may not have been so rare at that time. As surely as the sun rose each morning, there was work to be done. Running a household on the ranch demanded physical labor, and children were not exempt. We were expected to do our part. We washed dishes, swept and mopped the floors, made beds, helped with the laundry—a tremendous undertaking with an old wringer-style machine and clothesline in back of the house—and pressed everything with a sadiron heated on the wood stove.

When we had completed our chores, we mostly just stayed out of the way of the adults and entertained ourselves. This was not a child-centered culture. We had not yet learned to whine and felt that life was as fair as it was ever going to be.

Our greatest joy, as soon as the days turned warm, was the creek. Grandad would load us into his car, deposit us at the bank, and then find a good spot under a shade tree. While he dozed under his sweat-stained hat, the three of us, and any other child who happened to be in the vicinity, waded and swam in that friendly water, delighting in finding new deep holes and discovering fish, frogs, snakes, turtles, and other creatures.

We burned our skin as brown as biscuits and toughened the soles of our feet to the texture of sandpaper playing barefoot in the white gravel. No matter how long we stayed, we never got enough of the creek or the feel of the lovely, clear ripples splashing against our legs.

Sweet days of Independence.

"Time to go, girls."

"Just a little longer, please, please. We're not tired, Grandad."

In a childish way of thinking, I always assumed we were the only Chandler grandchildren to love the creek. It was a surprise, many years later, to hear Aunt Kat talk about her girls playing in that same beloved water with Uncle Clarence's and Aunt Iva's children. But that was before my time, and I hadn't yet discovered the amazing fact that the universe had existed before I entered it.

The creek was part and parcel of our lives. It seems we lived only from summer to summer. What happy times we had between those oak-lined banks. All the mystery, excitement, and adventure in the world were contained in that narrow corridor and in the words Independence Creek.

Back at the house we would have the simplest of suppers, more than likely whatever was left over from the midday meal. Grandad sat out under the trees in the yard and Ima Lou served him what he called his poverty bowl, usually toasted biscuits and milk or cereal. Doctor's orders—no big night meal, a faithfully followed regimen for most of his later years. The food served in that little house was as unadorned as the surroundings. Salt and pepper served as seasoning; bland was best, and fried was fine. Fried chicken, fried steak, fried catfish, fried bacon, fried venison, fried potatoes, fried pies.

An observant reader might note the absence of lamb in our menu. Grandad and all his sons were sheep men. The calendar of our year revolved around working sheep. While cattle and goats were part of the picture, the sheep business was our livelihood. But did we partake of lamb stew, lamb chops, and roast leg of lamb, all considered delicacies by the Yankees up north who bought our produce?

No. And to this day I don't know why.

Everything was prepared on the cast-iron cook stove, which was heated with wood of varied types, including mesquite. What labor and time went into preparing food, starting with the fire itself. Everything edible had first to be cut, diced, chopped, sliced, beaten, whipped, or mixed. Meat, milk, butter (fresh from the churn, another chore), and other perishables were stored in the "milk room," a small concrete space with a large vat of cold water that kept food relatively cool. Town dwellers had iceboxes by then for this purpose, but keeping ice on hand was impractical for us. Refrigerators came along later, of course, with rural electrification.

Red beans (pintos), cream gravy, and made-from-scratch biscuits or corn-bread were common dinner items, dinner being the main meal of the day, eaten at noon. We would not have recognized a salad and enjoyed fresh vegetables and fruits only in season; in winter we ate what had been canned in the summer.

Since the house had no dining room, we grew up eating in the kitchen. Trips to Sanderson to visit Grandmother Lena exposed us to a more genteel way of life, at least during mealtime. We chose from a larger and more varied menu in her dining room, and there was always a cloth on the table. Everything tasted better there; perhaps it was cooked with a little more imagination and skill, or maybe it was her German background.

JoBeth and I loved everything about Sanderson except getting there. We never balked when told we were going to town because we knew that visits with all the Stavleys and the delights of Kerr Mercantile and the Princess Theater lay ahead. However, there was a downside to all the pleasure.

The trip, over some fifty miles of unpaved road to Dryden with countless curves and ups and downs through draws and canyons, always made us sick. The smell of dust and greasewood through the open windows of the car mixed with wafts of my mother's cologne and cigarette smoke added to our queasiness, which was worse on hot summer mornings, as we sped away to the city. There was always at least one stop en route to throw up. "Mildred, get the water bag," Dad would shout as he threw on the brakes and got us out of the car while Mom retrieved the canvas water bag hanging on the rear-view mirror of the car. After a few sips of the cool, canvas-flavored water and a splash or two on our cheeks, we'd resume the trip, which was smooth sailing after we hit Dryden.

Sometimes a lively little Mexican lady who worked at the ranch came along on trips to Sanderson. She insisted that the smell of citrus would prevent car sickness, so she always peeled an orange or lemon and stuck the peel up her nose. She rode contentedly in the back seat, arms crossed, breathing deeply of her aromatic *remedio*. "Ahhh, *limón*," she would sigh. It must have worked, as I don't recall her ever joining us on our rest stops.

A NOTICE in the *Sanderson Times,* 1944, under the headline "Independence School News," marked the beginning of our school career:

> The following pupils are enrolled in the Independence School this year:
> First grade: Charlena Chandler, Virginia Chandler, Junior Rogers, Amelia Garcia, Bobbie Mancha
> Second grade: Felipe Mancha
> Third grade: Don McElhaney
> Sixth grade: Virgil McElhaney
> We have a good supply of new equipment including a blackboard, stove, Victrola records, library books, blackboard stencils, workbooks, songbooks, etc.

The other students called our teacher Mrs. Chandler, Jenny called her Mother, and JoBeth and I named her Moo, which sounds more like an affectionate nickname than it was in reality, for affection was not what we felt for this forbidding woman. Ima Lou's history with the family and the ranch is a strange one, a drama in itself. She came as a young woman, just out of teacher training at Abilene Christian, to serve as the Chandler children's school marm and ended up, after Grandad and Gran's divorce, as the second Mrs. Charlie Chandler.

She was not the first teacher who had tried to tame the wild children raised along the river and failed in the effort. There were many before her; they came and went with some regularity.

When Dad started first grade, the school was located in a grove of oak trees, now called Shady Oaks, accessible only by a footbridge across the creek. One freezing winter day when the air was especially dry and brittle and the unwilling children were pretending to smoke, puffing little bursts of steam from their mouths, as they made their way to school, the governess of the time fell into the cold creek water under suspicious circumstances. She departed soon after.

She was said to be sensitive about such things.

After the divorce of his parents, Dad and his brothers and sisters were sent away to school. At first, most of them lived in Abilene with Gran, but the two youngest were sent to boarding schools in San Antonio, Dad to Peacock Military Academy and Aunt Kat to Our Lady of the Lake.

Dad's enrollment at Peacock came after an incident involving a group of boys, Dad included, who decided to smoke forbidden cigarettes in the basement of Abilene Christian High School. Somehow, things got out of hand. A fire ensued, and Dad was dispatched to Peacock to "straighten him out."

Peacock, founded in 1894 by Wesley Peacock, enjoyed a fine reputation then and later, although its doors have been closed for a long time. It was one of the first private prep schools for boys in the state. The structured environment and individual attention turned school into a positive experience for the wayward boy from the creek who, after all, was only experimenting with cigarettes and never intended to burn the building down.

My dad's punishment became a reward. His years at Peacock were surely some of the best in his younger days. He made friends easily and took to the military camaraderie. Named to the honor guard, he fondly remembered marching with the Fiesta Queen's float in the Battle of Flowers parade and standing guard at the Alamo. A country boy who possessed physical strength and a competitive spirit, he excelled in athletics and became a close friend of the Peacock family. Colonel Peacock, one of the sons of the school's founder, made several hunting trips to the ranch. The institution came to an end in 1973 (it is now the home of the Salvation Army), but the school lives on in our family photo albums, and in those of many other old ranch families in Texas.

Dad's school years were not continuous, or else he was not a very diligent student, as he completed his senior year at Ozona High School in 1933 at the age of twenty-one. His best grades were in physical education—a natural athlete, he was a star on the football team and a member of the first OHS basketball team—and English literature. His performance in the latter was no doubt enhanced by the fact that he dated the teacher, a charming young lady about his age.

While in school, he "boarded out" with the Phillips family and was kindly treated by Mrs. Phillips. The Phillipses were Crockett County ranchers whose children were Arthur, Hillary, William (Babe), Lela Mae, and Emma Lou, most of whom were Dad's contemporaries.

During the summers in the early thirties, Dad worked for area ranchers performing any type of labor necessary to make a ranch function, from building fences and pens to working sheep and cattle. One of his most interesting jobs was driving sheep from Ozona to Barnhart, at the time a major shipping center. The route followed was called the Ozona-Barnhart trap, a corridor developed to allow the livestock to be driven some thirty-four miles without crossing fences or destroying the range. The Ozona-Barnhart Trap Company purchased or leased the land involved in 1924. Although the trap saw steady use for several years, the popularity of the drives dwindled with the advent of trucking. During the peak years, huge numbers of sheep were shipped from Barnhart. Twenty-nine boxcars were loaded in Barnhart in one day without making a dent in the number of sheep pouring through the trap.

During the drives, which took several days, Dad said the ewes and lambs were separated, and at night the air was filled with the sounds of the bleating mothers searching for their lambs under the vast West Texas skies. The arrival at Barnhart pumped energy into the tired riders as they drove their charges into holding pens or helped load them onto the waiting railroad cars, knowing that the little town held the novelty of rooming houses, hotels, and small cafes, with new people to meet and talk to and tales to share. The breaks were short, however, as the young men, many of them Ozona High School students, were needed for another drive, so after a night's rest in one of the hotels and a good meal or two, they'd mount up and point their horses homeward.

Active both in school and outside, Joe made many friends in those days. The families of Ozona welcomed him as one of their own. He was invited to all the lively functions in the small town and was honored at graduation parties. In fact, he received more support from these friends than from his own family. Joe's parents were not physically present in the life of their youngest son, and, although Dad was the only Chandler child to receive a high school diploma, not one member of his family attended his graduation ceremony.

During all this time, the presence of Joe's stepmother at the ranch undoubtedly made him feel as if he had no home there. A humorless woman, Ima Lou rarely smiled or took pleasure in anything. She served as cook, laundrywoman, housekeeper, babysitter, schoolteacher, and maid; these roles seemed to bring her little pleasure, and her situation was no doubt worsened by the fact that she was resented as the usurper of my Grandad's affection. If Grandad had married this younger woman to take care of him in his older years, a woman who addressed him as "Dear" and served him dutifully until he died, he chose well. Perhaps she felt that becoming Mrs. Chandler, rancher's wife, rather than Miss Echols, single woman, was worth the price.

Ima Lou was barely tolerated by the first daughters-in-law in the family. Once, after a disagreement over a pie pan, one of them attempted to stab her with an ice pick. Dad's intervention saved her; I don't know what happened to the pie pan.

My mother was a rarity, one of the few distaff members of the family who got along with Ima Lou. But then I never heard of anyone that Mom didn't get along with. Her easygoing, passive ways granted her exemption from familial turmoil and made everyone think she was on their side.

Ima Lou's methods of pedagogy suited her well. In her classroom, there was no delight in learning, no challenge, no reward. She was not there to inspire. We did as we were told during a short school day and followed a curriculum dictated by the Terrell County School District in Sanderson.

We started our quest for education in a one-room tin building located within spitting distance of Grandad's house. It was under a huge sycamore tree near the ditch that flowed from the springs in the hill through the yard and to the fields. But the little building burned one day after Grandad set some brush fires and then drove off to Sanderson with Dad. (This occurred when I was in second or third grade; by then our family had moved from the Stavley Place to the ranch on the creek, about a mile away from Grandad's, and we were living with our parents once again.)

Both Grandad and Dad burned dead brush and grass in the fields and pastures every winter. They didn't know they were practicing what was later recognized as an ecological method of brush control, but they did know that in the spring the grass grew back brighter and thicker and the livestock had more to graze. (The term used now is "controlled burning." Though there was nothing controlled about the Chandler approach, from across the years I can say that it worked and the land benefited.)

On this particular afternoon, the flames were whipped up by wind, and when we went to the main house to eat at noon, the little schoolhouse began to burn. The strange snapping sound from the vicinity of the school interrupted our meal before we smelled the smoke. From the porch we could see the blaze. "Run and get Mildred," Ima Lou commanded, and without asking for a moment what Mildred could do, I ran as fast as my legs could carry me. By the time my mother and I returned, the building was a smoldering mound of ruin and ashes. I breathed a sigh of relief, thinking my education was finished.

Our reprieve was short-lived, however. The Sanderson school system delivered books and desks, and we were back in business in what seemed like the blink of an eye. The furniture in the back bedroom was moved out of the house, and our lessons were held there until we made the move to town several years later.

An insert from the *McCamey News,* from September 1946, describes our unusual school:

> I want to tell you about a schoolmarm old timey Texas style. This schoolmarm has only ten students in her school, yet she teaches the first through the eighth grade. The school is in the family ranch house, one room serving as a spare bedroom during school months. This schoolmarm buys all her school supplies, paying for them out of her salary, which is something like $100 per month. It isn't necessary that this particular schoolmarm teach school. She and her husband are moderately wealthy. They have a greater sum in worldly goods than most. Perpetual springs of clear, cold, pure water flow from their land; wild turkeys and deer feed within a few yards of their door; tame ducks, guinea hens and fat hogs walk underfoot; figs, dates, and peaches grow in their orchard; their land is stocked with a goodly number of wool-bearing sheep. No, this schoolmarm is not lacking in worldly goods. Yet, each fall she takes down the big bed and moves it, along with dresser and chairs, into storage; and the bedroom becomes a seat of learning. All winter long she cooks for her family, as most ranch wives do, and teaches the little group of young Texans, and when school's end rolls around for another summer I should imagine that it is with regret that this schoolmarm says: "Class dismissed." This writer says, a Texas orchid to Mrs. Charles Chandler, Schoolmarm, Texas Style.

Modern educational methods were not applied in our little one-room school. We concentrated heavily on the three Rs, with a smattering of geography and history for the upper grades. We had no art, physical education, or music classes, although on rare occasions Ima Lou would crank up the Victrola and play some records for us. Our visual aids consisted of a globe of the world, the most interesting item in the room.

We had no indoor bathroom, and the run for the one-hole outhouse, complete with Sears and Montgomery Ward catalogs, was the first thing we did during recess. And we did run, especially if the weather was cold or rainy.

During recess, we played hide-and-seek, Red Rover, and other games of our own making, or we stood around or sat under the huge pecan and sycamore trees growing on the irrigation ditch and pretended. "Play like," it was called, and it did add some excitement to our days as we assumed the parts of characters and made up stories. For Christmas, we happily cut strips of green and red paper, glued them into chains, and decorated the classroom, and that was about it. I don't remember our extended family observing any of the other holidays that drive children into frenzies now. Certainly, the various generations of the Chandler family never sat around a turkey dinner Norman Rockwell–style.

Occasionally, on very cold days, Ima Lou would prepare warm Jell-O for us to drink during our breaks. We thought it was a real treat. On very hot days, we sweltered and drank cool spring water from the tin dipper hanging from the faucet in the front yard.

JoBeth and I walked or rode our bicycles to school most of the time after we moved to the ranch from the Stavley Place. We usually stopped off at a huge mesquite tree to enjoy a break in the shade on warm days. Our schoolmates varied from year to year depending on what families were working on neighboring ranches. Some I remember best were the Rogers and McElhaney brothers, who lived at the Hicks Ranch, and Janella and Juanita Morris, whose father worked for the county and lived at the head of Independence. But Virginia, JoBeth, and I were the mainstays.

Junior Rogers tells the story of how he and his younger brother, Butch, loved Grandad's hunting days. Grandad would burst into the classroom, shouting, "Ima Lou, I need those boys." Rescued from their lessons, the brothers would then run to help track a wounded buck or unload a deer from the trunk of the car.

The most pleasurable part of the day that I remember was Ima Lou's reading aloud to us after dinner. She read a chapter a day, leaving us with a cliffhanger at the end. My favorite books were *Elsie Dinsmore, Anne of Green Gables,* and all of Louisa May Alcott's works. We wept as Beth in *Little Women* became too weak to hold her needle and died, we hated the neglect

Elsie suffered at the hands of her father, and Anne was our heroine because of her plucky spirit. I also spent many hours living vicariously in the world of the *Bobbsey Twins* and *The Yearling.*

Since Moo read aloud in her low monotone to Grandad before naptime in the summer also, I listened in on all the westerns of Zane Grey, and then reread them several times on my own. Our book supply was so limited that I am sure I read everything we owned more than once, but I never was bored. All I wanted when my parents returned from one of their many trips was another book. Comic books and movie magazines were also treasured treats.

Mom was an avid reader, and she allowed me to read *Forever Amber,* which was considered shocking at that time but wouldn't bring a blush to the most innocent cheek now. She probably thought I couldn't understand it, and she was right, as I went back to the Bobbsey Twins right away.

At the end of my seventh-grade year, the Terrell County School District made a decision that had great impact on our lives. Our little school, along with the Dryden school, was to close; it was too costly to operate for so few students. So that chapter ended, but it would have soon regardless. I was now ready to enter the eighth grade and a new school. Jenny would go to school in Abilene, and JoBeth and I were headed to Iraan.

With no pomp or circumstance whatever, our education at the ranch was over and the Terrell County Independence School closed its doors, writing finis to a way of life for the children in the area.

WHY MY PARENTS CHOSE Iraan for our move into higher education is not clear. With so many Stavleys living in Sanderson and with Dad's many friends and good memories of Ozona, either of those small towns would have been a logical choice. But Iraan it was.

Without the oil underneath it, there would not have been a town of Iraan. It was named after Ira and Ann Yates, the owners of the land where oil was discovered in 1926. Subsequently, the Yates Field turned into one of the largest producers in the nation and put Iraan on the map for those knowledgeable of the oil industry. Samuel D. Myres, historian and author of *The Permian Basin,* notes that "the fact that the field had yielded more than a half billion barrels of oil and that it continued to produce in excess of twelve million barrels annually—after forty-six years of steady production—mark it as one of the great oil fields of all time. In prolific output and long life, Yates is truly a phenomenon of the first order."

At first, the town consisted of tents and rough shacks thrown up to accommodate the roughnecks and other workers who flowed in to seek their fortunes. When the Yates family donated the land for the town of Iraan, one of the stipulations was that the streets would be wide enough to accommodate the movement of drilling rigs and other equipment. To this day, the wide streets of the small town are unusual among the communities of West Texas.

When I see the Safety First sign made of white-washed rocks on the hill behind the school, I think about life in a small oil town in those days and wonder how it must have been. It was filled with hardship and inconvenience for everyone, men and women alike, but it also had its rewards. Myres describes the early days in McCamey, but could just as easily have been writing about Iraan: "A spirit of relaxation and camaraderie usually prevailed among the people. In almost all respects, they were equal: their Anglo-American background was the same, as were also their social standards and ways of life. In a sense, they formed one large family, open and friendly in their relations, enjoying the freedoms of a frontier society, stimulated by the daily news of gushers coming in and wealth being produced in abundance."

The boom was mostly finished by the time we got to town, but the friendly spirit prevailed. Iraan's peak as a rip-roaring town had come earlier when over 3,000 residents crowded into the Pecos Valley. While life was rough, those times were also marked by excitement and optimism, as each new discovery promised riches for both the landowners and oil companies, and good wages trickled down to the men who did the labor. Some of the charm was lost when times got easier, but Iraan was and still is an oil field town. And because of the five years I went to school there, it became my hometown.

Many men and women with ties to Iraan have become successful in various walks of life, but by the fifties, Iraan could boast of three names that had gained fame beyond its confines.

V. T. Hamlin, an early oilfield employee, envisioned dinosaurs roaming the surrounding hills and created the popular syndicated "Alley Oop" comic strip.

Elithe Hamilton Kirkland, who taught English and history in Iraan in the 1940s, wrote three historical novels that earned recognition nationwide, the most notable being *Love Is a Wild Assault*. First published by Doubleday in 1959, the novel has been translated into both Spanish and German and was serialized in Canada and Germany as well as in three U.S. newspapers. Recently, A. C. Greene listed it in the *The Fifty Best Books on Texas*.

Bud McFadin was a football star for the Braves and the University of Texas Longhorns, where he was named Iraan's first and only All-American, and later went on to play professional football. I didn't know the first two celebrities, but Bud was a frequent visitor to the ranch during his high school years.

Two other football players, Billy Pete Huddleston and Lloyd Hale, upperclassmen when I was in the eighth grade, gained recognition of another sort. Both were survivors of the infamous Texas A&M football camp at Junction. Perhaps this is not a claim to national fame, but in Texas it means something.

The Seals brothers, Jimmy and Dan, of rock-music fame are not on this list of Iraan notables because, as I was told, "Them Seals boys were the greatest celebrities Iraan ever produced, but ole Wayland [their dad] up and moved them to Rankin."

The majority of the student body in Iraan was made up of the children of employees of various oil companies, which have all now been bought out or merged into Marathon Oil Company. At that time, camps were maintained by Ohio and Mid-Kansas, which had four each, and by Shell and Gulf, which had two each, according to Mayme Young, who served as teacher and superintendent's secretary for an amazing tenure of over forty-five years.

My contemporaries were wonderful young men and women, and I was fortunate to have known them. They, and the school we attended together, represent a way of life built upon a solid foundation of American values. In retrospect, I can't imagine a better place or time to have spent my teen years than Iraan in the fifties.

We were not the first Chandler children to go to school in Iraan, as Uncle

Clarence and Aunt Lillie began taking their four children in from the ranch several years before JoBeth and I started. My cousins Mary Ellen, Clarence Jr., Gene, and Glynn were driven in every day by Aunt Lillie. She was the first of the Chandler daughters-in-law, a lovely soft-spoken lady with gracious ways. She still fits that description today at the age of ninety-two.

Clarence Jr., always called Brother, took over the driving as soon as he was old enough, at the grand age of twelve. He drove his older sister and two younger brothers to Sheffield each morning. From there, they took the bus into Iraan. This drive was much more arduous then than now, with unpaved roads, no air conditioning, and uncomfortable automobiles. Flat tires were common.

The two McGilvray girls, Jessie and Tootsie, Uncle Alvin and Aunt Kat's children, also went to school in Iraan during a brief period but finished high school in San Angelo. Aunt Iva, known as Sister, lived in San Angelo and sent her two boys, Sonny and Curtis, to school there. (These family names—an aunt named Sister, cousins called Brother and Sonny, sometimes Sonny Boy—identify us as real Texans. We're country people, and country people like those names.)

In Iraan Dad had rented us a small shotgun-style house behind the First Baptist Church and only a couple of blocks from the school. This nondescript, flimsy, white wooden building was called the Petty House and was a common type in the rough little boomtown. The name derives from the fact that you could have fired straight through it with a shotgun because all the rooms were in a line from front to back. The modest house consisted of a front room that served as a bedroom–living room for Mom, JoBeth and me, a short hallway with a bathroom, and a kitchen–dining room in the back.

Thus started a pattern of the three of us moving into Iraan each fall and going to the ranch every weekend and summer, while Dad struggled to make ends meet at the ranch. We were not so poor that we didn't know where our next meal was coming from, but we had little in the way of extra material possessions. I don't know how Dad paid the rent and utilities on the little house in addition to affording the extras that living in town involved.

There was little in the way of social hierarchy in the community, as far as whose father did what for a living. Practically everyone depended on the

Yates Field for an income. Most wage earners, many of whom were transients who followed the rigs, worked for one of the many drilling companies or for small businesses supported by the oil field.

And they had their own jargon. In Iraan new words entered my vocabulary, mysterious, powerful-sounding words. Men worked as *wildcatters, toolpushers, roughnecks,* and *roustabouts.* They used terms like *doghouse, morning tower,* and *graveyard; Christmas trees, derricks,* and *rigs.* Their work involved *fishing jobs, lowering casing,* and *skidding rigs.* It all sounded intriguing to me.

My friends' fathers worked for various oil companies and mostly lived in camps outside of town, but they were the settled ones. Others, and it seemed somehow romantic, packed up every so often and pursued their work in an itinerant fashion. They constantly moved from one small West Texas oil town to another. "We used to live in Crane," they'd say. Or Wink. Or Rankin. Or McCamey. Or anywhere the next job beckoned.

Few married women had jobs outside the home, other than the teachers at our school. Most were not expected to bring in a second income, and might have been considered unusual if they did. I did not have a friend whose mother had a "career," other than teaching or helping run a family business. We took it for granted that our mothers would be at home when we got there after a day at school.

Mom broke that mold one year by teaching tap dancing and ballet in a small building that Dad bought behind our second home in town. This activity lasted only a year, when the building was moved to the ranch and converted into a cabin, appropriately called the Dance Studio. Some of her students were children of the town's only doctor, Vincent Sherrod, and his two boys amused her when they rebelled. "We want to do the dancing where you put your arms around a girl," they informed her. She persevered, and all her students performed in a recital at the school auditorium at the end of the year.

Iraan was not totally alien territory for us when we moved there. Going to town on a Sunday afternoon to see a movie was a regular treat for us when we were younger. For me and JoBeth, there was no more enchanting place than the Texas Theater, where Hollywood entered our lives and dreams. After escaping into another world for a couple of hours, our family would have huge hamburgers and greasy french fries at the Lunch Kit Café, sometimes followed by a root beer float at the Corner Drug, and then drive home sated, the four of us packed into Dad's GMC pickup truck.

We had also gotten our first taste of live entertainment in Iraan when the Plunkett Show came to town. The immense tent erected on the town square was as magical as any Broadway theater, and the traveling show performed by the musical Plunkett family kept us and all of Iraan on the edge of our seats. We were so enthralled that we returned several nights in a row.

The teenaged daughter of the family, Jerry Plunkett, became my idol. I could imagine no life more glamorous that that of this lovely blonde girl, who was not much older than I was. Entrancing in her little white cowboy boots and jaunty white hat, she crooned romantic country love songs. She probably never knew how much she affected our young lives, spreading sophistication and dreams and giving us a glimpse of another world.

During those years, there were other musical events in our lives. Grandad's front porch became the scene for many impromptu fiddle concerts by Jimmy Seals of Rankin, who later became half the duo of Seals and Crofts. Jimmy could not have been over five or six years old at the time he began to play for us, but he would grab that fiddle and tune up and entertain us half the night.

At the age of nine, Jimmy won the state championship fiddling contest, the same year his father became the state champion guitar player. In the sixties and seventies, Seals and Crofts made many albums and were awarded both gold and platinum records, but I doubt that Jimmy Seals ever had a more appreciative audience than the Chandlers assembled on the screened-in porch. Seals said, "One place that I especially remember [in West Texas] is the Chandler Ranch at Sheffield, where we used to go fishing and camping. Dad [Wayland Seals] and I used to play for Mr. Chandler. He loved our music, especially 'Sally Gooden.' Dad was a friend of Roy Chandler's and of all the brothers, Clarence, Herman, and Joe." Both Seals brothers did well in the national music scene, as younger brother Dan became prominent in the world of country music.

We had also gone into Iraan for high school football games for years before we made our move. Dad was an avid football fan and would drive anywhere to see a high school game.

Iraan football has a colorful history. In the early days, according to old stories, Coach (Prof.) Williamson sometimes beefed up his team with roustabouts from the oil fields, enrolling them in a post-graduate high school course created for the purpose of football recruiting. Many of these ringers were grown men who just wanted to play for the home team. One of them was Jelly Alford, whose bald head would shine when he occasionally lost his helmet during the rough play. Some of the players never used helmets, as the school provided only uniforms, and one was known to have played barefooted. These stalwart heroes played in fields composed mostly of rocks and dirt; the letter *I* was earned with blood, sweat, and tears. Obviously, the now powerful University Interscholastic League did not govern early football in West Texas as it does today.

To go in on a Friday evening to watch the mighty Braves play Ozona or Eldorado or Rankin was great entertainment for Dad and his friends, and their celebrating usually ended in one of the beer joints nearby. But JoBeth and I knew what the real show was, and that was halftime. In the shaky wooden bleachers at the old football field, we sat through the first half, eagerly awaiting the appearance of the Iraan High School Band. The final scene of *The Music Man* always reminds me of the thrilling entrance onto the field of the red-clad musicians, led by the drum major in a tall white hat, who was followed by the loveliest and luckiest girls in the universe, the majorettes.

The cheerleaders were admired, but they did not match the radiance of the majorettes performing their intricate routines for the dazzled girls from Terrell County. Asking Mom and Dad for batons would have been pushing our luck, but we persuaded Dad to produce the closest facsimile he could. With two lengths of thin sawed-off pipe, we pranced up and down the dirt road in front of the house, twirling to our hearts' content as we pretended that the scarlet-coated Iraan band was stepping along just behind us. Our elbows were perpetually covered with bruises, but it was no matter—one must suffer for one's art—and we marched on.

For Christmas that year, two long, thin, cylindrical packages miraculously appeared under the tree. Santa had found us down on the creek and brought the gift we most desired. JoBeth later did gain one of those coveted majorette positions, both in high school and later at Texas Tech, but, alas, I never knew the thrill of leading the high school band onto the field.

IF MY FIRST DAY of school at the ranch was unnerving, my first day in Iraan seven years later can only be described as daunting. The old three-story building with the fire escape slide outside the third floor, long gone now, filled my mind with foreboding for days before we actually made the move. It was even more frightening when I actually entered its hallowed halls.

Clutching my schedule—first period, study hall with Mr. Charles Skipping—I slowly approached the first flight of stairs. There were other students there, people my age, but they were talking and laughing with each other in a way that let me know I was a country kid out of my element. The girls were all pretty (some of them even wore lipstick) and the boys handsome with their crew cuts and letter jackets; they belonged here. How would I ever fit in? The climb to the third-floor study hall loomed ahead of me ("I wish I were at the creek," I thought). First flight accomplished, I tackled the second ("What am I doing here?"), and then the third ("I want to go back to the ranch, I'm not dressed right, I'm not smart enough!").

I found a seat in the back row. All the students were deadly silent as the roll was called, but then a young man near me leaned over to whisper something. I never learned what he was going to say because Mr. Skipping leapt from his chair and barreled down the length of the room. Grabbing my neighbor by both shoulders, he shook him until his teeth rattled. Not a word was said as we all buried our noses in our books. If I had been intimidated going up those stairs, I was even more so going back down them.

The library was also on the third floor, and my first sight of all the books left me in a state of awe. I didn't know there were that many books in the world. Classrooms were on the second floor. There I encountered sophisticated Mrs. Jolly in English and knowledgeable Mr. McEwen in math, and later worldly Mr. Graham in social studies, gracious Mrs. Ballard in home economics, and self-assured Mrs. Reynolds in typing and shorthand. Then came Miss White and Mrs. Jerome, journalism teachers, mentors, and role models, who introduced me to another new world.

The gym occupied the first floor, and the rest of the campus was made up of the band hall and auditorium, the home economics building, and the football field. The elementary school sat nearby like a friendly neighbor, along with a small cafeteria, where motherly ladies dished out real food, including fluffy, made-from-scratch yeast rolls, whose aroma drove us crazy during the hour before lunch.

Leldon Clifton was superintendent, Jack Black was the principal, and Mayme Young was the school secretary. There were coaches all over the place, including Jones, Kitchens (who wrote the school song), Smith, and Burnett. Bill Tregoe was the band director.

The faculty at Iraan were the first adults I had contact with other than family, and they were the best. I can't think of one of them who didn't have a positive influence on me. They were professional, personable, and dedicated. (And to give the formidable Mr. Skipping credit, he headed the science department at Iraan—no, he was the science department in Iraan—and, although he ran a tight ship, he was never anything but fair to me and my classmates.) However, there was a certain formality or distance between teachers and students. What a surprise to learn they actually had first names and lives of their own and didn't sleep overnight in their classrooms, rising to greet us eagerly each morning.

As I was adjusting to eighth grade, JoBeth was making quite an impression in the fifth grade with her coonskin cap, fringed buckskin jacket, and friendly, outgoing ways. Eventually, my initial culture shock eased. Kindness from both faculty members and schoolmates made the transition easier, but my reserve stayed with me for all my school days.

The old three-story high school building was soon to become a thing of the past as a new high school and elementary school were built when I was in ninth grade. I remember every phase of the construction because C. L. Cunningham of Odessa, the building contractor, and his wife lived at the ranch during that period. The new building, one floor only, was constructed symbolically in the shape of an upper case I.

The academic transition for me, in that old building that smelled like a school is supposed to smell, was easier than the social one, as Ima Lou had prepared me to the best of her ability and mine. In any case, academic performance didn't seem to matter a great deal at the time. Good grades were nice, but not paramount, especially for girls. In fact, the kiss of death was to be labeled "too smart for her own good."

Slowly, I began to make friends with some of the girls. When Gayla Cauthen, Mary Alice Anderson, Jane Meyer, and Leta Sconiers asked me if I wanted to join the pep squad, I floated back to our little shotgun house on Cloud Nine. As a member of that elite group, I could wear a red skirt and white blouse and ride to out-of-town games on one of those packed yellow school buses, an adventure I had never experienced before. What bliss.

"We're from Iraan, couldn't be prouder, if you can't hear us now, we'll yell a little louder."

Over the next few years, I entered into all the activities that seem so stereotypical of the 1950s now. We decorated the football field goal posts, walked our boyfriends off the field arm-in-arm after games, fell in love regularly and "went steady," wore the boys' senior rings and letter jackets, danced at the Youth Center on Saturday nights, and wore bright, fluffy dresses of net and tulle and satin and sequins, most often made by our mothers, to the proms held in the old Ohio Hall. A notation in my diary in 1953–54 reads: "There were five red dresses at the Band Dance, but mine was the prettiest!" Mom had worked diligently on that dress and many others. She often said that her efforts were out of necessity, but she, a talented seamstress, truly enjoyed the creative effort involved.

"Memories are made of this," Dean Martin sang. But the times, of course, were not all good. I was vaguely aware that outside my little world there was war, crime, social injustice, segregation, and inequality for both women and minorities, but, in truth, I possessed little understanding then of the victims of racial injustice or other social ills. Our little space on the planet seemed wrapped in pink cotton candy, safely insulated from darker realities. I doubt if I could have named the president of the United States, but I knew the Braves' football schedule by heart.

After a couple of years of living in Iraan, my sister and I went back to boarding out, first with Wanda and Jim Watts, who ranched out of Bakersfield, and then with Babe and Olin Smith, ranchers out of Sheffield on the other side of Iraan. Both of those hospitable couples treated us as if we were their own, and I will always think of them with gratitude and affection.

It seems strange now, but we were following the pattern of many ranchers who boarded their children with other families for school purposes. Of course, a fee was exchanged, but it could not have been a large sum of money. This arrangement may have added some stress to our lives, and to those of the families we lived with, but it did not seem out of the ordinary at the time.

Mom moved back into town before my junior year in high school, so we returned to being a somewhat traditional family. While my education had begun in a one-room school at the ranch, it ended well for me. I have no feelings of deprivation, rather of privilege. When I finished school in Iraan, I had no idea where I was going, but I knew for sure where my journey had begun.

Chapter Seven

FISHING: THE FOUNDATION

When Zane Grey dipped his pen into Pecos River water, he dreamed up a stalwart, quick-on-the-trigger, slow-talkin' cowboy named Pecos and his lovely violet-eyed girlfriend, who disguised herself as a young man throughout most of the story because . . . well, you'll have to read West of the Pecos.

Together, these gallant protagonists had great adventures in the rugged hills and canyons of West Texas, adding to the now hyped mystique of the river.

When I put my hand into the same water, I pull up . . . catfish. Big cats, blue cats, yellow cats, channel cats, slick and shiny, with flipping tails and twitching whiskers. And I think of all the baited hooks and baited hopes, the aspirations of those who cast them into the deep holes, including my great-grandparents O'Bryant, who made a fishing trip to the ranch with their daughter Minerva and snagged a son-in-law.

WHILE THE HEROES of Zane Grey were only dreams, fishermen were a reality in our lives, a big part of the ranch and the river and all who settled along its banks. Bountiful Independence Creek and the deeper and longer Pecos River, which starts its 900-mile run to the Rio Grande in the mountains of New Mexico, have attracted fishermen for years. The shady oak trees and the scenic beauty of the Independence Valley, in particular, made the ranch an irresistible attraction for those who loved the outdoors. It was a baited hook that drew fishermen from miles around.

Bass and perch, along with the unwanted carp, suckers, gars, and eels, were abundant in both streams, but catfish were the big attraction and always the most sought-after catch. A story from *Land, Oil, and Education* by Berte R. Haigh, geologist for University Lands, relates a most unusual method of obtaining the big cats that lay along the muddy bottom of the river and the clear holes in the creek in the early days:

> In 1934 a crew was beginning the survey of four blocks in Terrell County. The starting point of the survey was an old established and recognized marker near the confluence of Independence Creek with the Pecos River. Independence Creek is a clear running stream that originates in a large spring located in Terrell County about five miles south of University Block 35. It flows eastward across the county and joins the Pecos River approximately 30 miles south of Sheffield located in Pecos County. About that time the Pecos River was running high from storms up the stream, and the water was muddy. The clear water of Independence Creek was entering the Pecos with considerable volume and creating a delta-shaped wedge of mud-free water that extended a considerable distance into the muddy Pecos. The wedge was filled with a mass of mud-fleeing fish, mostly catfish. The survey crew grabbed up tools and waded out into that clear water wedge, killing fish with axes and hammers. Enough fish were thus "caught" to nearly fill the bed of the crew's pickup truck and were transported to a nearby ranch where they were cleaned and canned.

The *Sanderson Times,* the newspaper of Terrell County, has run many early photos of camping, fishing, swimming, and wading in the creek, and the creek crops up in many tales in the county's history. It was always a popular recreational area despite the isolation and distance involved. There are few families that claimed the Trans-Pecos as home in the early half of the twentieth century who did not at some time journey to the creek.

Grandad never envisioned making any money from camping or fishing at the creek. He made his living from ranching, and that's what he was, a rancher. Even as a pastime, camping and fishing did not hold any allure for him. He had no hobbies, other than gardening when he grew older, and didn't know what the term *recreation* meant. As he grew older, he passed

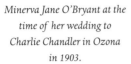
Minerva Jane O'Bryant at the time of her wedding to Charlie Chandler in Ozona in 1903.

The Chandler place around 1912. This house on the lower ranch replaced a primitive picket structure. Charlie and Minerva, holding Herman, are shown with Roy, Clarence, and Iva.

Charlie Chandler on the front porch of his house about 1950. This photograph first appeared on the cover of Frontier Times *in that year.*

Mildred, age sixteen, dressed for a tap dance performance in Sanderson.

Joe as a young cowboy in his early twenties.

Mildred and Joe Chandler, during their courtship, at the Stavley home in Sanderson. She is wearing his senior ring from Ozona High School.

The youngest children of the Stavley family with their parents in the newly constructed house in Sanderson in 1940. LEFT TO RIGHT: *Mildred, Ross, Lena, Frank, and Charlie Stavley.*

Showing off new dolls on JoBeth Chandler's third birthday, Mildred, JoBeth, and Charlena pose in front of a GMC truck at the Stavley place north of Dryden.

The author, age five (left), with her sister, JoBeth, and friend Jenny at the confluence of Independence Creek and the Pecos River.

*Mildred and Art Chandler, Charlie's brother, at the creek in 1940.
Note the lack of brush along the banks.*

Jenny and Charlena posing with Charlie and a ranch employee in front of two bucks shot on the ranch in 1946.

Joe with a big buck that he killed on the creek in the early 1950s.

"Letting 'er out." Joe Chandler opens a sluice gate to let fresh springwater into one of his well-stocked fishing lakes.
(Photograph and caption courtesy of the *Odessa American*, 4 August 1955)

Charlena and JoBeth holding a stringer of fish caught in the creek by
Joe and Clarence Chandler Jr., better known as Brother.
(Brother's letter jacket is from Marathon High School.)

Joe and Cleo Preas of
Iraan show off a big
yellow cat, a typical Pecos
River catch. The fish
weighed thirty to thirty-
five pounds. (The number
one tee box can be seen in
the background.)

Charlena on a hillside above Independence Creek valley.

Independence Creek.

Scenes of destruction at the ranch after the flood of 1954.
(Photographs by Johnson's Studio of McCamey)

The rebuilt pool, after the flood, in its original location.

Mildred assisting in serving a meal to a group of Tri-Hi-Y members from Odessa about 1960.
(Photograph by Thea-Delle Temple)

The Whetrock Gang of Odessa, which organized tournaments at the ranch for several consecutive years.
(Photograph by Joe Allen of Crane)

Golfers strolling past the canal and cabins on their way to tee off.
(Photograph by Covey Bean, courtesy of the *Odessa American*)

JoBeth and Charlena with Joe at the old wagon wheels near the entrance to the ranch in the mid-1960s.
(Photograph by Covey Bean, courtesy of the *Odessa American*)

Mildred, in typical high spirits, enjoying a visit with guests at the pool in 1966.

many long, drowsy summer afternoons sitting in his favorite chair under the shade of a large pecan tree in the front yard, dressed in his usual khaki shirt and pants with the legs tucked into high-topped black boots.

The fishermen and campers pulling up in front of the house on those quiet afternoons broke the monotony, and Grandad welcomed them sincerely, mainly for the opportunity of a little visit. Some he knew, some he didn't, but it didn't matter. He always refused payment. "Just go on down and have a good time," he'd say. If pressed, he would take a dollar for a week's stay. Of course, he would drive down to see how things were going during their time there and linger for a little more visiting, or they would come back up to the house to chat with "Mr. Charlie." Having these visitors at the ranch was commonplace, something the family grew up with and took for granted.

Some of those fishermen came so often that they seemed a part of the ranch and the family. It would be hard to reminisce about childhood times without thinking of Jess and Anna Morris of Iraan and their children Russell, Rose Mary, and Ruby Lee, who regularly enjoyed lengthy stays camping on the concrete slab. (The slab, the site of the dances during the Chandler Brothers rodeos, became the most popular camping spot on the creek.)

Rose Mary recalls how her dad and mine would make a cooler by digging a hole under the shade trees. They would line the hole with a tarp, fill it with ice, and cover it securely to keep the ice from melting quickly.

Rose Mary and her mother and sister once stayed up all night making blackberry jam after a visit to Grandad and Ima Lou yielded bushels of ripe blackberries. "Those blackberries made wonderful jam, and all the other fruit in the orchard," she said. "There was nothing your Grandad couldn't raise in his backyard orchard, and he loved to give it away to everyone who came down fishing."

What good summer times I remember on the slab, the picnics and fish fries, the long naps on the cots, playing Old Maid and Go Fish with Rose Mary and Ruby Lee, pretty teenagers then, who were often assigned the task of watching after me and JoBeth while the adults fished or made trips into town. We spent many long mornings and slow afternoons swimming and playing in the creek, with the breeze spreading cool relief and whispering through the leaves of the oaks.

I DON'T KNOW if visionary is the right term to use for Dad, but obviously the timing was right when he decided that there might be some profit in catering to the campers and fishermen. When we moved to the ranch from the Stavley Place sometime around 1945, Grandad had started dividing his land among his children. He kept only the Home Place for himself and Ima Lou. He also broke up the fields, giving each child a long, narrow portion of farmland between the creek and river.

It's an old story with farmers and ranchers of our country. One piece of land, too many children, and with each generation, more division and more difficulties, both personal and financial.

I don't know how Grandad arrived at his decisions or how much land each child received. Nor do I know how much land he owned, although Marvin Hunter's article in the *Frontier Times* gave the size of the original ranch as 18 sections. Grandad's obituary in the *San Angelo Standard-Times* said that he eventually owned 34 sections. I never knew, never heard it mentioned, never thought about it.

(It's no more polite to ask a rancher how much land he or she owns than to ask someone how much money he or she makes. Yet traditional Texas etiquette holds it as unmannerly to answer such questions as to ask them. Consequently, ranchers have learned to evade questions like "How big is that place?" as politely as possible. The answer "not as big as it used to be" has become as mythic in its reticence as the Texas of Edna Ferber's *Giant*.)

I'm not sure why Dad got the land he did, the area of the old goat camp at the entrance to the ranch, and the site of the Church of Christ encampment, but that's the way it worked out. We've often repeated the story that Dad was the last to receive since he was the youngest son, and that was all that was left. True or not, he gratefully took what was given and began to transform the use of the land. From the time he started to realize that recreation was marketable, we were never the average ranch family again. For better or worse, the place became a guest ranch, and we never went back to being real ranchers again.

While Dad was leaving ranching to earn a living in another way, our friends and neighbors were still struggling through the long-lasting drought. As late as January 1952, according to an article in the *San Angelo Standard-Times,* those who depended on rainfall continued to suffer: "Almost 400 ranch people from all over West Texas gathered here Monday for the Texas Production Credit Association meeting. But the principal subject was not loans or credit. It was dry weather, heavy feeding and short cattle and sheep numbers. On every hand, from almost every part of West Texas, the story was the same. Ranchmen told of livestock numbers cut 25 to 50 percent. They told of constant heavy feeding, high feed prices and the difficulty of getting enough feed at any price."

All the reasons for making the move back to the Chandler Ranch added up. My parents were young and healthy, and both had the kind of personalities that would make them likable hosts. The ranching industry was at one of its lowest ebbs, and in addition, the debt from the Stavley Place was pressing and had to be reckoned with.

So, one of the biggest decisions in Dad's life was made because of the drought. He said in an interview in his later years, "I loved ranching and would have stayed with it if it had rained." He told a reporter for *West Texas Livestock Weekly,* "We'll be back in it someday. We love the ranch business. But we want to get back in on a little different basis, where we don't have to borrow money every year just to pay the interest."

I disagree with William O. Douglas, author of *Farewell to Texas,* who wrote in 1967: "The land continues to depreciate. The time may come when present owners (and their bankers) will want to be 'bailed out.' It is probably only then that the land can be put to its highest use—recreation." It would seem to me that the highest use of the land must be agriculture, if citizens are to be fed and clothed. However, recreation and preservation also have to be considered, as it becomes more difficult to farm and ranch, except for those fortunate few who possess oil and gas resources. More than fifty years after we made our move back to the creek, ranchers are turning to other uses of the land, such as tourism and development, not always by choice but from necessity. I feel a certain nostalgia here, as an old way of life slowly disappears, but also admiration for the resilience and ingenuity of the ranching community.

In addition to the decline in the ranching industry, the oil boom in the Permian Basin also played a role in my parents' successful move into recreation. The oil industry throughout West Texas was flourishing, with a wave of big money bringing prosperity to every bank and small business in the area. The crest was reached in the early 1980s when, with OPEC controlling the oil market, the price of crude went to thirty-five dollars a barrel. During the forty or so years before the boom reached its peak, the working man in the Permian Basin was earning enough to take his family on weekend camping trips.

I don't believe Dad ever had a great epiphany about the project. He never said, "I have a dream of building a guest ranch." We didn't even use the term *guest ranch* until much later. We started as a fishing camp, and that was the basis for everything else that followed.

Between 1945 and 1950, Dad embarked on several major projects at the ranch. One of the first was the construction of a swimming pool, which he said he built for me and JoBeth, but we were pretty content with swimming in the creek. His brother-in-law from Sanderson, Francis Mansfield, who was married to Mom's oldest sister, Bertha, was in the construction business, and he brought down a crew with a cement mixer to build the walls and foundation after a bulldozer dug out a hole. The idea was to fill the pool using the irrigation ditch, which was full of creek water that had been diverted from Independence about a mile up into the Hicks Ranch, with full cooperation from both Hicks and subsequent owner Bill Roden. The plan was to build the pool just below the ditch, insert a large pipe with a cutoff valve to fill the pool, and then drain it back into the creek via another large pipe in the bottom end when it was time to be cleaned.

It was simple and it worked. Knowing nothing of filter systems or chlorination, Dad built a beautiful spring-fed pool that served as the center of the business until the flood destroyed it in 1954. (It was later rebuilt in the same spot.) When he started this project, some of his family members were skeptical.

"Joe, can you build a pool?"

"Hell, I can build anything."

Knowing that campers and fishermen always needed bait and supplies, he next built a small store out of cinder block he made himself and stocked it with all kinds of goods including live bait and stink bait, canned goods, Coleman fuel, candy bars, and "Cokes," which in Texas means any type of bottled soft drink. Our best-selling drink was not always Coca-Cola but sometimes Delaware Punch, Big Red, Orange Crush, or the ever popular Dr Pepper, a longtime favorite in the Lone Star state.

We never sold beer, although we could have gotten a license and "made a mint," as many advised us. It was a wise decision. Selling alcohol on the premises would have changed the entire atmosphere of the ranch. It was a place for families and family recreation. That's not to say people who came to camp, fish, or later golf didn't bring their own drinks, but they knew it was not available at the ranch and that Dryden was the nearest "wet" stop if the supply ran low. While there were those who enjoyed a drink, school organizations, Boy Scouts, Girl Scouts, and church groups outnumbered the drinkers by a long shot. (Years later, some of our lessees obtained a liquor license and sold beer for a short period of time.)

And now to the most important merchandise, bait. The original Chandlers in England sold candles, but we sold worms and minnows and also the less attractive blood bait, stink bait, cut bait, chicken liver and gizzards, and even canned corn—anything that could be put on a hook. Regardless of the goods, we were still merchants at heart.

We bought the worms from various suppliers, including a mail-order business called Rex Worm Ranch, and then Dean Watson in Iraan, and later Alex Castaneda in Sheffield. We had a worm bed in the front yard where most of our normal friends had flowerbeds. We kept it full of cool, moist soil for the night crawlers, earthworms, and red wigglers.

We trapped the minnows ourselves. We seined them with a long net attached to two poles, with one person on each end, always working upstream. One person remained stationary while the other moved in toward the bank for the catch. Then we ran as fast as we could with the minnow bucket to get them to the vat in front of the store.

We also "jarred" the minnows. This job involved putting bait, crackers or dry dog food, into clear glass Mason jars with lids designed for the entry of the minnow. The jars were filled with water and pushed firmly into the gravel of the creek with the lids pointing downstream. I could do this in my sleep today, even though it's been a coon's age, as country folks say.

Once inside, the minnows could not escape. It was a simple operation that worked when they were "jarring." I never figured out why they swam into the jars some days and ignored them on others. But I do remember the thrill of holding up a jar full of shiners against the blue sky and seeing the sunlight bounce off their darting silvery bodies in the clear water.

One of the minnows we sold was the proserpine shiner *(Notropis proserpinus)*, a rare species prized by conservationists, but ignorance was on our side. We seined them and jarred them and sold them, and it seems their number has not diminished, so I believe we did little damage.

A barracks building was moved in at about the same time the store was built to provide the first recreation room with our first pool table. A bathhouse was built by the pool, along with the first two cabins, all built of the homemade cinder block.

All the buildings, including the house we lived in, were white with red roofs, and they formed a little cluster around the pool. This painted a pretty picture under the huge oak trees, and it wasn't long until we actually had paying guests. The structures were utilitarian, but the natural beauty of the setting more than made up for their lack of elegance. In fact, the ruggedness of the buildings added to the atmosphere. We did offer indoor bathrooms, hot and cold running water, and a stove and refrigerator in the kitchen, quite a step up from camping on the riverbank.

"Daddy, what are you building?"

"Just wait and see, girls. I can build anything."

The first lake, as we called it, was constructed in the late forties. It was really more of a pond, but we are Texans and given to exaggeration. We also call the hills surrounding the ranch mountains.

The dam was built by a crew of four to six men from Odessa, and we had the responsibility of feeding several of them until the job was done. Mom was recuperating from major surgery, and the job of camp cook fell to me even though I could not have been more than eleven or twelve. JoBeth and I were still going to school at the ranch, so I would return home each afternoon and head for the kitchen. The men were kind enough not to complain, or at least not to me, and they survived without any drastic results.

I got up early and, with Dad's help, prepared a big breakfast for our boarders. He cooked for them at noon, in addition to working alongside the crew. Then a bountiful supper had to be ready for those workers at the end of the day. Those must have been exhausting times, but there was an air of adventure about everything we did then, and we just plowed ahead from one project to the next.

The end result of all the physical work and expense was a scenic little body of water set like a pale blue Easter egg in the Independence Valley. It had the cleanest and clearest water for miles around and was a real oddity in our arid area. Dad stocked the pond with the help of the state of Texas, and it proved to be a great attraction for anglers, along with the creek and the river. Dad constructed two more ponds later, one below the original and one across the creek. (Grandad was ahead of him in this venture as he had built a pond years before where the springs flowed out of the hill above his house in the valley.) All this water in the midst of the arid Trans-Pecos made the ranch a blessed oasis.

Dad was happiest when involved with a project, whether building a cabin, constructing a pond, or putting in a field. He was always a farmer and rancher at heart, and for several summers, in addition to everything else he was doing, he decided to raise alfalfa and bale hay in the irrigated fields along the Pecos. Not having the cash available to purchase the necessary equipment, he approached a neighbor and friend, Keith Mitchell, and they worked out an agreement. Keith would buy the equipment and be repaid in bales of hay. After the debt was paid, thousand of bales were taken out of the fields over several years; some went to Grandad, while others were sold to area ranchers.

During this period, farming became an obsession with Dad. He worked from daylight until dark and would not have stopped then if he'd had lights on the tractor, as farmers do today. His boundless energy and self-confidence made for high periods when he thought anything was possible, and it usually was. Moderation was not a word generally applied to my father, in any aspect of his life.

Dad would have been at a loss if asked for his philosophy of life, but he was fond of a few maxims, some borrowed, some original, that became a part of his identity:

> *People who stay in bed all day never amount to anything. ("All day" meant anytime after sunrise.)*
> *Don't like my peaches, don't shake my tree.*

If a man pays you wages, make him a good hand.
I'm a cowboy in cow country.
The sun's gonna shine in my back yard someday.
You can run but you can't hide.
It's hell when it's like that, and it's like that now.

As word spread about our new facilities, more and more people came to the ranch. But Dad's next idea proved to be even more successful than the guest ranch. He formed a club for fishermen. It was called the Independence Lake Club, and a year's membership sold for $25.

I believe this was the first venture of its kind in our area, although ours was not the first recreational ranch. That honor went to the Prude Ranch at Fort Davis, which had a totally different type of operation. The Prudes offered city folks a real ranch atmosphere, complete with horseback riding and cowhand activities. We did have horseback riding at the ranch for a few years, but later let it go since fishermen didn't come to the ranch to be cowboys. We also decided the horses were just too much trouble with everything else going on. (When I use "we," I usually mean "he," as decisions were normally not made by majority vote in our family.) But something else surely took its place, as there was never a lack of activities for the increasing number of guests discovering the ranch.

During the building years, Dad's restless nature pushed him constantly. The end of one project only meant that another could be started. But no small part of my parents' success was their "natural liking for people," as one reporter put it.

In Mom's neatly kept membership book, she listed each new member's name, occupation or company, and address. The various occupations of the first members give an idea of the diversity of those attracted to the ranch. They were business owners, tool pushers, ranchers, farmers, bank presidents, salesmen, geologists, doctors, truck drivers, lawyers, preachers, and men who kept the trains running, literally. They came from all walks of life, but there were two characteristics most of them had: they were family people, and they liked camping and fishing.

The first year's roster, for 1953–54, had over 120 names (which are listed in Appendix B). As I look at those names, many questions arise. How did they decide to invest $25 in a fishing club, obviously a greater amount then than now? How did they hear of us in the first place? How did Dad sell them on the idea? What memories do they and their families have of their times at the ranch? These names represent not only customers but friends. We never advertised; many guests kept returning, and word of mouth brought in new members.

I was recently asked if ranch membership was exclusive. Never. Mildred and Joe were about the most inclusive people I've ever known. However, as one early member told me, there was a certain cachet attached to "belonging" to Chandler's. "It was kind of a special thing to do. . . . We liked to tell our friends we were members of a great fishing club and invite them down with us. Half the time they ended up as members, too. It was a bond, and when we'd get together in town, we'd talk about our latest adventures at the ranch."

During those years, we also started catering to high school groups and private parties. On some weekends and during summer months, as many as 200 high school students and sponsors would visit the ranch at one time. Some of these groups were high school classes, while others were organizations. The latter included Tri-Hi-Y clubs from Odessa, FFA and 4-H members, Boy Scout troops, and church groups from all over the area.

One group from Crane met with tragedy when a young man named Ray Omo fell from one of the lower bluffs on the river. Several young men had gone hiking, and as darkness fell, Ray separated from his friends to take a shortcut. No one actually saw his fall, but when they came to get Dad, their faces told the story.

When Dad arrived on the scene, he realized the young man was dying. Ray was mortally injured, but conscious and praying. Dad knew immediately that Ray could not be moved, so he sent for Uncle Herman and Aunt Myrtle to come and stay on the scene while he drove into Iraan to get medical help. When Dad returned, after carrying Dr. Vincent Sherrod across the river piggyback, Ray was pronounced dead. His mother came down later to see the site where her son had died. This was the most tragic accident and the only death that ever occurred at the guest ranch. It made an impact on all of us and left us with sad memories.

Countless family reunions were held at the ranch during those busy years. It was satisfying to see family groups of several generations enjoying being together in a carefree atmosphere. There were other groups, too, ranging from Parents Without Partners to university classes to teachers and coaches holding workshops.

It would have been an entirely different picture at the ranch without the help of our workers from Mexico, who caught bait and maintained the pool, golf course, cabins, and grounds. Their labor was available and affordable, and it was a mutually beneficial arrangement. The men sent their wages home to their families in Mexico and were well fed, decently housed, and fairly treated by everyone they worked for. Their greatest fear was of the *chotas*, their word for the green-clad officers of the U.S. Border Patrol. We tried to learn their language, and they attempted to learn some words in English. They also made us fine chile and tortillas, and sang "Jalisco" and "Rancho Grande" for us, and we gave them *comida* (food) for their daily board and shiny Brilliantine for their hair and roll-your-own pouches of tobacco, with an occasional pack of Camels thrown in.

Most of our workers were illiterate, and Mom put her Spanish to good use when they received letters from home, which were written by paid writers and began formally with "Mi Estimado Esposo" (my esteemed husband) or "Mi Querido Hijo" (my dear son). Often these letters brought sad news of a sick child, a failing older parent, or the death of a loved one, of empty pantries and loneliness. Dad used to drive these workers back to the bridge in Del Rio and once even took a longtime employee back to his hometown in Mexico, where Dad was a welcome guest in his family's home.

Life at the ranch had a certain rhythm during the spring and summer months. Monday was laundry day. Immense mounds of sheets and towels were stripped from cabins on Sunday evenings and washed in a Maytag. The pieces were individually fed through the wringer with soapsuds flying, rinsed in big tubs of clear water, wrung out twice more, and then hung on long clotheslines near the ditch to dry.

With up to a hundred or more sheets and as many towels, we didn't always have enough line space, so we'd end up with baskets of wet, clean laundry ready to be snapped onto the lines as soon as the first load was dry. The dry climate and plentiful sunshine made this a fairly quick process; if there was a breeze it was even faster. The flapping and billowing of dry sheets on the line signaled lots of activity. They were then taken down, folded, and distributed to the cabins, and another load was hung up to dry.

We didn't consider this much fun. At the end of washday, we felt as if we, too, had been put through a wringer.

Once, at the end of a long Monday, Grandmother and Aunt Bertha, who treasured every drop of water on their dry place, told Mom they couldn't understand why she didn't have a garden. "Just look at all that water going to waste," they said. My tired little mother just smiled, wondering when she would have the time or energy to tend to one more chore. When you take care of people, someone else had to take care of vegetables, she decided.

On Tuesday we started cleaning the cabins and making the beds. This task often continued through Wednesday, depending on the number of cabins that had been rented the weekend before. Everyone knew that Thursday was pool-cleaning and Friday meant filling the pool, cleaning the game room, or clubhouse, as we called it, and the dressing rooms, setting out the minnow jars, bagging ice, restocking the shelves of the little store, and in general everything else we had to do to get ready for company.

Dad always reminded us that these folks weren't coming to see *us* and, to make his point, noted, "We didn't have half so many friends when we lived at the Stavley Place." But we knew better.

Starting early Friday afternoon until Sunday, we checked in river fishermen, rented cabins, sold bait and ice, kept the pool area clean, and enjoyed the company of every living soul who drove over the cattle guard in front of the house. When I was asked if I ever got lonely growing up at the ranch, the answer was negative. Loneliness was not an option.

During busy weekends in the spring, summer, and fall, there could be as many as fifty or sixty vehicles in the camping area, which was open to the public. We started out charging a dollar per person, but inflation hit us, too, and by the time we closed the business in 1990, the charge was five dollars per person and five per vehicle.

Dad normally kept an eagle eye on checked-in vehicles to make sure they were paying customers, but there were exceptions. After Dad's funeral, a man I didn't recognize said to me, "Your daddy was good to me. Once when

I had lost my job and was flat broke, he told me to bring my family and camp on the creek as long as I wanted and he wouldn't charge me a dime. I did, and I never forgot it, either."

Just about dark on Friday and Saturday evenings, Dad loved to drive around the creek and river, just as Grandad used to do, ostensibly to check for poachers, but I think he just loved the sight. So did I. The campfires glowed up and down the banks, and the aroma of cooking food, usually fried fish and potatoes and onions, wafted on the gentle evening breeze as campers of all ages welcomed us to view the catch or hear another fish story or just visit.

It seems that Mom and Dad always had a special fondness for young fishermen.

Mr. Chandler, will you show me how to put this worm on my hook? He won't hold still.

Look at my finger, Mrs. Chandler, my fish bit me.

Mr. Chandler, I only have a nickel. How many minners can I buy?

Look, everybody, I caught a fish. My mom said we'd have to have a big salad to go with it.

Look, Mrs. Chandler . . .

Look, Mr. Chandler . . .

Got a whopper, did you, son?

No, sir, he's a catfish.

The Hundleys of Fort Stockton told the story of giving their children the choice of a trip to Hawaii or a week at the ranch. The ranch won out in a second.

A common surgery performed by Dad, more often than one might imagine, was the removal of a hook from the tender flesh of a fisherman. He would push the barb all the way through and clip it to allow the hook to be pulled out. This type of first aid was finished up with words of comfort and a generous splash of alcohol.

Sarah Schaub, a fishing friend from Odessa, remembers her experience as a patient of this type of surgery. When she showed my dad a hook embedded in the palm of her hand, he asked her if she had any "alcohol." She procured a bottle (of the drinking type), and they each took a swig. The hook was out in no time. "You know," she said, "I hardly felt it." A really deep hook might call for a trip to the emergency room in Iraan, where Dr. Ed Franks would perform the same operation under more sterile conditions.

Bait sales provided good income and some good stories. Frances Chandler, widow of my Uncle Roy, also charged campers and anglers at her place below us on the Pecos. Frank Schuster of Iraan recalled the time he and Thad Morrow were fishing down at Frances's place and ran out of bait: "So we went up to Joe's to buy some worms. Mildred asked us where we were fishing, and when we told her she told us to buy those (expletive deleted) worms from Frances, that she wasn't going to sell us her worms. So we got out of there in a hurry, but Joe caught us and said to come on back and he'd sell us some worms, that Mildred was just joking."

The story is true except for the raw "expletive," as that was not Mom's way. She did, however, have a legendary recall for jokes, some of them off-color, and a way of telling them that could have made her an entertaining comedian.

Another time, one of our customers, a woman of some financial means, thought we were cheating her on the number of worms in a container. (This was when we were charging twenty-five cents a dozen.) With Mom and a dozen fishermen as her witnesses, she dumped the worms on the counter and began to count, her diamond rings sparkling as she lifted each worm from the container. We breathed a sigh of relief when she counted to fourteen, disgustedly put them back into the cup, and left.

Mom was constantly being asked the question, "Do you have worms?" She finally had a shirt made up that was printed with the question and her answer: "No, I just act this way." A sense of humor is essential in the bait business.

Mom's good humor, however, was pushed to the limit when Dad painted a sign on the side of the house that said "Bait." This was going too far and looked tacky, she thought. JoBeth and I saw it as perfectly normal and thought everyone would want to let the world know about a worm bed in their front yard.

Observing normal hours was out of the question when the fish were biting, so we were open twenty-four hours a day and had a bell installed for service if we had gone to bed. The customer came first, and the bait had to be there on demand. How many dozens of worms and minnows did we sell at the ranch during those years? A lot, but who was counting?

JoBeth and I learned from early on how to put a "minner" on a hook, how to thread a wriggling worm, how to put the catch on a stringer, and never to leave it in the water overnight or the raccoons would have a feast and we'd be left with fish heads. We grew up assuming these were life skills, that everyone grew up fishing because we had.

A CONSTANT FISHERMAN, Dad planned every trip around a good fishing spot, never mind the locale or type of fish. But one of his favorite forms of fishing was setting trotlines (often mispronounced "trout lines") for the big cats. In this method, the dedicated fisherman strings hooks along the line, baits them with minnows, goldfish, or cut bait, and then positions the line across the river, anchoring it to a branch on the bank on one end and a rock or weight on the other. This is how the big ones were caught. Weighing from thirty to eighty pounds, these were the grandaddy catfish of the Pecos. (Jug lines and throw lines were other forms of fishing in the river.)

The Rio Grande, which forms part of the boundary between Mexico and the United States, was only a few hours' drive from us, and it seemed that Dad was always planning, away on, or just getting back from a fishing trip to the Rio Grande. He had friends who ranched along the river, and for several years Uncle Herman had a ranch in the Dryden area.

Mom went along most of the time, somewhat reluctantly, and spent her hours reading in the pickup or on one of the cots under the shade of a tarp while Dad set trotlines. JoBeth and I accompanied them when we were younger, but as teenagers our interests turned away from days of camping in the summer heat and scrambling up and down steep riverbanks.

We couldn't keep up with Dad anyway; he never seemed to tire of the hard work of fishing, while we'd be exhausted by the middle of the day. So he'd run the lines time after time by himself, and we'd go home supplied with catfish as fresh as they get. Those trips back to the ranch were an adventure in themselves. JoBeth and I, sunburned and tired, sat in the back of the pickup or Jeep, crowded in among the wet tow sacks that held the flopping catfish while Mom sat next to Dad in front, reading her book.

Drinking icy cold Delaware Punch purchased in Comstock, we were glad to be headed back to running water and a comfortable bed.

Dad found an enthusiastic fishing friend in Frank Green of Odessa, and they made several trips down to the Mexican border to fish the murky and sometimes dangerous waters of the Rio Grande together. They always came back loaded down with big ones and tales of even bigger ones that broke the line. (Frank and his wife Katherine were founders and owners of the historic Barn Door, still one of Odessa's best-known restaurants.) Frank recalled first going to the ranch in 1946, when he and Johnny Harris went down to get permission to hunt javelinas. "I fell in love with the place and used to go down in the middle of the week when no one was there, and Joe and I seined, grabbled, and gigged fish up and down the creek."

Another acquaintance of my dad's during these years was Cuthbert Carll, owner and editor of the *McCamey News,* who reputedly once said, "Nothing is duller than the pure, unadulterated truth." I don't know if he liked to fish as much as he liked to just visit the ranch and talk to Dad, but he was a good friend.

Of course, we fished every spot the ranch offered. We also fished up the creek on our neighbor Lindsey Hicks's property (now the Oasis Ranch) for years. He and his family were welcome to do the same on our part of the creek. Fence lines and boundaries between neighbors were not so intimidating then.

Grappling (also called grabbling) was another fishing method of which Dad was a master. I have seen others do the same thing but not so skillfully. He would find a deep hole in the creek that goes back under a rock formation or bank, reach in as far as he could stretch, and pull out a slippery cat with his bare hands. Years later, Lee Casstevens of Odessa, who grew up on the creek, was driving his family to the ranch for a fishing trip when one of his young daughters asked him to tell the story of Joe Chandler "pulling catfish out of the creek with his teeth." He might have tried that also. But stories tend to get bigger and better as time goes on, and I think most used their hands when grappling.

Billy Pete Huddleston of Iraan and aforementioned football fame recalled this type of fishing on the ranch: "We knew your grandfather, father, and mother well and spent many a splendid day on their places on the lower Independence and Pecos back in the late forties and fifties. One of my most memorable sunburns was collected from grappling fish all day one cool May day with a minimum of clothes about one-half mile down from the house."

The story of one fishing trip didn't need much embellishing. Dad and several friends were running trotlines in the river one midwinter evening. One of them, who had just gotten a new set of dentures, was in the boat with Dad when it capsized. The friend was plunged into deep water, and as he swam to the surface, inhaling deeply and sputtering out river water, he managed to eject his new dentures. He and Dad, assisted by others standing on the bank with flashlights and lanterns, repeatedly dove into the cold dark water to search for the teeth. They returned home wet and cold, with some nice cats but no teeth. Those dentures are probably still buried deep in the thick mud of the Pecos River bed. "My wife won't believe how I lost my teeth, but that's the gospel truth," he said. And in these parts, truth can't get much purer.

Many skilled fishermen visited the ranch, but one of the names that always comes to mind when fish are mentioned is that of Mickey "Doc" McGuire of Odessa. An optometrist who practiced his profession to support his habit, he thought that every hour in the city was wasted. He loaded up his family, assorted relatives, and fishing gear every weekend for years on end to head to the creek, and the weekends got longer and longer in the summer. When others complained, "Those danged fish just aren't biting," Mickey would strike out for the hole of the day with a sly smile and bring back a full stringer.

Fishing was our life and our livelihood for a long time. It was the foundation of the recreational activities at the guest ranch and enabled us to meet many fine people, who enriched our lives in countless ways. Many West Texans were in the vanguard of visitors and were primarily responsible for the success of the business. The ranch became especially popular with Odessans and Midlanders. (This period was before Amistad Lake was put in at Del Rio, and other than Nasworthy at San Angelo, there just wasn't much water in West Texas.) There's hardly a veteran fisherman in the area today who didn't fish at Chandler's at some point. These folks, and those from every other small town in the area, became acquainted at the ranch and formed friendships sitting around the pool and telling fish stories. Some lived blocks from each other or went to the same church, but had never met. They all spread the word that Chandler Ranch was a good place to go.

Slowly we added the modern conveniences that city folks took for granted. We didn't have electricity at first; our power came from a generator Dad operated until rural electrification finally reached us. We thought we were "uptown" then, at least until a storm knocked out the lines and we were left with food going to ruin in the freezers and no water or lights in the house or cabins. At those times we'd employ a bucket brigade to flush the toilets with water from the ditch, unless the storm had also flooded out the ditch, and then we had to go back to Mother Nature until current was restored. But this was just part of life at the ranch and pretty much taken for granted.

Highway 349 was a graded dirt road with countless cattle guards for many of the guest ranch years. We now only have seven miles until we get to the heavenly feel of pavement.

For many years we had no phone service at the ranch, which suited us just fine at the time. Even after we finally had a phone installed in the house, we never had them in the cabins. Dad's contention, as he once told a reporter, was that "most of the people who come down here don't want to be bothered with telephones; they want to get away from town." But that didn't stop us from getting calls in the middle of the night.

"Are the fish biting?"

We never said no.

Chapter Eight
INDEPENDENCE RISING

On Sunday, June 27, 1954, our beautiful and benign friend, Independence Creek,
turned on us with a fury. In a cruel bit of irony, our family had been through a
natural disaster in the form of lack of rain just a few years earlier, and
we were now hit by another, in the form of too much rain.

AT THE RANCH, having little direct communication with the outside world, we had no way of knowing that on June 25 Hurricane Alice had come ashore south of Brownsville. The remnants of that storm were slowly crawling up the Rio Grande and into the Pecos and Devils River basins and had dumped as much as thirty-five inches of rain over the Howard and Johnson Draws. Sixteen people would lose their lives in the flooding that the *San Angelo Standard-Times* called one of the worst natural disasters of the century, the Crockett County Flood.

To us, the creek on a rise, while not a common occurrence, was not unprecedented either. Once or twice a year, a good rain would cause an overflow that quickly ran into the Pecos, cleaning out underbrush and moss and leaving the gravel beds clean and clear. Therefore, we had no sense of foreboding, no feeling of anything out of the ordinary, when it started to rain on Saturday, June 26, and continued unceasingly on into the night. The guest cabins and the campgrounds were full, but no one felt alarmed enough to leave the area. A little shower in West Texas was not going to ruin the weekend.

However, we soon knew that this was no ordinary rain. Whether it

---

rained 24 inches in 18 hours or 18 inches in 24 hours, I don't know, but at the crest, the water flowing into the creek covered the electric poles on the ranches upstream. Those of us miles below didn't know that. Nor could we picture the hundreds of dry draws and canyons around us filling with swirling water in amounts unheard of and rushing into the creek or the river.

According to Jack Skiles, a Langtry native and Trans-Pecos historian, "the average rainfall in Roy Bean country is about fourteen inches, but that figure tells only part of the story. Some years, only three or four inches of rain falls; conversely, in June 1954 much of the region was inundated with rain, receiving more than twenty-four inches in one night."

There was no wall of water, just a steady increase of volume as the bank of the creek moved closer and closer to us. By mid-morning on Sunday, we were wading in the yard. Uneasiness began to spread among our guests, as well it should have.

At Dad's suggestion, the campers and those in cabins packed their cars and moved to higher ground near the entrance to the ranch. They could not leave, as by now all the draws were running and blocking the small roads leading out of the ranch. We had no idea how the fishermen and campers across the Independence were faring. We had no way of communicating with them or the outside world. The only indications that this was more than just another rise were the steadily falling rain, the ominous thunder, and the swiftly rising creek.

We had time to take some belongings, but we didn't. There was such a sense of unreality to it all that by the time we realized we were in danger, it was too late to think of material things. Dad drove the ranch vehicles to higher ground and then, at the last moment, remembered his prized hunting rifles and ran back into the house to retrieve them.

It was too late. The building was breaking apart. Dad escaped the rising water with only seconds to spare. The guns, along with all the memorabilia of family life, were gone. We stood in the pounding rain in almost total silence as we watched our home and our livelihood wash away in the swollen, swift-moving creek.

A vivid memory is that of our bedroom walls buckling with the force of the water and a baby crib loaded with dolls and stuffed animals practically exploding out of the house. Raggedy Ann and Andy floated quickly to the top, smiled, and then were gone. Baby dolls in pink blankets blinked their blue glass eyes at us before they, too, were submerged.

The destruction at the ranch was accomplished in a matter of minutes. Water and more water rushed through the parts of the house that miraculously were still standing. The slide at the pool had crumpled into a mass of twisted metal, the concrete walls of the pool had collapsed, and the clubroom was gone except for the foundation, roof, and partial walls. Pieces of the pool table were scattered for miles downstream.

Grandad had been on the ranch for half a century and there had never been anything like this in his memory, possibly not in hundreds of years. The worst storm he could recall was in June 1909, when heavy rainfall sent Independence on a huge rise, destroying the ranch home and several windmills of a man named Wes Wade, who lived upstream. But the 1954 flood undoubtedly caused the heaviest damage ever inflicted on the Chandler Ranch. Oak trees that had taken many decades to reach their present size were snapped and gone. The devastation left Grandad shaking his head in disbelief.

The cresting Pecos pushed torrents of muddy water filled with debris toward the fields below the Home Place. The sight of so much water left an indelible impression, but the sound also remains, the dull but powerful roar of a river out of control.

Although we were too far away to have seen it, the small white house that was Mom and Dad's first home was destroyed. It was built so near the junction of the Pecos and Independence that it didn't stand long when the creek and river rolled together. Gone also was the fishing pond built with so much hard work and financial sacrifice and enjoyed by so many. Its dams could not withstand the raging waters of Independence.

We were stranded between the high water of two streams, the creek to the south, the river to the northeast. The roads leading out had been destroyed by the raging water in the draws. There was no way to know if our uncles and their families downriver had escaped the fury of the flooding water. We learned later that Herman Chandler's house had been flooded by the Pecos but not totally destroyed and that Roy's house had been demolished and he and Frances had escaped with minutes to spare. Aunt Myrtle, in the final moments, tried to save her baby chicks and turkeys, but the water had already reached their coops. Herman, Myrtle, and little Cathy, along with seventeen guests, sought higher ground on the surrounding hills and waited until the water subsided. Upon their return, they found that much of their furniture had been destroyed along with all the family photos and mementos.

Of the four families living on the creek, only Grandad's house remained untouched. Three sons saw their homes destroyed or severely damaged. None of them had imagined that their houses were close enough to the creek or the river ever to be affected by such an event.

The night of the disaster is a blur. Darkness descended to the sound of running water. We undoubtedly ate, listening to the running water. We undoubtedly slept, listening to the water. We were left with only the clothes on our backs but were thankful that there had been no loss of life, not on our side of the creek or the other, where the campers had been able to reach higher ground.

Carlene Cooper, the wife of Dr. James Cooper of McCamey, and her children were camping in the grove of oak trees below the pool when the water began to rise. Carlene had decided to take the family on a vacation trip in their new Cadillac sedan and had a last-minute change of plans as they drove out of McCamey. Originally headed for Ruidoso, Carlene asked the children which way to turn as they left the city limits, west for Ruidoso or east for Chandler's. They unanimously chose the ranch, but didn't inform James of their destination.

When it was determined that they couldn't move the car or trailer due to rising water, some of the men at the ranch chained the car to a tree so that it wouldn't be swept away. It stayed there, all right, but was battered to pieces by the powerful current. The trailer was gone before their small dog that had been left inside could be rescued.

I'm sure there were personal prayers of thanksgiving before the uncomfortable rest that night, but mainly it seemed that everyone wanted only to be dry and warm and out of the rain that still fell intermittently from leaden skies.

The following newspaper article gives a brief account of the flood. The writer was Larry L. King, then a reporter for the *Odessa American,* who later went on to write *The Best Little Whorehouse in Texas*. This account was written after we had made it to safety and were staying in Odessa with James and Earlene Newton, whose cabin across the creek had also been destroyed.

FISHING RANCH SWEPT AWAY

The flood cost Joe Chandler $100,000 and half his toenails.

That huge amount of money was lost when waters tore away Chandler's fishing club 17 miles south of Sheffield.

And the toenails were lost as Chandler led a caravan of weekend guests—many of them Odessans—out of the flooded area, constructing 30 miles of road as he went.

Today at the home of Odessa friends, Mr. and Mrs. James Newton, 620 North Belmont, Chandler said he wasn't very worried about the loss.

"Naturally, it hurts and I have a tough time making myself believe it happened," he said, "but I'm going to build it right back. I talked to Pat Simmons down at the First National Bank today and made arrangements to start constructing again right away."

Chandler said when the waters recede at the ranch, "We'll still have some fishing and a few trees."

But his loss included 18 of 25 big oak trees in a park, the Chandler house, all the cabins, food and equipment—valued at about $100,000.

Some 35 guests were gathered at the ranch last weekend when the heavy rains started.

"Nobody thought much about it at first," said 16-year-old Charlena Chandler today. "The kids laughed and had a lot of fun.

"Then the water started to get up and we worried a little. Some of the folks got in their cars and drove up to the top of high ground. We stayed in the house and it rained for 15 or 16 hours. Then about 20 minutes before the flood hit its peak, we got out in the car and got to higher ground, too."

The rains continued and the house was swept down. Down tumbled cabins, big trees, automobiles. Higher climbed the marooned weekenders.

"We got hungry," Charlena said. "My sister JoBeth, who is 13, and Jimmy Newton helped me hunt for food. We found some canned goods that had washed away from the house.

"The grown folks didn't eat anything. They gave all the food we found to the little kids."

And plenty of "little kids" were in on the wet, miserable experience.

There were Ed and Fred Hanley, five-year-old twin sons of Mr. and Mrs. Edward Hanley of Odessa. And four-year-old Susan Tilson and 14-month-old Jan Tilson, daughters of Mr. and Mrs. Jim Tilson, Odessa. Several other small children made up the party.

The 14-month-old Tilson baby girl was flown to Medical Center Hospital here with 105 degrees of temperature during the rescue work Monday, but was reported in good condition today.

As cars overturned, waters churned and the rains continued, Chandler decided to try to work his way out of the flood.

He organized a caravan of eight cars, a jeep, a pickup truck and two tractors.

"I got in front," he said, "and when we came to a place we couldn't cross we all piled out and worked on the road.

"We dug up brush, rocks, anything at all to help make a bridge. That's where I lost the toenails and hurt my feet—walking in those old shoes, digging and kicking at the road."

It took the group nine hours to go 30 miles, finally reaching low water country Monday. Then the big ordeal was about over, after warm clothing and food with medical checkups for the youngsters.

The caravan coming out was met by Mr. and Mrs. James Newton of Odessa, who started to the ranch to hunt [for] their 12-year-old boy after the flood. The Newtons got as far as Sheffield and had to stop Sunday until Monday when they met the weary survivors of the flood coming out.

One of the first people to make it out ahead of the caravan made a list of names and phone numbers of those involved and helped to inform family members that everyone was safe. Dr. Cooper was probably one of the most surprised recipients of a phone call, as he had assumed his family was safe in Ruidoso. He immediately left for the ranch; we met him as we were heading for higher ground.

We also encountered the Newtons. They must have been sick with worry over their son, Jimmy, who had been spending part of the summer with us. Babe and Olin Smith of Sheffield were also on their way down, to see about us, and we met them on the highway before the turnoff to the ranch. They had heard the terrible news about Ozona, where many had died in the rampaging floodwater of Johnson Draw, more than a hundred homes had been destroyed, and the Red Cross had been called in with medicine, cots, blankets, food, and water-purification units.

There was more bad news in other places. Miles downstream from us, the Pecos River High Bridge near Langtry had been pushed from its foundations when the flood crested at some ninety-six feet, according to Verne Huser, Pecos River historian. Dr. Mary Nan Aldridge of Sul Ross and her husband had just driven over the bridge minutes before the wall of water hit. They noted the irony of the destruction happening on a warm day "with the sky as clear as a bell, seemingly perfect weather for driving in a convertible."

The Mexican town of Ciudad Acuña was reported completely under water. Some four to five thousand citizens were stranded, and nearly 200 were evacuated from the water by U.S. Air Force helicopters from Del Rio, according to reports in the *Odessa American*.

Traffic between Eagle Pass and Piedras Negras was cut when the international rail bridge was washed out and water flowed over the highway bridge as well. More than 300 persons were forced from their homes in Eagle Pass, and damage was greater across the border.

Many fences were damaged by the flood as well. Because of the danger of quickly rising waters in all the draws and canyons during storms, ranchers normally left one end of the fence sections that crossed these gaps loosely connected. Water from a heavy rain would then just push the water gap open, rather than destroying the entire fence. After the flood of 1954, however, all the water gaps were gone, adding to the problem of lost livestock.

But the loss of life in so many places overshadowed any loss of property we experienced. We considered ourselves fortunate. When we returned to the ranch a few days later, we were prepared to begin rebuilding.

And we had plenty of help. Sanderson rancher Sid Harkins arrived on the desolate scene with a check in his hand, renewing his membership in a recreational club that no longer existed. Gail Henson from Odessa and Grandmother Stavley moved in with us and helped us get through those first days. Odessans James Newton and Roger Ashford wrote letters of recommendation to help us get bank loans. W. T. Hutchinson, owner of H and H Food Store in Iraan, carried my family on credit for months and never sent a bill. Bill Casstevens, owner of Casstevens Furniture in Odessa, gave Dad credit for bunk beds and other furniture for the cabins. "We'll talk about that later" was their reply when Dad tried to make financial arrangements.

The owners of a department store in McCamey, Victor and Alma Baron, gave us new clothing, as did the owners of Jacobsen's in Iraan. Mary Beth Turner came from Sanderson with boxes of dishes and kitchen utensils. The outpouring of assistance was heartwarming. I hesitate to mention names for fear of omitting many; the numerous acts of kindness overwhelmed us.

We set up basic housekeeping as we cooked over the remains of the fireplace and slept on the floor in the clubroom. Leldon Clifton, superintendent of the Iraan-Sheffield Schools, drove down to offer assistance and to find out if I would attend the SMU cheerleading camp, scheduled for the following week. The other members of the squad, all good friends of mine, realized that I had nothing to wear to camp and offered to share their clothing if I decided to go. Despite their kind offer of help and the superintendent's encouragement, I refused. I felt I would be letting my family down if I left under such conditions. In retrospect, I am sure that I needed them more than they needed me.

We did return to Iraan for school that fall to a life that seemed surprisingly routine after our summer of upheaval, with classes and football games and other school activities. But the event stayed with us for years after the fact.

As I think back now, it seems incredible that Dad rebuilt the place. Many people simply would have given up. But he was determined, and he never expressed any self-pity, even on the first day, never asked, "Why did this happen to me?" His positive attitude must have been contagious, because it never entered our minds, either, to give up on the ranch.

Rebuilding began almost immediately, with help from so many. The following letter was written by a friend from Odessa on August 17, 1954, to assist my dad with loan applications:

To Whom It May Concern:
   I, and my family, have been members of the Independence Lake Club, owned and operated by Joe Chandler, for the past four years and being well

acquainted with Joe Chandler and his fine family socially and in business, I wish to make the following statement:

The Independence Lake Club is one of the finest lake clubs I have ever had the pleasure and opportunity to belong to. It is a place that any family with children (I have three) can go and feel perfectly safe, as Mr. Chandler does not allow wild parties or any undesirable characters on his place.

He keeps the premises in excellent shape.

It is the only place of its type that I would consent for my family to go without me. This is not only my personal opinion but also that of my friends and other lake members.

When the lake club was washed away in a flood about two months ago, many friends and business acquaintances offered Mr. Chandler their support of money and materials so he could rebuild the club, without collateral. I believe that that alone speaks very highly of his honesty and integrity.

I personally take pleasure in recommending Mr. Joe Chandler as a good man and an excellent business risk.

> Signed: Roger F. Ashford, Ashford Lumber Co.,
> Odessa, Texas

During the years of rebuilding, the strain of debt incurred from the Stavley Place still remained, and there were the new flood-related debts. One loan from 1955 covered a payment of $11,000 for the following work performed by George Reynolds, an Iraan building contractor:

The construction and repair of improvements as follows: Repair and modification of Club House; complete construction of one 14 x 25 dressing room, frame stucco; complete construction of one 16 x 22 cabin with siding, repairing one 13 x 13 cabin; addition of 13 x 13 to present cabin; 1050 square feet of concrete sidewalk; repair of living room floor; painting of buildings outside and inside; complete electrical and plumbing for new installation and repair of existing construction; floor repairs and covering; complete installation of air-conditioning units; 5 1000-cubic-feet units; 2 diving boards; complete installation of one Music Box; all according to plans and specifications heretofore and now agreed upon by and between the Parties hereto.

There were other structures that had to be repaired or rebuilt as well, such as the pool, the store, and other cabins. Dad secured money for the rebuilding and did much of the work himself.

In less than a year, we were again in business. There is no record of the exact date, but a full-page article on the ranch titled "A Good Spot for Just Relaxin'" appeared in the *Odessa American* on August 4, 1955. It describes the visit of a group of Tri-Hi-Y girls from Odessa High School, and one photo shows the group at the rebuilt pool with the slide in the background, almost as if the flood had never happened. Some excerpts from the story follow:

> About three hours drive into the rugged Terrell County where Independence Creek meets the Pecos lies the Joe Chandler Fishing Club.
>
> The club is run on a membership basis and presently has 100 families on the roles. The membership—$50 a year—gives the fisherman exclusive fishing rights on a mile and a half of creek and three miles of the Pecos.
>
> In addition, there's plenty for the non-angler to do. There's horseback riding, swimming in a spring-fed pool, hiking, volleyball, tennis and basketball. The only extra charge is for the horses and fees for the cabins, each of which is furnished with gas range, electric refrigerator and cooking utensils.
>
> There's more fishing in store for the members this fall. Joe Chandler, the amiable operator of the club, says a well-stocked lake will be opened in October, and another will be completed next summer.
>
> Last year's treacherous flood took the Chandler fishing ranch down the Pecos. But a winter of hard work has put the place back in top shape and more expansion is planned. . . .

The flood was a benchmark for us for years afterward; everything we talked about was "before the flood" or "after the flood." We will always be indebted to those who supported us, not only financially but also with their friendship and encouragement. Many good memories began to take the place of the bad ones. JoBeth and I never fully appreciated our parents' efforts until later in life. Now that we have struggled against some hard times ourselves, we have much more empathy for what our parents went through back in the fifties.

Rain has fallen many times since then, and we have seen many rises on Independence. But if the good Lord's willing, we won't see the waters of '54 again.

OUR FAITHFUL GUESTS continued to come when there was not much to come to, and new ones started arriving during the rebuilding years. While the structures were in a state of shock, the creek and river settled back into their placid beauty. In fact, because so much brush had been uprooted and swept downstream, the creek bed became wider and cleaner, with long, pristine white gravel beds that were more inviting than ever. The old deep pools were gone, but they had been replaced with new ones. And fishing only got better in both the Independence and the Pecos. The natural appeal of the confluence of these streams was undiminished.

After the ranch was rebuilt, there were several offers to buy it, but none more serious than the one made in 1961 by J. C. Williamson, a geologist and independent oil operator from Midland. The old axiom that everything is for sale if the price is right was proven true, and Dad, with mixed emotions, considered the offer. He and Mom also visited the Williamsons' ranch, Tres Valles, in Colorado, and Dad was so impressed he began to talk of buying "a little place up in Colorado."

Williamson was a legendary oilman and, according to his obituary in the *Midland Reporter-Telegram* in August 2001, was personally responsible for drilling over a thousand oil and gas wells in West Texas, and more than ten thousand wells had been drilled as a result of his exploration. When author James Michener visited the area to do research for his novel *Texas,* it was J. C. Williamson, the epitome of a Texas wildcatter, whom he interviewed.

I don't know what happened to cause the deal to fall through, but Dad, with relief, returned to work at the ranch, which remained his occupation and preoccupation for the rest of his life. "I don't think I would have been happy in Colorado," he said.

Many members have a story about how they first started coming to the ranch after the flood. The following is one of the most unusual because a membership at Chandler's was crucial in making the decision to move to West Texas. Joyce and Tom Freeland of Odessa started visiting the place with their friends, John Guffey, who owned an advertising agency, and his wife, Gayle, in 1957. Joyce later recalled: "Chandler's was instrumental, four years later, when Tom decided to accept a partnership offer from John and we moved to Odessa from Dallas. John's offer sounded great, but neither of us cared for Odessa the first time we were there so the clincher was this: Let's make ourselves a promise. Let's find the money for a membership at Chandler's, and every time we get stir crazy in Odessa, we'll have a place to go and get away from it all."

After the rebuilding, river fishermen continued to stream down the old dirt road, check in with us, and hurry off to wet a hook. One constant in our lives was having fishermen come up from the river at midnight to buy bait. When we heard the bell sound at any hour after the sun went down, we knew the fish were biting and we rolled out of bed to accommodate our guests. I must admit there were times I resented having to count out worms and minnows, or check in campers, but I can now look back with great appreciation for those fishermen who helped us make a living in such a special place.

We received lots of strange requests from guests, but nothing topped this one. A young man interrupted his fishing to jump in the car and drive his wife up to the store. Running in, he informed Dad that he needed help right away as he thought his wife was having a baby. He was right. By the time they got out to the car, she had.

Class parties were held every weekend during the spring, and I don't know who enjoyed the trips more, the students, their sponsors, or Mom and Dad, who called them kid parties. Many adults today remember having good times in their younger years at the ranch. Back then, most teenagers found all the fun they wanted lying by the pool working on their tans in the strong West Texas sun, eating cold candy bars (they were always kept refrigerated) or drinking Dr Peppers, and listening to their favorite music blaring from the jukebox. When the buses loaded up at the end of the day, everyone seemed to go home tired, sunburned, and happy.

Lynn Casstevens Bromley, daughter of Bill and Frances, who had a cabin at the ranch for many years, said that she remembered the jukebox, table tennis and pool tables, the rinky-tink piano, and cold Zero candy bars that never tasted as good anywhere else. She also recalled watching the pool being drained on Thursdays and being surprised at how big it was when it was empty. Bill, better known as Cass to us, and Frances were frequent visitors. So were Bill's younger brother, Kenneth, his wife, Dee, and their children, who spent every summer vacation for twenty-seven years at the ranch—surely a record—always accompanied by Bill and Kenneth's mother from Lubbock.

Every visitor seems to have a memory of his or her favorite song blasting from the jukebox, our only source of musical entertainment. Marge and Frank Downs of Midland, owners of Lifetime Lawn Sprinkler, said they could never hear "Proud Mary" or "C. C. Rider" without thinking of Dad and the ranch. We kept all the latest hits, and JoBeth and I were pleased when we got to choose the new 45s and change the labels on the jukebox. When Dad was feeling generous, he handed out quarters to the entire young bunch. We all had favorites that we played over and over. I, for one, fell in love with Elvis Presley the first time I ever heard "Don't Be Cruel" booming out of the game room through the speaker attached to an oak tree by the pool.

My mother documented many busy weekends at the ranch. In May 1970, she wrote, "I'm trying to write this letter in spurts between waiting on customers. [We've been swamped] since Thursday (50 seniors from Ozona), Friday (50 seventh and eighth graders from Sanderson), Saturday (15 teenagers from Grandfalls plus 61 Boy and Girl Scouts from Midland), plus our regular customers." In the same year she wrote, "This was the weekend that was. John Cummings, who is general manager for New York Life in Midland, brought employees and families down from San Angelo, Midland, Odessa and Abilene. They had fly-in catering service yesterday. Flew the food in and left—now ain't that something? All cabins full, so I have 82 sheets to wash plus everything else. Have two good Mexican boys to help me."

Getting up early and cleaning the cabins was another constant at the ranch, as brought home by this story from Betty Dishong Renfer, JoBeth's good friend from Odessa:

Once JoBeth and I were at the ranch with our dates and, after much begging, won permission for a trip to Acuña on condition that we'd not be out too late.

The promised time of return was long gone and the eastern sky was pink as we arrived home, creeping over the gravel road, hoping the car would not wake Mildred and Joe—especially Joe. JoBeth and I tip-toed onto the porch. . . . So far, so good . . . [We were] thirty minutes into a good sleep when Joe, who hadn't been fooled for a moment, hustled us out of bed and into the kitchen, where Mildred was fixing a big breakfast to fortify us for a day of cabin cleaning.

Mom and Dad were always hospitable to our friends, both male and female, but were never shy about putting them to work either. Chris Downs, Marge and Frank's son, once took a couple of friends to the ranch to go fishing. When they stopped at the house to pay their fees, Dad made a deal with them. If they'd rake a few leaves around the pool, he wouldn't charge them anything. After several hours of raking and piling and hauling leaves, the boys wearily approached Dad again: "Joe, couldn't we just pay you and go on down to the river?" Recalling this, I hear echoes of Grandad's "Just step right over there and do it, won't take you a minute."

DURING THE YEARS after the flood, several universities chose the ranch as a location for field studies. However, it was not the first time that parts of the region had been studied. The earliest record I found of such a visit is that of William L. Bray of the University of Texas, who conducted an intensive ecological investigation of a neighboring area in 1905. It appears that he confined his research to the areas around Langtry and Sanderson. In 1944 Benjamin Tharp reported on the vegetation of the northern edge of the Stockton Plateau, which may have included the ranch area. However, Grady L. Webster of the University of Michigan reported in 1950 that "the region in northern Terrell County has scarcely been mentioned except for a few observations by Havard (1885) who remarked that the valley of Independence Creek was an excellent grazing district."

Dr. Webster made a visit to the ranch again in the spring of 2003 and discussed his field trip there in 1949 when he was a student at the University of Texas. "We camped at the Blackstone Ranch, but spent a lot of time at the Hicks and Chandler ranches." He said the biggest changes he could see, after half a century, were the heavy vegetation along the creek and the proliferation of the star thistle, an aggravating little plant that he found everywhere he looked.

Professors and students from Sul Ross University in Alpine were probably the most frequent visitors in my memory, but I also recall groups from the University of Texas at Austin, Odessa College, Texas Tech, and Tulane University. The diversity of biological life on the ranch produced findings of great interest to us. We were living in a haven of wildlife but never imagined there were so many different species of animals, birds, reptiles, fish, and insects. Some of the research was done at night. I recall the hill behind our house covered with twinkling lanterns and headlights all through the night as students delved for specimens ranging from beetles to toads and bats to snakes. It's too bad that some of these groups did not come in September or October to witness the migration of the Monarch butterflies on their journey to Mexico. This is a beautiful time of year at the ranch, and the bright clouds of Monarchs descending from the autumn skies to the willow trees around the ponds make the season even more memorable.

Dr. Royal D. Suttkus of Tulane University directed one such field trip and left us a record of his evaluation of the creek and river done on July 12, 1966 (the measurements were made by Clyde D. Barbour):

Independence Creek: H_2O temp 27 degrees C; pH—7.4; dissolved O_2 = 7.4 mg/liter; total acidity = 9.0 mg/l; total alkalinity = 159.0 mg/l.

Pecos River above Independence Creek: H_2O temp 20 degrees C; pH—7.4, O_2 = 5.0 mg/l; total acidity = 19.0 mg/l; total alkalinity = 164.0 mg/l

Pecos River below Independence Creek: H_2O temp 28 degrees C; pH—7.4, O_2 = 6.5 mg/l; Total acidity = 11.0 mg/l; total alkalinity = 159.0 mg/l.

While these figures may signify little to the layperson, they will be of interest to those of a more scientific bent.

James F. Scudday of Sul Ross, whose study and evaluation of the creek as a potential natural landmark is found in Appendix A, was a frequent visitor to the ranch during the 1970s. When I wrote to him requesting his permission to use his paper, he readily consented and added the following note of interest:

> Your father was always the perfect host. He was most accommodating to all of our needs on every trip I made to the ranch over the years. He seemed to welcome me bringing students to the ranch for fieldwork. The students always enjoyed the trips there, and we greatly enjoyed visiting with your dad. He always had some interesting tales to relate about the history of the ranch and things that had occurred there, particularly some of the tremendous flash floods that rolled down the creek. Three of my students ended up specializing in fishery science and are now employed as fisher scientists, two by Texas Parks and Wildlife and one by New Mexico Game and Fish Department. They have always credited their experience with the great variety of fish found in Independence Creek and the Pecos River with getting them hooked on studying fish.

Two interesting observations concerning poisonous snakes in the area were made by William W. Milstead of the University of Kansas City, Missouri, during a field trip in 1957. He noted, "The Independence Creek population of copperheads was one of the greatest aggregations of poisonous snakes ever recorded outside of a den, but it was all extirpated by a flood in 1954. Collections along Independence Creek in 1957 yielded only a very few specimens." His second comment was that Independence Creek in 1950 was one of only two places in the Chihuahuan Desert where the Texas Coral Snake was found.

Of the three poisonous snakes found on the ranch, the one I remember as most common was the rattlesnake, with the coral snake being the most uncommon, as I recall seeing only one or two in my personal experience. We did have copperheads in more abundance in the past, so perhaps the flood contributed to their present rarity.

One father and daughter had a frightening experience with a copperhead as we were gathered around the pool one summer day. The little girl found a small copperhead in the oak leaves nearby, picked it up, and took it to her father to examine. As he bent over to look at it more closely, the snake simultaneously struck the hands of both the father and daughter. Dad took them to the Iraan hospital immediately, where they received competent medical attention. The daughter was released with no ill effects, but the father remained seriously ill for several days, possibly as a result of an adverse reaction to the serum.

CANOEING ALSO BECAME a part of the scene at the Chandler Ranch. The ranch was and is a popular spot for canoeists who want to take the Pecos down to the Rio Grande. One such expedition was described by Paul Montgomery in *Texas Highways* in September 1979. Montgomery was also a photographer, and the magazine featured a beautiful cover shot he took of the bluffs of the Pecos in Crockett County when his group reached the ranch. The story begins, "None of us knew what the Pecos River had in store for us as we pushed our four overloaded canoes from under the Sheffield Bridge and headed for the Amistad Reservoir 120 miles south."

The trip was sponsored by the Texas Natural Areas Survey, an organization based at the University of Texas, Austin, that identifies and documents primitive areas of Texas still unaffected by urban growth and spreading population. The party included botanists, zoologists, an archeologist, and a student of field geography. They may have gotten more than they bargained for as portaging the canoes was more frequent than anticipated in the shallow areas of the river.

"For most of the journey, the Pecos was little more than a creek, and normal canoe travel was virtually impossible," Montgomery writes. He also describes the thunderstorms that can transform the tranquil Pecos into a dangerous torrent and how flash flooding often comes swiftly and unannounced: "One particularly vicious thunderstorm dumped two inches of rain on our campsite early one morning. Later we found out this same storm had claimed four lives on the Devils River south of us by creating a flash flood."

The acknowledged dean of Texas writers, John Graves, author of *Goodbye to a River*, took a similar trip on the river several years ago, departing from the ranch to head south to Pandale, a popular destination for canoeists. Graves's book was indirectly referred to in an article by John Karges of the Nature Conservancy of Texas titled "Hello to a River," which appeared in the Conservancy magazine *Horizons* in the summer of 1994.

Karges describes some of the wildlife he encountered along the shore in the area of the confluence of the creek and river: "In a single view, the 'red boys'—a cardinal, summer tanager, vermilion flycatcher and painted bunting—were all visible in a stunning array, each a proud male attempting to fulfill seasonally motivated needs and obligations. The incessant babbling of yellow-breasted chats and Bell's vireos, even in the midday heat, rang out of every other bankside thicket and a pair of nest-building greenbacked herons was startled off their rickety stick platform overhanging the river."

He tells of sighting soft-shelled turtles the size of dinner platters, big beavers on the banks, and salt cedars, buttonbush, western soapberries, sumacs, junipers, and live oaks growing along the canyon walls. He also describes changes in the Pecos as he travels downstream:

> The water reveals few secrets and except for an occasional splash, I see nothing of the fish-life of the river. The water is the color of Thai tea, deeper than the height of my canoe paddle here, a shallow gravel-bottom riffle there. . . . Downstream in the direction of Amistad, the canyons become even steeper and deeper, and the river grows even larger from springs. A huge rapid through a boulder field, just above the slack water of the lake, serves as a remote final exhibition of free-flowing wildness and as a thought-provoking filter from the greatly changed landscape downstream.

The ranch was sought out by an incredible number of people during the years since Grandad made his start there on the Pecos and Independence. But whether their aims were recreational or academic, their diversity contributed to a fascinating way of life for those of us who called the place home.

The following note was received with a photo after a visit in 1991 from Mickey Lavy, one of those who knew the ranch as a child: "You never know who is going to show up at Joe Chandler's. They come from miles away and years ago. I've wanted to come back since 1957. Maybe it won't take me another 34 years." Another note, written after a recent visit by another "kid" who grew up there, Janie Harris Henderson of Dallas, reads, "I feel calmer when I think of standing on the road and seeing and hearing Independence Creek run beneath my feet."

Chapter Nine

GOLF: A DREAM COURSE

Dad never heard of Kevin Costner's movie, but in the mid-sixties he built his own "Field of Dreams"—a nine-hole golf course in the middle of a cow pasture. For nearly twenty-five years, our lives revolved around greens and grass, bogeys and birdies, tournaments and teams.

It was truly a dream course and our pride and joy. We thought life was one long tournament, and that golf was eternal. But it ended, just as all dreams eventually do.

The cow pasture has reclaimed the course, and nature is daily taking back the unnatural, forced elegance of mowed greens, fairways, and tee boxes. The ground squirrels and rabbits move freely over their domain, undisturbed by the rumble of golf carts, the laughter of players, the crack of hard-hit balls.

It's over, but what memories it left behind, that improbable little course on Independence.

DURING THE ENTIRE TIME of rebuilding after the flood, Dad was still struggling with debt from the drought at the Stavley Place. A short letter from Phil Lane of the Texas Production Credit Corporation in San Angelo, dated July 9, 1963, marked the end of that era: "We are pleased to enclose receipt and small overpayment of loan. I know that you are relieved to get this debt paid and I want to add my thanks for your cooperation, integrity, and ingenious efforts in getting the job done. I always felt that you would work this out and I am particularly pleased that my faith in you was justified."

In September 1964, I went to Germany as a civilian employee of the U.S. Army. When I departed, golf was as foreign to Mom and Dad as Europe was to me. Dad often smiled at golfers as he drove by a course, seeing the players as men pursuing a foolish sport.

Through letters, I learned that changes were taking place at the ranch. I wrote back, "Dad, can you build a golf course?" I could rest assured that his answer was, "Hell, I can build anything."

When I came home two years later, the scene at the ranch had changed, and that's putting it mildly. There, nestled on the banks of the creek and the irrigation canal, where once existed a fishing pond and pastureland, sat a sparkling green jewel of a golf course. I had envisioned some sort of miniature course with little Dutch windmills, based on Mom's letters, but this was the real thing. It was the first and only golf course ever constructed in Terrell County and the only privately owned course in West Texas. But it didn't happen overnight, and it didn't happen without the proverbial 1 percent inspiration and 99 percent perspiration.

There were long fairways of smooth mowed turf, greens as lush as thick carpet, and treacherous sand traps and water hazards. The land looked completely different. But just as surprising to me was the change in my parents. Dad, now wearing shorts and golf shoes, and Mom, whose previous idea of strenuous sport was table tennis or floating around the pool in an inner tube, had been transformed into avid golfers. They were up with the sun, teeing off in the dawn's early light, and talking the remainder of the day of that long tee shot on "Old Shady" or the birdie on "Short and Sweet." They didn't remain hackers for long either. Taking to the sport like ducks to a pond on a hot summer day, they were soon amazingly proficient and could hold their own against more experienced players.

How had this change taken place? Jimmy Attaway of McCamey, a young man with a love for the sport, had planted the seed. He had a vision of a golf course at the ranch, and Dad became caught up in that vision. The more Jimmy talked, the more Dad liked the idea. With Jimmy's ideas and the help of Bennie Adams, a pro at the McCamey course, the plan took shape. Dad's friend Bill Casstevens also was in on the picture, adding ideas, encouragement, and support from the very beginning.

But after the dream and all the talk came the hard part—making it happen. With the help of laborers from Mexico and a neighbor from Dryden, Wayne Rogers, Dad hauled tons of soil to spread on the fairways and greens, using a dump truck and a power loader. Good ranch land was becoming good golf land.

According to an article in *West Texas Livestock Weekly* in July 1968, Dad reported the course cost about $30,000 to build, with most of that going for the pump and underground sprinkler system. Without his doing a large part of the physical labor, the cost would have made the project impossible. At the time the article was written, the course was valued at $90,000 (or $10,000 a green), so the investment had been a good one.

For most of his remaining years, the golf course was Dad's reason for living; he expended time, money, and labor on it in a way that we are only now beginning to appreciate. I can remember him mowing and fertilizing all day and then staying up until midnight watering. He drove himself harder than any employee we ever had. No detail was too small, no job too large. Only a person with an abundance of physical stamina would have attempted such a task, and he never tired of it.

Over a twenty-five-year period, business got better and better, and the golf course became the main attraction at the ranch. It surpassed everyone's expectations.

There were various problems in maintaining the course, however. Ground squirrels delighted in burrowing into greens, and one of Mom's favorite chores was to jump onto a golf cart with a .410 shotgun and see how many of the little damage-makers she could get rid of. This sight sometimes startled observers, for some reason. Frances Casstevens, who was Mom's faithful golf partner, remarked that she had never seen a golf cart so well equipped, with a gun for the ground squirrels and poison for the red ants. Mom was always prepared.

Jackrabbits and cottontails, who loved the verdant grass, were also frequently seen on the course, along with a lively parade of skunks, possums, porcupines, raccoons, armadillos, and an occasional herd of javelinas, all of them no doubt thinking they were in paradise.

A newcomer entered the scene during this time, the homely nutria. Nonnative animals, the nutrias swam up the Pecos and inflicted all kinds of damage on the ponds, ditches, and creek as they dug their burrows. Snakes of all sorts could be found along the ditch on the golf course, having come down from the hills for water. Most of these did not present a problem except for the rattlesnake. And the deer? They thought all that grass had been planted just for them.

Birds in abundance added to the golfers' enjoyment, and we took pleasure in their beauty. But we never knew there were more than 200 different species until years later when the Nature Conservancy of Texas did some research and supplied us with a list.

Drought was still a tremendous problem. With a reasonable amount of rain, which is not very much in the Trans-Pecos, the fairways had a chance of staying green without constant irrigation. But when the rain didn't fall, an inordinate amount of time and labor went into watering. We never quit thinking of rain, either as ranchers or golf-course caretakers. Even now that we no longer depend on heavenly precipitation for our livelihood, whenever I see clouds gathering and hear the rumble of thunder, I wonder (echoing Isak Dinesen's thoughts of her beloved farm in Africa) if it's raining at the ranch.

Dad did love his golf course, and he would sometimes just ride over it on a cart to savor its beauty. He once remarked to Mom, "I just wish Dad had lived long enough to see this. He wouldn't have believed it." She replied, "Maybe it's best he didn't. He would have thought you'd lost your mind."

The course had nine holes and was laid out like this:

The tee box on the first hole was just below the pool. Named "Hooker's Hollow," it was a 265-yard, par-4 hole with the irrigation canal to the north and the creek to the south, with formidable oak trees almost dead center. The sound of a ball bouncing off a tree trunk or into the waters of Independence was not unusual on the first hole. (A note from Mom, sometime in 1968, says: "Yesterday when Joe played golf, he teed off at the first tee box and his ball went *past* the second tee box! Herbert and Sid were so impressed, they were raving. To say the least so was your dad. I imagine that's really about the longest drive that has ever been made here, especially on that particular hole, due to the trees and water.")

Then came "Short and Sweet," only 140 yards long and one of my favorites because I had some success, as many women did, with its par 3.

The third hole was called "The Needle." This 360-yard, par-5 hole featured a long narrow fairway with ditch water on the left and a pond at the end, and the green was practically on the dam of a well-stocked fishing pond.

The 180-yard fourth was "The Monster." It was the most cursed hole on the course, as the drive had to cross about 140 yards of clear blue water to get to the fairway on the other side. We pulled hundreds of golf balls a year from the pond when it was drained, not to mention a few clubs tossed in anger into the middle of it.

The first grandchild in the family was honored with the fifth hole, "Jana Babe." (By the time the next three grandchildren came along, Joell, Anne, and Joey, there were no more holes left to name, so Jana was the sole recipient of this recognition.) It was a straight par-4, 375 yards long, north of the canal. A sand trap lay to the right, and a holding pond for the pump sat just past the green.

"Long Knock" was the 300-yard-long sixth hole, lined with fruitless mulberry trees on each side. A sand trap awaited many luckless players before they got onto the green.

Then came "Runway." Covering 360 yards with a dogleg to the left, this hole had a sand trap to the left and the canal just past the green.

"Old Shady," the eighth hole, was a short one (145 yards) named for the big mesquite tree to the left of the green. A large sand trap in the right corner saw its share of balls. When JoBeth and I, as children, rode bikes or walked back and forth to Grandad's, the oversized mesquite was the perfect place to take a break. We never envisioned its future or its name.

"Journey's End" was the ninth hole, 350 yards long. The fairway doglegged to the right along the canal for about 200 yards. A large water hazard protected the green, and the rough to the right was a common source of frustration.

Not long after the golf course opened, the tournaments started. It was all so new and quite incredible to us that people actually drove so far and paid us to play golf on a course that hadn't existed two years before. One of the early tournaments took place on August 20, 1967. Appropriately, the first entry registered for this tournament was the team of Lee Casstevens and Mike Curry of Odessa. Lee had helped his dad name the greens and had watched the course being built from the first day. Fifty-two teams registered for $18 each, and the prizes were golf merchandise.

The following story from the *Iraan News,* dated August 8, 1968, describes a typical meet: "The Independence Creek Golf tournament will be Sunday, Aug. 11, at Joe Chandler's. The first 50 teams to sign up will make up the field for 27-hole low-ball partnership. There will be trophies awarded along with merchandise prizes. Chandler's nine-hole course is laid out along Independence Creek, less than a mile above the point where it empties into the Pecos River. Chandler reports that the greens are in top shape for the tournament. Chandler's Guest Ranch is located 30 miles south of Sheffield."

Women's tournaments also started about this time. Gay Emery of Iraan, a devoted golfer and Chandler friend, announced the first one in the *Iraan News:*

> Joe Chandler stopped by yesterday evening to let me in on the fact that he had given in to the ladies for a tournament on the cutest course in Texas. Just too many of us have hounded Joe to give his one lady golfer a tournament. Isn't it great to have only one lady golfer on the spread and get to hold a tournament? Iraan can't hold one and they have at least five or six hackers. You don't give a tournament just to make money; it's a purely social thing to show off your course and be neighborly to the surrounding towns. This is just what the Chandlers are doing. Just lots of women golfers have never played his course and they have missed some beauty if they haven't. We hope the Chandlers' tournament comes off just fine.

Dad did enjoy showing off the course, but he discovered that the tournaments were money makers as well. The income from cabin rentals, golf-cart rentals, and camping and fishing mushroomed on tournament weekends. We'd gather in Mom and Dad's bedroom upstairs on Sunday nights after everyone was gone and spread the cash and checks out on the king-sized bed. After we had stacked, sorted, and counted, we were always somewhat stunned by the total. For a man who had worked for a can of corn and a dollar a day on neighboring ranches, learned to do without and use things up, and "slept with the banker" most of his life, Dad can be forgiven for proudly saying, "This is a moneymaking little son-of-a-bitch!"

Tournament time also meant huge food preparations. I can't taste barbecue today without thinking of those days. Brisket and chicken never tasted so good as when we fed all those hungry golfers and their families. On Saturday nights before the tournaments, we prepared tubs of potato salad and pinto beans. We would sometimes have a kitchen full of friends chopping onions, dicing pickles, peeling potatoes, and seasoning beans until the early morning hours.

Sunrise always seemed to burst over the hills too early the next morning, but we had to prepare breakfast for the directors, who had either spent the night or driven down early in the day. There would be a stream of headlights cutting through the dark on the dirt road leading in to the ranch, as most of the golfers drove down in time for an early tee-off. We didn't have the cabin space to accommodate that many, but part of the fun for them must have been getting up at four or five and setting off on the road. (Golfers, like fisherman, are sometimes irrational.) Some guests flew down in their private planes and landed on the graded strip adjacent to the golf course. The buzz of the planes as they circled the ranch added to the excitement. A big coffee pot was already perking in the clubroom for the early arrivals.

The amount of food served at Sunday's lunch grew along with the crowd. With an average of more than 100 players per meet and with each of them having three to four family members or guests, we sometimes served more than 400 barbecue plates. Eventually, we turned to catering services, from Underwood's or Jack Jordan's of Odessa and others, and mealtime became less of a chore and more of a pleasure.

The directors in the early years were Carson Montgomery and Allen Perry of Iraan. Later Bill Goldwire of Sanderson and John Guffey of Odessa helped out, along with Tommie Williams, also of Sanderson, who was an outstanding woman golfer. They gave many hours to help us out during these weekends.

As the popularity of the course grew, so did the publicity. Numerous articles appeared in area newspapers and, Dad, never averse to the limelight, was invited to appear on the sports briefs on Midland and Odessa television stations before tournament time.

Mom and Dad never directed their own tournaments, but they were busy and visible all day long on tournament days. Mom checked teams in and collected fees before tee time, answered the phone, supervised the food preparation, and entertained one and all. Her warm personality was a fundamental part of these gatherings, and her quick wit, noted by guests, added spice. Once, Joe and Doniece Allen of Crane had observed a new drilling rig near the entrance of the ranch. Joe said, "You got a well!" Mildred replied, "No, I'm still-a sick!" Another time, a golfer introduced himself by saying, "Hello, I'm Jack Frost" (it was really his name), to which Mom replied, "Hello to you; I'm Mother Nature!" She had a deadpan delivery and perfect timing.

Mom was able to make use of life itself for her fun, and we all had to laugh at this one. Her telephone friend from downriver called one day to complain about the Sanderson Bank. "I'm changing banks," she said. "Those people in Sanderson don't know shit from honey." The next time Troy Druse, one of the bankers from Sanderson, drove in to play golf, Mom met him with a clearly labeled jar of honey.

"Troy, do you know what this is?" she asked.

Realizing he was being set up for something, he carefully examined the jar and replied, "No, Mildred, I don't believe I do."

"It's honey, and you can keep it," Mom said. "Now I've got to go and make a phone call." No doubt to share a laugh with her Pecos River friend.

Dad was in his glory during tournaments. His golf cart never stopped roving as he replaced flags, moved cups, and took up sprinkler heads. He checked on the smallest details, always aiming to please. Nothing made him, or any of us, happier than departing golfers telling him what a great time they'd had. We basked in the goodness of those days.

We averaged four or five tournaments a year, one a month from May to September. There were private tournaments also, for family, community, and business groups, including an annual event held by the Odessa Junior Chamber of Commerce. One of the most unusual groups was the Whetrock Gang from Odessa. A loosely organized bunch of men connected with the oil-field industry, including Dad's good friend from Iraan, "Rye" Rylander, they gathered a couple of times a year to play golf and raise money for worthy causes. The highlight of their Saturday nights was an auction where they sold everything imaginable and donated all the proceeds to charity. An all-night poker party followed, but some hardy souls could still be seen teeing off early Sunday morning.

When the golf course was no longer maintained, several of the gang called and asked to come back, saying they didn't care what condition the course was in. That was impossible, but it hurt to say no. One of the gang said, after we closed the course, "Well, our favorite watering hole in Odessa, the Blue Max, closed down and then Chandler's up and quit. Life's just not worth living!"

Two other groups dear to us were the hometown people from Iraan and Sanderson. They were loyal supporters from the beginning. Hardly a day went by during the summer months when several of them didn't show up to play. Since Iraan had its own nine-hole course, the Sanderson players were probably more frequent visitors. A special group from Sanderson was made up of Sid Harkins, Herbert Brown, Lee Dudley, and Herbert Cates. They were Dad's contemporaries and shared lots of years and many good experiences, and they loved golf and being outdoors together.

So many of these players were employees of the Southern Pacific Railroad that we had a special board in the clubroom where we posted the train schedule. They would often play nine holes and then rush to call the Sanderson Depot to get an update on the trains. Unfortunately, the Southern Pacific often took precedence over a good round, and they would have to load up and rush back into town to keep the trains moving.

Membership fees had gone up to $200 by 1974, but a special price of $150 was available to Terrell County golfers because of their frequent visits and lack of a golf course in their vicinity. Golf-cart rental was $5 and the greens fee for nonmembers $7. Tournament entry fees per team had increased to $20 in the seventies. These prices were considered reasonable at the time. Cabin rentals, fishing and camping fees, and sales from the store were still steady sources of income. However, golf had become the big attraction at the ranch (though fishermen may disagree).

A faithful twosome, once awarded prizes at a tournament for being the most "senior" players present, was Dewey Sconiers and Travis Curtis of Iraan. These two gentlemen always had such a good time that everyone enjoyed being around them. We all loved the story of Mr. Curtis going into the pond by the green at the third hole to retrieve a ball and disappearing under the water until only the top of his hat was visible to those on the bank. One good laugh followed another for those two.

Gay Emery, in her *Iraan News* column "Off the Tee Box," covered a typical tournament in June 1975 in which they, and many others, were recognized:

> Dewey Sconiers and Travis Curtis failed to place in regulation play this past Sunday in Joe Chandler's Partnership with 66 golfers teeing off. The pair won a different kind of honor, a special sportsmanship award. They were awarded keen putters.
>
> Bill Estes and Steve Cranfill of Crane won the Championship Flight and beautiful trophies. Ken Stout of Big Lake and Ross Wortham of Iraan teamed to take the runnersup honors by defeating Gerald Burnett and Ronnie Huckaby of Monahans on the second hole of the sudden-death playoff.
>
> Playoffs were required of the top three places in the First Flight. Troy White and Norman Guess of Big Lake were victorious over John Whistler of Sanderson and Bruce Adams of Del Rio.
>
> Don Love and James Wright of Odessa defeated Steve Chandler and Bob Little also of Odessa for the third place. All fired 107's.
>
> Second Flight saw Skipper Harris and Bill Mott of Sanderson win with 113. Mike Butler and Dennis Riley took the second place with 115 with Ron Maedgen of Mesquite and Ron Hall of Sanderson having the third spot with a 116.
>
> Chandler's next tournament will be hosted by the new lessees, Mrs. and Mrs. Phil Jones of Midland, and will be held on Sunday, Sept. 1.

The largest tournaments on the books list up to 63 teams, but most averaged around 50. Players came from Odessa, Midland, Crane, McCamey, Iraan, Sanderson, Ozona, Sonora, Big Lake, Rankin, Ft. Stockton, and other neighboring towns.

Par for men on the 2,500 yards was 34 (40 for women), and hotshot golfers blasted that on occasion. And then there were many who never got close to making par but still came back for more. Maybe it was Mom's potato salad or Al Hood and John Guffey's succulent chicken or John Smith's brisket sizzling on the pit that drew them. Or the enjoyment of sitting around the pool and watching the kids splash in the cool water under cloudless summer skies. Or spending a pleasant day with friends outdoors in a beautiful natural setting.

WHILE BIRDIES were being made on the course, real birds went on making their home at the ranch. They were an attraction in themselves. Birders had always been drawn to the ranch, and we had a great fondness for these naturalists.

Midland and Odessa birders were frequent visitors. Joan Merritt, Mavis Murphy, and Bill Edwards recorded two trips for posterity in 1983 in reports for the *Phalarope,* the newsletter of the Midland Naturalists. They reported spotting forty-six species in April, fifty-three in May, and sixty on another trip in May. Two excerpts from their reports follow:

> A great horned owl sat atop an oak tree and hooted as we arrived. Later that night another owl joined in for a duet. . . . The biggest surprise was the turkeys roosting in the trees next to us. We had stayed at the golf course until well after sundown to see if the turkeys were roosting there, but no luck. Early next morning we were awakened by a loud gobble-gobble-gobble. We quietly dressed and made our way around the hill so the sun would be at our back and were rewarded by seeing four gobblers with tails fanned and wings spread. . . .
>
> A circular hike through the ranch produced yellow-throated vireo, black-capped vireo, Bell's vireo, hooded and orchard orioles and courting vermilion flycatchers. The most common bird was the brilliant painted bunting. Green kingfishers were in abundance on the creek and river.

Other birders mentioned on these trips were Don Merritt, Rose Marie and Mary Frances Stortz, Mike Murphy, Pauline Warren, and Dorothy Harris, who were kept busy recording all the species spotted.

Birding, golfing, camping, fishing, and hunting sometimes occurred simultaneously at Chandler's. The ranch was alive with visitors for so many years. One of the most notable was a future president of the United States, who did not come to fish or hunt but just to visit. George W. Bush, then known only as a citizen of Midland, was a friend of Hal Dean Jr., who had a pasture lease with Dad. Hal Jr., known to most as Rocky, and his wife Evelyn lived in the house we call the Home Place, and their now prominent guest enjoyed a hamburger in the kitchen of that humble dwelling.

In the early eighties, another great adventure took place at the ranch in the form of a summer camp for children. The ranch had always been a wonderful place for children. For six sessions, the attendees took part in every healthy and enjoyable outdoor activity associated with summer camp. Many of those who came, adults today, still say it was the best time they ever had.

Diane Cantrell and Jovita Aguilar were camp nurses, and Oleata Westbrook and Judy Turner were camp cooks, four of the most indispensable folks around. There were two innovative and dependable head counselors, Elaine Odom of Midland and Ruthie Fortune of Sheffield. Elaine's father was a Boy Scout leader and Ruthie's a Baptist minister, so they were veteran summer campers, well-prepared for their roles. Of course, there were many others—counselors, junior counselors, teachers, dishwashers, and campers —who made those summers special. I remember red-shirted campers all over the place, paddling their canoes up the Pecos, sleeping outdoors at Shady Oaks, hiking through the hills, and singing silly songs around a campfire under a waning moon.

AN UNUSUAL PROPOSAL came our way in the early eighties. A retired Midland lawyer approached Dad with the idea of selling water to the city of Midland. Paul F. Power Jr. of the *Odessa American* reported on the city's response to the idea:

> A retired attorney says he can provide Midland or other cities up to 19 million gallons of water daily from a ranch 110 miles south of Odessa, but so far has found few takers for the project that could cost $30 million or more.
>
> "We might be interested in the water if it wasn't so costly," Assistant City Manager Fred Poe said today. "The big bugaboo about this proposal is the water is so far away."
>
> Midland already is under contract to receive water from the proposed Stacy Dam, but that doesn't faze 74-year-old Hal Rachal from looking for a

buyer for the water. A renewable aquifer below the Joe Chandler ranch near Sheffield could be tapped with water wells and pumped north through a 36-inch pipe, Rachal said.

He has already taken his proposal to the Midland City Council and proposes selling the water for 25 cents per 1,000 gallons and said reports from the U.S. Geological Survey, the Texas Water Commission, and the Texas Water Development Board suggest the water—which flows from underground springs in the vicinity of Independence Creek near the confluence with the Pecos River—could provide millions of gallons of good water for decades to come.

The idea was discussed during a city council meeting but rejected almost immediately due to the prohibitive costs.

THE WATERS of the Pecos and Independence have continued to flow, but the character of the river and its plants and animals have changed in response to both natural and human causes.

The first major change came to our attention in the mid-eighties when large numbers of fish in the Pecos River began to die. Turning to the fresh water in Independence for survival, many began to swim upstream to escape a deadly plague, which was identified by state authorities as toxic algal bloom. In the first kill in 1985, the number of fish affected was conservatively estimated at 110,000; over half a million were reported dead the following year. The main area of concern was between Iraan and the upper regions of Amistad Dam near Del Rio, which put the ranch right in the middle of the phenomenon. Over half the fish killed were reported to be minnows and sunfish, but we saw carp, gars, bass, and catfish floating with their white bellies turned up. Both these kills happened about the same time each year, in October and November.

Different varieties of toxic algae are always present in the Pecos, according to those who study the river, but usually in small concentrations that are not harmful to fish. However, sometimes a certain combination of sunlight, water chemistry, and temperature causes the algal cells to reproduce rapidly, and their toxicity increases to levels high enough to kill fish.

Another slowly creeping problem is the salt cedars. These invasive trees now line the banks of the Pecos in Texas and have made the river inaccessible on most of the ranch today. In addition to choking the stream, they produce salt and therefore take up water. One tree can drain up to 200 gallons of water a day—a sad fact, as the Pecos needs all the water it can get. Plans for intensive spraying began in fall 2003.

Patrick Dearen, a Midland author who has done extensive research on the Pecos, summed up its current condition in a statement to *Dallas Morning News* reporter Bryan Woolley:

> For several decades, dams and irrigation farming have reduced it [the Pecos] to a vestige of its frontier self, a mere trickle in places, no longer a killer of men and destroyer of dreams. Truckers and travelers crossing its bridges barely notice it. . . .
>
> It's hard to believe it's the same stream. Now it's shallow, it's smothered in salt cedars, it's polluted with oil. It's hardly a river anymore. You have to look deep to find the sweat and blood of the cowhands and immigrants and pioneers who saw in it a challenging obstacle.

As for those who live on its banks today, he continues, "Living along the Pecos still requires a certain strength, stamina and a sense of humor. If, as they say, Texas ain't for amateurs, the Pecos is strictly for the hardiest professionals. Even for them, unless they were born there, life on the river is an acquired taste."

Our land has also been invaded by thousands of willow trees, scientifically called *Baccharis,* which have taken over the creek and surrounding land along ditches and draws. Between the willows and the salt cedars, neither native to the area, the view and access to both the creek and river have become more obstructed. We have been asked why we allowed this to happen. My answer is that we didn't really "let" it happen. These unfriendly trees, whose roots can reach down fifty meters or more for groundwater, just slowly entered the area over a period of years. It would take an overwhelming effort, in the form of spraying, burning, or root plowing, to control these innocuous-looking little intruders.

The combination of water-draining vegetation, long hot summers, and periods of drought all threaten the flow of the creek and river. In figures supplied by Jimmy Pond of the U.S. Geological Survey, the highest flow in Independence was recorded in 1974 by a gauge that was operated and checked periodically until 1985. (A new measuring device was installed in 2002.) The average flow during those years was approximately 12,477 gallons per minute or 750,000 gallons per hour.

Although water levels in the Independence fluctuate, it remains healthy. However, I fear for the future of all natural free-flowing streams and springs in our state. Gunnar Brune, whose work *Springs of Texas* was the source for my description of springs on Independence Creek, does not paint a hopeful picture. Since the book was written, in 1981, many of the springs he describes are now dry or producing less water. The failure of most of Texas' springs has multiple explanations but is especially caused by the drilling of flowing wells and pumping of groundwater for irrigation. He cites the destruction of Comanche Springs at Ft. Stockton as an example of human mistreatment of water in this area. The pollution of many remaining springs has been caused by substances such as oil-field brine, sewage, herbicides, and insecticides.

Concern for the future of the creek was behind one of the most painful decisions our family ever made. In June 1991 we placed the golf course land and most of our part of the creek into a conservation easement held by the Nature Conservancy. This arrangement, the first of its kind in Texas, was more acceptable to my family than an outright sale, which was the original proposal of the Conservancy. Selling the easement meant that we retained ownership of the land along the creek banks but gave up certain development rights in order to preserve its special environmental qualities. In essence, we sacrificed the saddle to keep the horse.

Under different circumstances, we might not have taken this course of action. But subsequent events have shown that the agreement with the Conservancy in Dad's last years was a good move at the time. After a lifetime of having our father make every decision concerning the ranch, JoBeth and I were forced finally to step in. We convinced him that the easement was good for the family financially and for the future of the creek, and it allowed him to feel that he was still holding the reins. I personally doubt that he fully understood the terms of the easement, as his grip on reality had begun to weaken much earlier. Dad's deteriorating physical and mental health over several years and his family's blindness to the situation had led to poor business decisions on his part and denial on ours. In his last years, Dad was unaware of events beyond his control, and neither the course nor the ranch nor our family would ever be the same again.

Dad had borne the physical work and mental strain of managing the ranch for most of his life, and we realized we could not carry on business as usual without him. Even if we had tried, I can see now that we would not have succeeded. His gregarious, untamed personality and unlimited energy were so much a part of the ranch that our efforts to maintain the status quo could not have measured up.

His eighty years on the creek far outnumbered those of other dwellers on its banks, including Grandad, and you couldn't tell the story of one without the other. Today, the ranch is closed (except for a deer lease), but the creek continues on its course into the Pecos, and we still call this place on Independence home.

Perhaps a hundred years or so from now, some naturalist or archeologist will be walking in the area and unearth a battered golf ball. I can see him now, scratching his head and wondering about such an unusual artifact.

It seems fitting to end the story of life on the ranch with an imaginary scene from the golf course, a field of dreams if ever one existed. I approach the first tee, freshly mowed and smooth as lush carpet, just below the pool. I tee up, and in memory of all the events that have transpired on this place and all the people that have gone before me, I hit the ball, cleanly and surely.

It sails over the oak trees lining the fairway and heads straight into the brilliant Texas sky, drives the green by a hundred years . . . and soars.

EPILOGUE
From the Nature Conservancy of Texas publication *Horizons*, Spring 1992:

We extend our deepest condolences to the family of Joe Bailey Chandler, who passed away on January 6, 1992. Joe Chandler and his wife, Mildred, owned the Chandler Ranch on Independence Creek in Terrell County, which is now operated by their daughters, JoBeth Holub and Charlena Vargas-Prada. Joe Chandler was born in 1912 and lived on the ranch his entire life with the exception of his school years. During the 1950s, Joe and Mildred developed the Joe Chandler Guest Ranch, which has provided a beautiful retreat and happy memories to many Texans over the years. Joe had a special commitment to Independence Creek and the land around it, and shared his love of the land with all who knew him. The Nature Conservancy owns a conservation easement over a portion of the Chandler Ranch.

State Senator Bill Sims of District 25 sponsored a Texas State Senate Proclamation in Dad's memory that recognized his achievements and extended sympathy to his family. Mildred died on July 1, 1999. Her passing did not bring the accolades that Joe received, but those who knew them would agree that she deserved all the praise he received, and more.

Both she and Dad are buried at the ranch.

EVALUATION OF INDEPENDENCE CREEK, TERRELL COUNTY, TEXAS

as a Potential Natural Landmark
(Abridged)

Evaluator: James F. Scudday, Ph.D., Professor of Biology, Sul Ross State University, Alpine, Texas 79830. 8 April 1977

Consideration for designation of Independence Creek as a natural landmark is based upon published reports of the relictual species of vertebrate animals found there (Milstead, 1960), and upon an assessment of the area's biota by Dr. Fred Gehlbach (1966) of Baylor University. Additional published reports of the area's biota are those of Webster (1950), Milstead et al. (1950), and Scudday.

This evaluator has conducted a great amount of field work in the area, beginning in 1960. The Independence Creek area has always been a favorite site for conducting vertebrate biology field trips by the Biology Department at Sul Ross State University. Consequently, a great wealth of material is available in the Sul Ross Vertebrate Collection from the Independence Creek area as well as from field notes of the evaluator.

Great changes have been wrought by man along the course of Independence Creek. When I visited the area in the early 1960s, Lindsey Hicks owned the big springs that supplied much of the volume of water that flowed into Independence Creek, and Mr. Hicks did little in modifying the springs and upper part of the creek. The Chandler family owned the lower end of the creek, including the mouth of the creek at the Pecos River. Some water was taken from the creek to irrigate a small amount of farmland, but little else was done to change or alter the natural communities along the drainage. The Chandlers charged fishermen to fish the Pecos River and the creek.

By the late 1960s, Lindsey Hicks had sold his upper part to W. F. Roden, who greatly modified the springs and upper drainages into a manageable but unnatural setting. Joe Chandler . . . [developed] a recreational resort on the lower end of the creek. This included the construction of a nine-hole golf course, cabins, a swimming pool, ponds and canals, and a developed campground for visitors.

The effect of these recent changes upon the biota has not been assessed. It can be assumed that certain fish species may suffer because of loss of habitat and pressure of fishermen using the small forms for bait. Some reptiles, such as the Trans-Pecos copperhead and mottled rock rattlesnake will suffer because of an increasing number of people that will kill snakes.

The avifauna, on the other hand, appears to be enriched because of the greater diversity of habitats available. Whereas only a few teal ever visited the area before, large flocks of canvasbacks, scaups, and mallards were seen in February 1977 on the large ponds at the Roden Ranch and Chandler's. A thorough biological survey needs to be conducted at this time to document changes now taking place, and assess the status of relict species recorded there during the early 1950s.

Joe Chandler supplied me with most of the historical data. Mr. Chandler has always been very open and friendly and is justly proud of his family's historical association with the area. Mrs. Dunn of the Brewster County Soil and Water Conservation Service was most helpful in locating landowners and determining the section lines. . . .

SIZE

Independence Creek contains running water only in the lower eight miles of creek bed. A very small segment of running water is found west of State Highway 349. This segment should be excluded from the proposed area. The area of greatest significance begins at the Oasis Ranch of W. F. Roden where the large springs supply most of the water for the creek from this point to its mouth on the Pecos River, a length of about five miles.

I propose a maximum acreage of 2,383 acres be included in the Natural

Landmark site. A minimum of 783 acres could be considered, which would include only the land owned by the Chandlers from the mouth of the creek on the Pecos River to a point two miles upstream from the mouth (all of block 313). . . .

OWNERSHIP

. . . Mr. Joe Chandler was the only owner that I contacted. Mr. Chandler lives on his land and is easily accessible. He indicated interest in the Natural Landmark Program and would most likely be favorable to such designation for his property. Mr. Roden has not been contacted. He lives in Midland and is at the ranch only occasionally. [Other owners listed in this report were Clarence Chandler and Mrs. Herbert Brown.]

LAND USE AND INTEGRITY

The area has always supported an agrarian economy. The presence of running water in an arid environment long attracted stockmen to Independence Creek. First cattle and horses, later sheep and goats, were introduced to the rangelands of Terrell County by the turn of the century. Some land near the Pecos River was put into cultivation by Mr. Charles Chandler, who purchased the land from the state of Texas around 1900. Cotton and watermelons were produced on this land until the mid-1950s. Some of the cultivated land has since been restored to range land, while other acres recently have been cleared and planted to oats and other grazing crops. These newly cultivated areas are just outside the proposed boundaries.

Extensive acreage has been placed into irrigated pastureland by W. F. Roden on the upper part of the area. Another smaller area was cleared and planted to oats between the road and the creek about halfway between the Roden and Chandler ranches. This field was not planted in 1976–1977, and appeared to be returning to a native weedy vegetation. Mr. Roden does not allow any hunting, and fishing is provided only for invited guests.

The Chandler Ranch is now fully committed to a resort type development which is functional and operating. Commercial deer hunting and fishing are conducted during seasons.

THREATS TO THE AREA

Continued development of the upper end of the creek area into permanent irrigated pasture or cropland, and the impact of greater numbers of people visiting the Chandler Guest Ranch are the most direct threats. In spite of the fact that the Roden Ranch does not allow anyone but invited guests, and enforces strict no trespass policy, the extreme alteration of habitat for increased livestock production poses even a greater threat than the resort development on the Chandler Ranch. The habitat has not been altered nearly as much on the Chandler Ranch in order to accommodate guests. Instead, most of the guest facilities have been built to utilize and blend into the present habitat as much as possible. For this reason, the designated area could well include only block 313.

DESCRIPTION OF NATURAL VALUES

Independence Creek is a tributary of the Pecos River in northeastern Terrell County. The creek ultimately drains a very large watershed in both Pecos and Terrell counties. Physiographically, Independence Creek is one of the major drainages of the great Stockton Plateau (Milstead, 1950). The Stockton Plateau is considered to lie within the Chihuahuan Biotic Province (Blair, 1950), but shows transitional characteristics with the Balconian Province to the east (Milstead, 1950).

Independence Creek is dry most of the year, except for the lower end. From its mouth at the Pecos River to the great springs on Roden's Oasis Ranch, a distance of about six miles, the creek perennially flows a great volume of water. Another two miles west of the Oasis Ranch's giant springs and numerous small springs contribute to a continuously flowing creek of lesser volume. Beyond this point, about eight miles from the south of the creek, water flows in the creek bed only during heavy rains on the watershed. The flowing lower six miles of Independence Creek support a riparian association dominated by large live oak trees *(Quercus fusiformis)*. This site represents the most westward extension of this species of oak (Webster, 1950).

Because of the large area drained by Independence Creek, disastrous floods periodically occur, sometimes when no rain at all falls on the lower part of the creek. This presents a constant hazard to both wildlife and people, particularly campers and fishermen, during the rainy time of the year (late summer and fall).

The most disastrous flood of recent history occurred in 1954. Joe Chandler has numerous photographs and newspaper clippings of that event. This flood occurred at a time when a prolonged drought had gripped southwest Texas, and the rangeland was denuded of vegetation. This, coupled with a record rainfall of as much as 22 inches within a 24-hour period, produced a flood that greatly altered the creek bed and the riparian vegetation as it had existed since anyone could remember. Many great live oak trees that bordered the creek were washed away, and the creek bed was greatly widened and became somewhat braided in nature. Floods that put the creek out of its banks still occur almost annually, and evidence of such floods are a constant reminder of the danger of flash floods. Milstead (1960) commented on the irony that the greatest danger of extinction of species here is by either too little or too much water.

The very fact of the existence of such a large, free-flowing creek of pure, high-quality water in the arid Chihuahuan biotic province is in itself a unique natural feature. But more than that, Independence Creek provides an important clue to the formation of the Chihuahuan Desert in time and sequence. The area is represented by a relictual biota that has been partially stranded by the encroaching desert since the more pluvial periods of the late Pleistocene. The valley containing Independence Creek today represents a mesic corridor that thrusts, fingerlike, into the most arid Chihuahuan environs from a larger mesic corridor, the Pecos River. Other corridors once existed, but now have become fragmentary, leaving isolated populations of an earlier, more mesic adapted flora and fauna as relicts in a vast desert area. Milstead's (1960) study of 14 relict species of reptiles and amphibians in the Chihuahuan Desert revealed more relict species (9 of 14) existing along Independence Creek than elsewhere, and attributed this to its proximity to the eastern edge of the desert.

The present status of the nine relict species discussed by Milstead is not presently known. Milstead suggested that the flood of 1954 had decimated these populations and perhaps extirpated some species. My own field work in the area in the 1960s indicated that six of the nine species were at least present, but may exist in diminished numbers. Milstead listed the barking frog *(Hylactophryne augusti–Eleutherodactylus latrans)* from the Stockton Plateau on circumstantial evidence only, but Scudday (1963) discovered the species to exist rather abundantly among the limestone cliffs above Independence Creek on the Joe Chandler Ranch. The cricket frog *(Acris crepitans),* ground skink *(Scincella laterale),* blotched water snake *(Natrix erythrogaster transversa),* and Trans-Pecos copperhead *(Agkistrodon contortrix pictigaster)* were commonly encountered in field work, but the cliff frog *(Syrrhophus marnocki),* gulf coast toad *(Bufo valliceps)* and Texas coral snake *(Micrurus fulvius tenere)* have not been reported recently in the area.

In addition to reptiles and amphibians, the area supports a number of peripheral and relict populations of plants, fish, birds, and mammals. Large mottes of plateau live oak *(Quercus fusiformis)* attract a number of avian species that normally do not nest this far west. The Rio Grande perch *(Cichlasoma cyanguttatum)* reaches its westernmost and northernmost distribution in the creek here. A rare green kingfisher was sighted near the Chandler headquarters in February, 1977.

Beaver have always existed here in the Pecos River and the lower end of Independence Creek. Nutria, on the other hand, represent a recent invader along the watercourses, and according to Joe Chandler, are not common enough to be a pest. This is the only place west of the Pecos River where fox squirrels are commonly seen.

Thus, the most biologically significant aspect of the area as a natural landmark is its role as a mesic corridor into an arid desert environment that allows two somewhat distinct biotic communities to exist side by side. This provides for the westernmost range extensions of some eastern species and gives some insight into the development of the Chihuahuan Desert. A striking contrast is presented where the dry rangeland suddenly merges with the greenery of the riparian community. Another contrast is seen in comparing the juniper-grasslands of the mesa tops with the slope and valley floor communities. . . . Geologically, the area represents an eroded plateau of Cretaceous limestone, leaving behind flat-topped mesas dissected by numerous arroyos and valleys. Fossils of gastropods, cephalopods, and echinoderms are abundant. An abundance of chert nodules imbedded in the limestone strata provided a basic material from which early man fashioned his tools.

SIGNIFICANCE STATEMENT

The free-flowing lower end of Independence Creek provides a refugium for a number of species of mesic adapted plants and animals surrounded by a hostile arid environment. The area displays sharp contrasts between the surrounding Chihuahuan Desert vegetative communities and those of the valley floor with its lush riparian habitat. Large live oak mottes, now only a remnant of a once extensive gallery forest bordering the creek, provide a setting that attracts avian species not normally found this far west. Milstead discussed the relict amphibian and reptilian species represented in the area. Beavers, fox squirrels, armadillos, and nutria are mammalian species commonly occurring here that are not normally found west of the Pecos River. The Rio Grande perch *(Cichlasoma cyanoguttatum)* is a common fish in the creek, but is found nowhere else north or west of this site.

Geological and archeological aspects are also important. Independence Creek has cut a deep valley through the cretaceous limestone of the Stockton Plateau, exposing a representative sedimentary sequence. Fossils of the Cretaceous age are abundant. . . . Although the surrounding terrain has been altered somewhat by man, the floral and faunal assemblages still found along the lower end of Independence Creek are of national significance.

RECOMMENDATION

It is my opinion that in spite of much habitat alteration that has occurred over the past decade, the valley containing the lower end of Independence Creek still maintains a high degree of its natural integrity, and I recommend it be designated a national natural landmark.

REFERENCES

W. F. Blair, F. R. Gehlbach, H. McClintock, J. S. Mecham, W. S. Milstead, J. F. Scudday, and G. L. Webster

MEMBERS OF THE INDEPENDENCE LAKE CLUB

First Year, 1953–54

Names are grouped by hometown and listed in order of registration. Members' professions or company affiliations are included, a good indication of the different walks of life represented in the club.

ABILENE: Dale Allen, Sun Electric

BEST: James Watkins, Ranching

CRANE: Durwood Gaines, Gulf Oil; Marion Brunette, Crane Sweet Shop

FT. STOCKTON: E. A. Robertson, D.D.S.; Aubrey Price, Assistant to Dr. Robertson; Hart Johnson, District Attorney; G. E. Porter, Barbecue

GRANDFALLS: Homer Nettleton, Sunbeam Food Market

IRAAN: Jim Watts, Ranching; Jimmie Jacobsen, Jacobsen's Dry Goods; Clyde Shahan, Building Contractor; W. T. Hutchinson, H & H Food Store

LUBBOCK: J. E. Hammond, Frito Company; Jack L. Brown, Decal Oil Company

MCCAMEY: C. C. Carll, News Publishing Company; V. P. Baron, Baron's NuWay; Bill Tidwell, News Publishing Company; Sherrill Davis, Baron's NuWay; Clarence Powell, Baron's NuWay; Olen Pigford, Traveler's Liquor Store; Lelan Haren, Farming; "Sandy" Sandlin, Coca-Cola Bottling Company; Jack Edwards, Stock Farmer; Marshall Neville, Stock Farmer; J. M. Slaughter, D.D.S.; James L. Cooper, M.D.

MIDLAND: Herbert Franklin, Superior Oil; Don O. Crookham, Superior Oil; Baird Neville, Superior Oil; Bud Frizzell, Independent Oil Operator; Bob Taylor, Shell Oil; G. P. Crawford, Superior Oil; B. W. Burkhead, Superior Oil; Martin Johnson, Stanolind Oil; John H. Hughes, Hughes Jewelry Company; Dean Chase, Lario Oil and Gas; Stan Collins, C and H Appliance; Bob Maberry, Milwhite Mud Company; W. L. Morrison, El Capitan Oil; Gene Brewer, Brewer's Hardware; Joe Starnes, Abstracts; J. K. Easterling, S. W. Wholesale Drug; J. D. Martin, Building Contractor; W. T. Moore, C. L. Cunningham Building Contractor; "Red" Smith, Red Smith Tire Company; Tom Cline, Frank Frawley Drilling; L. S. Melzer, Statex Explorations; Robbie Robinson, Pittsburgh Plate Glass; Bill Price, Attorney; D. S. Elmore, House of Beauty; Stanley Weiner, Texas Crude; Jack Garrett, Gulf Oil; Billy Adair, Club Manhattan; Jack Ptosky, Independent Oil Operator

ODESSA: James Newton, Newton Lumber Company; Gene Shreve, Shreve Tire Company; Neal O. Nichols, D.D.S.; Frank Russell, Royal Cleaners; H. E. Rydell, Mid-Continent Supply; H. H. Hughes, Harry's Liquor Store; Ollie Blanks, Waddell & Blanks; Blake Sweatt, Mgr., Lincoln Hotel; Adell Laird, Texas Music Company; Lang White, Reliance Lumber; B. B. Strahan, D.D.S.; Conally Evans, Pastor, Belmont Baptist Church; Matt Mabry, Wayside Paint and Body Shop; Jim Bunch, Bunch Construction; Howard Fallin, Visco Products; J. A. Smethers, Superior Paraffin Scraping Company; J. F. Harrison, West Texas Concrete; N. N. Miller, Gulf Oil; R. D. Guthrie, Powell-Gruthrie Engine Service; Roger Ashford, Ashford Lumber Company; Lee Bromley, Texas Music; Jim A. Tilson, Plains Machinery; John Neely, Frito Company; W. M. Baron, Newton Construction; John Hallum, Writer; Geo. V. West, Stanolind Oil and Gas; R. N. Whiteside, Caser; Mickey Lavy, J. C. Penney; Boaz Hoskins, Victory Home Equipment; M. P. Gillis, Wholesale Electrical and Mechanical; Mutt Hunley, Frito Company; Harold C. Powell, Powell's Service Station; Bob Kelly; Kelly's Food Market; Lynn Hunt, M.D.; Jack Faulkner, West Texas Insurors; L. B. Henson, Henson's Garage; Don Bright, Friday, White and Donk; J. H. Chrietzberg, Choya Drilling; Billy Joe Buster, Mary Lou Pie Shop; W. C. Peer, Axelson Manufacturing; Ashley Lawson, Lawson Food Market; Ned Woolley, Woolley Tool Company; Bob Hart, Woolley Tool Company; C. L. Cunningham, Building Contractor; J. H. Ulrich, Woolley Tool Company; Don Hampton, Cactus Rental Company; J. C. Foster, Theaters; Gene Luna, Lucey Products Corporation; Frank Green, Green's Restaurant; Johnnie Adams, A&B Company; "Cotton" Clover, Public Accountant; Geo. W. Horton, M.D.; Fred M. Perry,

Reed Roller Bit; Glen Flournoy, Ector County Airport; Duke Samson, K & S Construction; Dan Garrison, K & S Construction; Bill Casstevens, Casstevens Furniture

RANKIN: Joe W. Powell, Rankin Gas Company; Horace West, Haliburton

SANDERSON: H. W. L. Johnson, Southern Pacific Railroad; Keith Mitchell, Ranching; Clarence Jessup, Ranching; Jimmie Hanson, McKnight Motor Company; Sid Harkins, Ranching

SHEFFIELD: Olin Smith, Ranching; Henry Sandel, Sandel's Mercantile

STANTON: Harry Dobbs, Texas Crude

Appendix C
GOLF TOURNAMENTS

A newspaper clipping from the sports pages of the *Odessa American* in the late sixties recounts a typical golf tournament at the ranch and highlights the names of many regular participants. This story by Carl Dingler appeared under the headline "Repeat Champions—Gibbs Wins Tourney":

> Sandford Gibbs hopes June will never end. The young Odessa golfer and his father, Buddy Gibbs, shot nine under par Sunday to win the Independence Creek Golf Tournament at Joe Chandler's Guest Ranch.
>
> The duo had a low-ball 28 on the first nine of the par 34, 2,450 yard course and followed up with rounds of 34 and 31 for 93 and a three stroke victory to successfully defend their championship. . . .
>
> Meanwhile the other two flights ended in a tie for first place with Tommy Warner and Don White of Odessa winning a sudden death playoff with a par on the first extra hole from Jack Vail and Mike Werst of Odessa. Both teams ended with 107.
>
> In the second flight, Jim Young and Neil Collins of Odessa had a par to beat Jim Rapier and Max Jarrell of Odessa. These two teams also finished with 107.
>
> Also there was a playoff for second place in the championship flight with J. Neville and G. Johnson of Sonora getting par on the first extra hole to beat Boots Armstrong and James Bird of Big Lake. They ended with six under par, 96.
>
> There were 52 teams entered in the second tournament with most of

the golfers running into trouble during the tough first three holes of the plush course which were lined with trees and water hazards.

Also there were 10 teams who shot sub par golf over the 27 hole, one day tournament.

Championship flight—Buddy Gibbs–Sandford Gibbs, Odessa, 93; J. Neville–G. Johnson, Sonora, 96; Boots Armstrong–James Bird, Big Lake, 96; George Kyle–Brooks Dozier, Ozona, 97; Troy White–Eddie Burkett, Big Lake, 98; Irby Gleaton–Mike Kropp, Odessa, 98; Tommy Wagoner–David Matezowsky, Odessa, 98; Stan Pulley–C. Sizemore, Odessa, 98; Arnold Chambers–Red Grant, Odessa, 100; Johnny Martin–Dennis Hinkle, Odessa, 101; Don Hall–Terry Tuggle, Odessa, 105; Neal Wright–Willie Roberts, Iraan, 107; Ralph Chalfant–Charley Smith, Iraan, 109; P. B. Brown–J. B. Hutchins, Rankin, 109; Wes Whitefield–Doug McAnally, Iraan, 109; Harlan Smith–K. Allerding, Odessa, 111; W. Wilson–Harold Smith, Odessa, 120. (Neville–Johnson won sudden death playoff with par on first hole.)

Other players listed that day:

First Flight—Tommy Warner–Don White, Odessa; Jack Vail–Mike Werst, Odessa; L. Bryant–Clayton Kennedy, Iraan; Gene Swindle–Johnny Adams, Odessa; Kellus Turner–Paul Tittle, Odessa; Neal Nichols–Larry McKinney, Odessa; Junior Whitefield–Royce Whitefield, Iraan; Jack Sigman–Bud McAnally, Iraan; Don Gracey–Harrell Sanders, Iraan; Chuck Grigson–Bobby Bassett, Odessa; Troy Druse–Curley Kyle, Sanderson; Horace Zellers–D. L. Darley, Odessa; Bill Beckett–I. O. Smith, Iraan; Allen Harrison–D. Modisette, Odessa; Jerry Hudson–Doyes Allen, Odessa; Ken Johnson–Lewis Woodson, Crane; Doug Newton–Bob Davenport, Del Rio, withdrew. (Warner–White won sudden death playoff with par on first hole.)

Second Flight—Jim Young–Neil Collins, Odessa; Jim Rapier–Max Jarrell, Odessa, C. R. Rylander–Earl Morris, Iraan; Paul Dobbs–Kevin Dobbs, Odessa; V. Harris–David Pinard, Odessa; Don Reekman–Gary Dugan, Big Lake; Carter Garland–Johnny Scott, Iraan; Howard Morgan–Benny Houghton, Odessa; Batts Friend–James Trainer, Sonora; Charlie Hale–Brian Edmiston, Rankin; Joe Earnest–Gerald Patterson, Odessa; S. Culpepper–D. Crawford, Odessa; Jerry Payne–Bruce Fletcher, McCamey; Curtis Witt–Bill Norman, Odessa; Selwyn Smith–Travis Curtis, Iraan; H. G. Barbee–Bobby

Locker, Ozona; E. J. Holub–Bob Hammond, Odessa, withdrew; Buddy Brown–Darey Carroll, Sonora, withdrew. (Young–Collins won sudden death playoff with par on second hole.)

NOTES

INTRODUCTION

(p. 5) Charlie and Bill Chandler: W. H. "Coon" Chandler, personal communication.

(p. 6) Return to Junction: "Charlie Chandler's Memories of Dryden Country Go Back to 1890," *West Texas Livestock Weekly,* 31 October 1957.

(p. 6) Open range drawing to a close: R. D. Holt, "Vanished Empires," in *Terrell County, Texas: Its Past, Its People* (1978), p. 47.

(p. 6) I stood there that day . . . : "Charlie Chandler's Memories."

(p. 7) Centuries past: Leon Pope, *Archeological Report on the Chandler Ranch,* 41:TE.

(p. 7) Early predecessors: Pope, *Archeological Report.*

(p. 7) Native tribes: Alice Evans Downie, "Indians," in *Terrell County, Texas,* p. 24.

(p. 7–8) Native diet: Larry Bleiberg, "Indian Legacies," *San Angelo Standard-Times,* 6 April 1997.

(p. 8) Cooler conditions: Pope, *Archeological Report.*

(p. 8) Cabeza de Vaca: Anna Lee Allen, "The History of Terrell County," in *Terrell County, Texas,* p. 9.

(p. 8) Journals of Juan Mendoza: ibid.

(p. 8–9) Comanche War Trail: Clayton Williams, *Never Again* (1969), p. 160.

(p. 9) Ibid., p. 156.

(p. 9–10) Government Survey: William H. Emory, *Report on the United States and Mexican Boundary* (1857), p. 75.

(p. 10) Lieutenant Bullis: Jim Fenton, "John Bullis Always Meant Business," *Permian Historical Annual* 33 (December 1993), p. 1517.

(p. 11) Doomed from beginning: David G. McComb, *Texas: A Modern History* (1994), p. 22.

(p. 11) Evidence of primitive man: Bleiberg, "Indian Legacies."

(p. 11–12) Description of fetish: Franklin Barnett, *A Dictionary of Prehistoric Indian Artifacts of the American Southwest* (1973).

(p. 12–13) Description of Dryden: Lela Neal Pirtle, *Life on the Range and on the Trail* (1936).

(p. 13) Land owned by D. Hart: R. D. Holt, "Early Day Stockmen of the Lower Trans-Pecos," in *Terrell County, Texas*, p. 52.

(p. 15) Independence Cattle Company: Pirtle, *Life on the Range*, p. 49.

(p. 15) Hicks Ranch: Marjorie Canon Brown, "The A. M. Hicks Family," in *Terrell County, Texas*, p. 452.

(p. 15) Robert McCurdy: Ralph Hauritz, "Preservation Deal Is Made for a West Texas Oasis," *Austin American-Statesman*, 25 January 2002, p. 1.

(p. 16) Enormously important watershed: James King, Nature Conservancy of Texas, press release, 2003.

(p. 17–18) Camels in area: Frank Bishop Lammons, "Operation Camel: An Experiment in Animal Transportation in Texas, 1857–1860," *Southwestern Historical Quarterly* 61, no. 1 (July 1957), p. 41.

CHAPTER 1: CHARLIE

(p. 20) Dress of an old-time cowhand: Pirtle, *Life on the Range and on the Trail*, p. 60.

(p. 24) Obituary: "Charles Chandler, Ranch Pioneer, Dies," *San Angelo Standard-Times*, 11 November 1957, p. 6.

(p. 24) Birth date: "Dryden Rancher Recalls Wild Early Days of State," *Fort Worth Star-Telegram*, 25 March 1956, Section 2, p. 11.

(p. 25) Jackson, Mississippi: Hackberry Johnson, personal communication.

(p. 26) Hamp's children: Personal communication.

(p. 26) First job: "Dryden Rancher Recalls," p. 11.

(p. 26) Age of ten: Ibid.

(p. 27) Quanah Parker: Ibid.

(p. 28) Start as a rancher: Will Adams, "Woman, Age 71, Completes Work on Texas Pioneers Book," *San Angelo Standard-Times*, 14 September 1952, p. C5.

(p. 30) Price of Bullis purchase: Clayton Williams, *Texas' Last Frontier: Fort Stockton and the Trans-Pecos, 1861–1895* (1982), p. 299.

(p. 30–31) Description of Sulphur Springs: Gunnar Brune, *Springs of Texas* (1981), p. 423.

(p. 31–32) Panthers, wolves, etc.: J. Marvin Hunter, "Charley Chandler, A Rancher of the Pecos," *Frontier Times*, May 1950, p. 211.

(p. 32) Cotton: "Dryden Rancher Recalls," p. 11.

(p. 33) German trapper: Hunter, "Charley Chandler," p. 215.

(p. 33–34) McKay: Ibid., p. 214.

(p. 34) Dunlap Ranch: Terri Pease, "A Terrell County, Texas, Ranch," *Permian Historical Annual* 40 (December 2000), pp. 60, 65.

(p. 35) Great Depression: Joe Chandler, personal communication.

(p. 35) Federal program: Paul Patterson, *This Place of Memory: A Texas Perspective* (1992), p. 31.

(p. 36) Big Bend: Joe Chandler, personal communication.

(p. 37–38) Model-T Ford: Hunter, "Charley Chandler," p. 212.

CHAPTER 2: MINERVA

(p. 39) Divorce: Joe Chandler, personal communication.

(p. 40) Paul Patterson's quote: Bryan Woolley, "A Legend Runs Through It," *Dallas Morning News*, 28 June 1998.

(p. 42) Marriage: Crockett County records.

(p. 44–45) O'Bryant family: Minerva Chandler, personal records.

(p. 45–46) Fort Lancaster: Allan R. Bosworth, *Ozona Country* (1964), p. 20, and Harry Wood, "Knowledge of Old West Texas Fort Scant, and Most Is Bad," *San Angelo Standard-Times*, date unknown.

(p. 47) O'Bryantville: Mary Ellen Chandler Kimball and W. D. O'Bryant, "The W. D. O'Bryant Family," in *Terrell County, Texas*, pp. 567–68.

(p. 47) O'Bryants in Comstock: Comstock Study Club, *Comstock Friends and Neighbors*, pp. 146–148.

(p. 47) Picket house: Alice Evans Downie, *Terrell County, Texas*, p. 297.

(p. 48–49) Death of Fernando Brittain: Letter reprinted courtesy of Norma Fisher, relative of Fernando Brittain, and T. J. Holmes, Sheffield.

(p. 50) Early neighbors: W. F. Adams, "Kerr Woman Writes Book," *Kerrville Times*, 1952.

(p. 50–51) Effie Turk: Mildred Chandler, personal communication.

(p. 51) House in Kerrville: Adams, "Woman, Age 71," p. C5.

(p. 52) Obituary: "Services Thursday for Mrs. Chandler," *San Angelo Standard-Times*, 21 October 1970.

CHAPTER 3: SAINTS AND SINNERS

(p. 53) Black Jack Ketchum: W. H. Joyce, Virginia Madison, and Hugh B. Wilson, "Train Robberies," in *Terrell County, Texas*, pp. 91–93.

(p. 54) Hole in the Wall Gang: Henri Bob Russell, "West Texas Outlaws Era Viewed in 'Gunfighters,'" *San Angelo Standard-Times*, 26 August 1951.

(p. 54–55) Boone Kilpatrick: Joe Chandler, personal communication.

(p. 55) Kilpatrick and Welch: Jack Skiles, *Judge Roy Bean Country* (1996), p. 106.

(p. 55) David Trousdale: "Train Robberies," in *Terrell County, Texas*, p. 93.

(p. 56) "To see about a horse . . .": Elmer Kelton, personal communication.

(p. 56–57) Description of Herman: Paul Patterson, personal communication.

(p. 57) Hoover cattle: Joe Chandler, personal communication.

(p. 57–58) Rodeos at ranch: Joe Chandler, personal communication.

(p. 60–61) Herman and Myrtle in Mexico: Jay Walley, "Eighty-One Years West of the Pecos," *Ranch and Rural Living*, February 1996.

(p. 61–62) Church of Christ encampment: The Welch sisters, personal communication.

(p. 62–63) Early families at encampment: Susan Hayre, "Encampment's 50th Year," *Iraan News*, 17 June 1993.

CHAPTER 4: THE STAVLEY PLACE

(p. 65) Wedding: Mildred Chandler, personal communication.

(p. 66–68) Stavley family: Howard Stavley, "The Charles F. Stavley Family," in *Terrell County, Texas*, p. 638.

(p. 67) Juno: Comstock Study Club, *Comstock Friends and Neighbors*, p. 201.

(p. 70) Brown-Bassett: Gaye Ten Eyck, "Block Y Ranch," in *Terrell County, Texas*, p. 55.

(p. 71) Dancing lessons: Mildred Chandler, personal communication.

(p. 71) Introduction: Ibid.

(p. 76) Wreck on Pecos High Bridge: Mike Turk, "The C. J. 'Doc' Turk Family," in *Terrell County, Texas*, p. 658.

(p. 79–80) Drought: "Joe Chandler Rides Range in Golf Cart or, at Worst, a Jeep," *West Texas Livestock Weekly*, 11 July 1968, p. 6.

(p. 83) Bob Wills: Mildred Stavley, personal communication.

(p. 84) Shearing: Walter G. Downie, "Early Day Shearing Crews," in *Terrell County, Texas*, p. 61.

CHAPTER 5: HUNTING: DEER TALES

(p. 86) A close call: Mildred Chandler, personal communication.

(p. 88) Average buck deer: Ilo Hiller, *The White-Tailed Deer*, p. 28

(p. 89) Hole in the living room floor: Betty Dishong Renfer, personal communication.

(p. 91) Abandoned fawns: Hiller, *White-Tailed Deer,* p. 11.

(p. 92) Javelinas: David J. Schmidly, *The Mammals of Trans-Pecos Texas* (1977), p. 160.

(p. 94) Reasons for hunting: Rick Bass, *The Deer Pasture* (1989), p. 59.

CHAPTER 6: ONE-ROOM SCHOOL

(p. 99) School enrollment: "Independence School News," *Sanderson Times,* 1944.

(p. 100) Peacock: "PEACOCK MILITARY ACADEMY." The Handbook of Texas Online.<http://www.tsha.utexas.edu/handbook/online/articles/view/PP/kbp9.html> [Accessed Mon Feb 15 1999].

(p. 101) Joe's diploma: Ozona High School records.

(p. 101) Phillips family: "Jan. 19 Services for Lela Mae Nussbaumer," *Ozona Stockman,* 20 January 1999.

(p. 101–102) Driving sheep to Barnhart: Burr Williams, "The Ozona-Barnhart Trap Company and 'The Golden Hoof,'" *Ranch and Rural Living,* April 2003, pp. 12–14.

(p. 102) Graduation ceremony: Joe Chandler, personal communication.

(p. 103) Brush control: Diane Murray, "Brush Problems Rooted in History," *San Angelo Standard-Times,* 16 May 1999, pp. 1–4.

(p. 106–107) Yates Field: Mella McEwen, "Officials Gather to Celebrate Legendary Field," *Midland Reporter-Telegram,* 4 November 2001; Samuel D. Myres. *The Permian Basin: Petroleum Empire of the Southwest* (1973).

(p. 108) Elithe Hamilton Kirkland: Sylvia Ann Grider and Lou Halsell Rodenberger, eds., *Texas Women Writers* (1997), p. 121.

(p. 109) Clarence Chandler children: Glynn Chandler and Mary Ellen Chandler, personal communication.

CHAPTER 7: FISHING: THE FOUNDATION

(p. 118) Unusual fishing methods: Berte R. Haigh, *The Frank Friend Survey: Land, Oil, and Education* (1986).

(p. 120) Size of ranch: "Charles Chandler," *San Angelo Standard-Times,* 11 November 1957, p. 6.

(p. 121) Love of ranching: "Joe Chandler Rides Range," p. 6.

(p. 121) Depreciation of Land: William O. Douglas, *Farewell to Texas* (1967).

(p. 121–122) Oil boom and bust: Susan Orlean, "A Place Called Midland," *New Yorker,* 16 October 2000, p. 129.

CHAPTER 8: INDEPENDENCE RISING

(p. 137) Amount of rain: Skiles, *Judge Roy Bean Country,* p. 41.

(p. 138) Flood of 1909: Hunter, "Charley Chandler," p. 214.

(p. 139–141) Newspaper report: Larry L. King, "Fishing Ranch Is Swept Away," *Odessa American,* 29 June 1954.

(p. 142) Crest of Pecos: Verne Huser, *Rivers of Texas* (2000), p. 139.

(p. 142) "Sky was as clear as a bell": Russell Ashton Scogin, *The Sanderson Flood of 1965* (1995), p. 95.

CHAPTER 9: GOLF: A DREAM COURSE

(p. 166–167) Proposal to sell creek water: Paul F. Power, "Midland Man Offers to Sell Water to Area," *Odessa American,* c. 1985.

(p. 167) Fish kills: Ric Jensen, "Pecos River Fish Kills," in "What's Killing the Fish?" Texas Water Resources 13:1 (1987): 7-8. <http://twri.tamu.edu/newsletters/TexasWaterResources/twr-v13n1.pdf>.

(p. 168) Salt cedars: Greg Harman, "Pecos River Tangled Up in Green," *Odessa American,* 19 September 1999.

BIBLIOGRAPHY

While not all of the following sources are directly quoted, they each contain material relevant to the history of the Chandler Ranch and were read in preparation of this book.

REPORTS, MAGAZINE AND NEWSPAPER ARTICLES

Adams, W. F. "Kerr Woman Writes Book." *Kerrville Times,* 1952.

Adams, Will. "Woman, Age 71, Completes Work on Texas Pioneers Book." *San Angelo Standard-Times,* 14 September 1952.

"A Good Spot for Just Relaxin'." *Odessa American,* 4 August 1955.

Banner, Nicholas Paul. *Jeff Davis' Camel Corps on the Western Frontier.* Odessa: University of Texas of the Permian Basin, 1994.

Bean, Covey. "Joe Chandler: An Innkeeper-Rancher." *Odessa American,* 23 July 1966.

Billingsley, Sandra R. "Group Works to Record Rock-Shelter Paintings." *San Angelo Standard-Times,* 10 January 1999.

Bleiberg, Larry. "Indian Legacies." *San Angelo Standard-Times,* 6 April 1997.

"Charles Chandler, Ranch Pioneer, Dies." *San Angelo Standard-Times,* 11 November 1957.

"Charlie Chandler's Memories of Dryden Country Go Back to 1890." *West Texas Livestock Weekly,* 31 October 1957.

Cline, Harry. "He Quit Livestock; Ranch Now Playland." *San Angelo Standard-Times,* 2 June 1968.

Dick-Peddie, William A. *Survey of Potential Natural Landmarks of the Chihuahuan Desert–Mexican Highlands Region: Landform and Biotic Themes.* Prepared for the National Park Service, United States Department of the Interior, August 1882.

Dingler, Carl. "Repeat Champions—Gibbs Wins Tourney." *Odessa American,* 20 June c. 1970.

"Dryden Rancher Recalls Wild Early Days of State." *Fort Worth Star-Telegram,* 25 March 1956.

Emory, William H. *Report on the United States and Mexican Boundary Survey* (1857). Survey made under the direction of the Secretary of the Interior, Vol. 1. Austin: Texas State Historical Association.

Fenton, Jim. "John Bullis Always Meant Business." *Permian Historical Annual* 33 (December 1993).

Harman, Greg. "On a Course with Danger: The Changing Face of the Pecos River." *Odessa American,* 14 March 1999.

Harman, Greg. "Pecos River Tangled Up in Green." *Odessa American,* 19 September 1999.

Hauritz, Ralph K. M. "Preservation Deal Is Made for a West Texas Oasis." *Austin American-Statesman,* 25 January 2002.

Hayre, Susan. "Encampment's 50th Year." *Iraan News,* 17 June 1993.

Hunter, J. Marvin. "Charley Chandler, A Rancher of the Pecos." *Frontier Times,* May 1950.

"Independence School News." *Sanderson Times,* 1944.

Ivy, Charles E. "Iraan's First Touchdown." *Iraan News,* 6 September 1979.

"Jan. 19 Services for Lela Mae Nussbaumer." *Ozona Stockman,* 20 January 1999.

Jensen, Ric. "Pecos River Fish Kills." In "What's Killing the Fish?" *Texas Water Resources* 13, no. 1 (1987): 7–8. <http://twri.tamu.edu/newsletters/Texas WaterResources/twr-v13n1.pdf>.

"Joe Chandler Rides Range in Golf Cart or, at Worst, a Jeep." *West Texas Livestock Weekly,* 11 July 1968.

Karges, John. "Hello to a River." *Horizons,* Summer 1994.

King, James. Nature Conservancy of Texas Press Release. 2003.

King, Larry L. "Fishing Ranch Is Swept Away." *Odessa American,* 29 June 1954.

Lammons, Frank Bishop. "Operation Camel: An Experiment in Animal Transportation in Texas, 1857–1860." *Southwestern Historical Quarterly* 61, no. 1 (July 1957).

McDonald, Bud. "Deerless Venture in West Texas." *San Angelo Standard-Times,* 7 December 1986.

McEwen, Mella. "Officials Gather to Celebrate Legendary Field." *Midland Reporter-Telegram,* 4 November 2001.

Montgomery, Paul. "Odyssey on the Pecos." *Texas Highways,* September 1979.

Murray, Diane. "Brush Problems Rooted in History." *San Angelo Standard-Times,* 16 May 1999.

Orlean, Susan. "A Place Called Midland." *New Yorker,* 16 October 2000.

"PEACOCK MILITARY ACADEMY." The Handbook of Texas Online. <http://www.tsha.utexas.edu/handbook/online/articles/view/PP/kbp9.html> [Accessed Mon Feb 15 1999].

Pease, Terri. "A Terrell County, Texas, Ranch." *Permian Historical Annual* 40 (December 2000).

Pope, Leon. *Archeological Report on the Chandler Ranch,* 41:TE. 1991.

Power, Paul F. "Midland Man Offers to Sell Water to Area." *Odessa American,* c. 1985.

Russell, Henri Bob. "West Texas Outlaws Era Viewed in 'Gunfighters.'" *San Angelo Standard-Times,* 26 August 1951.

"Services Thursday for Mrs. Chandler." *San Angelo Standard-Times,* 21 October 1970.

Smith, Rick. "Oldtimer Spins Yarns of Epic Past." *San Angelo Standard-Times,* 28 February 1992.

Spragg, Arthur. "Desert Oasis." *Odessa American,* 3 August 1987.

Templeton, Bob. "West Texas Hideaway." *M Magazine,* July–August 1992.

Turpin, Solveig A. Letter to JoBeth Holub, 28 September 1992.

Walker, John. "Take a Ride to the Chandler Ranch." *San Angelo Standard-Times,* 15 September 1991.

Walley, Jay. "Eighty-One Years West of the Pecos." *Ranch and Rural Living,* February 1996.

Williams, Burr. "The Ozona-Barnhart Trap Company and 'The Golden Hoof.'" *Ranch and Rural Living,* April 2003.

Wood, Harry. "Knowledge of Old West Texas Fort Scant, and Most Is Bad." *San Angelo Standard-Times.* Date unknown.

Woolley, Bryan. "A Legend Runs Through It." *Dallas Morning News,* 28 June 1998.

BOOKS

Allen, Anna Lee. "The History of Terrell County." In *Terrell County, Texas: Its Past, Its People,* ed. Alice Evans Downie. San Angelo: Anchor Publishing Company, 1978.

Barnett, Franklin. *A Dictionary of Prehistoric Indian Artifacts of the American Southwest.* Flagstaff, Ariz.: Northland Publishing Company, 1973.

Bartlett, Richard C. *Saving the Best of Texas.* Austin: University of Texas Press, 1995.

Bass, Rick. *The Deer Pasture.* New York: W. W. Norton & Company, 1989.

Bedicek, Roy. *Adventures with a Texas Naturalist.* Austin: University of Texas Press, 1961.

Bosworth, Allan R. *Ozona Country.* New York: Harper & Row, 1964.

Brown, Marjorie Canon. "The A. M. Hicks Family." In *Terrell County, Texas: Its Past, Its People,* ed. Alice Evans Downie. San Angelo: Anchor Publishing Company, 1978.

Brune, Gunnar. *Springs of Texas.* Fort Worth: Branch-Smith, 1981. Reprinted, College Station: Texas A&M University Press, 2002.

Connelley, William E. *A Standard History of Kansas and Kansans.* 5 vols. Chicago: Lewis, 1918. Biography index prepared by Carolyn Ward, instructor from USD 508, Baxter Springs Middle School, Baxter Springs, Kansas. <http://skyways.lib.ks.us/genweb/archives/1918ks/biondx.html>. [Accessed Sun Jun 27 1999].

Comstock Study Club. *Comstock Friends and Neighbors.* Waseca, Minn.: Walter's Publishing Company, 1978.

Douglas, William O. *Farewell to Texas; A Vanishing Wilderness.* New York: McGraw-Hill Book Company, 1967.

Downie, Alice Evans. "Indians." In *Terrell County, Texas: Its Past, Its People,* ed. Alice Evans Downie. San Angelo: Anchor Publishing Company, 1978.

———, ed. *Terrell County, Texas: Its Past, Its People.* San Angelo: Anchor Publishing Company, 1978.

Downie, Walter G. "Early Day Shearing Crews." In *Terrell County, Texas: Its Past, Its People,* ed. Alice Evans Downie. San Angelo: Anchor Publishing Company, 1978.

Dugger, Ronnie, comp. *Three Men in Texas.* Austin: University of Texas Press, 1967.

Fulcher, Walter. *The Way I Heard It: Tales of the Big Bend.* Austin: University of Texas Press, 1959.

Green, Ben K. *The Village Horse Doctor: West of the Pecos.* New York: Alfred A. Knopf, 1971.

Grider, Sylvia Ann, and Lou Halsell Rodenberger, eds. *Texas Women Writers.* College Station: Texas A&M University Press, 1997.

Haigh, Berte R. *The Frank Friend Survey: Land, Oil, and Education.* El Paso: Texas Western Press, 1986.

Hiller, Ilo. *The White-Tailed Deer.* College Station: Texas A&M University Press, 1996.

Holt, R. D. "Early Day Stockmen of the Lower Trans-Pecos." In *Terrell County, Texas: Its Past, Its People,* ed. Alice Evans Downie. San Angelo: Anchor Publishing Company, 1978. First published in *Cattleman* (November 1937).

———. "Vanished Empires." In *Terrell County, Texas: Its Past, Its People,* ed. Alice Evans Downie. San Angelo: Anchor Publishing Company, 1978.

Huser, Verne. *Rivers of Texas.* College Station: Texas A&M University Press, 2000.

Joyce, W. H., Virginia Madison, and Hugh B. Wilson. "Train Robberies." In *Terrell County, Texas: Its Past, Its People,* ed. Alice Evans Downie. San Angelo: Anchor Publishing Company, 1978.

Kelton, Elmer. Foreword to *Judge Roy Bean Country.* Lubbock: Texas Tech University Press, 1996.

———. *The Time It Never Rained.* New York: Doubleday, 1973.

Kimball, Mary Ellen Chandler, and W. D. O'Bryant. "The W. D. O'Bryant Family." In *Terrell County, Texas: Its Past, Its People,* ed. Alice Evans Downie. San Angelo: Anchor Publishing Company, 1978.

King, Dick. "Excerpts from *Medina Electric News,*" October 1976. In *Terrell County, Texas: Its Past, Its People,* ed. Alice Evans Downie. San Angelo: Anchor Publishing Company, 1978.

McComb, David G. *Texas: A Modern History.* Austin: University of Texas Press, 1994.

Myres, Samuel D. *The Permian Basin: Petroleum Empire of the Southwest.* El Paso: Permian Press, 1973.

Newcomb, W. W. *The Indians of Texas.* Austin: University of Texas Press, 1961.

Patterson, Paul. *This Place of Memory: A Texas Perspective,* ed. Joyce Gibson Roach. Denton: University of North Texas Press, 1992.

Pirtle, Lela Neal, ed. *Life on the Range and on the Trail, as Told by R. J. (Bob) Lauderdale and John M. Doak.* San Antonio: Naylor Company, 1936.

Schmidly, David J. *The Mammals of Trans-Pecos Texas.* College Station: Texas A&M University Press, 1977.

Scogin, Russell Ashton. *The Sanderson Flood of 1965: Crisis in a Rural Texas Community.* Alpine, Tex.: Sul Ross State University, 1995.

Skiles, Jack. *Judge Roy Bean Country.* Lubbock: Texas Tech University Press, 1996.

Stavley, Howard. "The Charles F. Stavley Family." In *Terrell County, Texas: Its Past, Its People,* ed. Alice Evans Downie. San Angelo: Anchor Publishing Company, 1978.

Ten Eyck, Gay. "Block Y Ranch." In *Terrell County, Texas: Its Past, Its People,* ed. Alice Evans Downie. San Angelo: Anchor Publishing Company, 1978. First published in *Texas Historian* (May 1972).

Trousdale, David. "Train Robberies." In *Terrell County, Texas: Its Past, Its People,* ed. Alice Evans Downie. San Angelo: Anchor Publishing Company, 1978.

Turk, Mike. "The C. J. 'Doc' Turk Family." In *Terrell County, Texas: Its Past, Its People,* ed. Alice Evans Downie. San Angelo: Anchor Publishing Company, 1978.

Wilbarger, J. W. *Indian Depredations in Texas.* Austin: Hutchings Printing House, 1889.

Williams, Clayton. *Never Again.* San Antonio: Naylor Company, 1969.

————. *Texas' Last Frontier: Fort Stockton and the Trans-Pecos, 1861–1895*. College Station: Texas A&M University Press, 1982.

SCIENTIFIC REPORTS

Cole, Charles, J., and Laurence M. Hardy. "Systematics of North American Colubrid Snakes related to Tantilla Planiceps." *Bulletin of the American Museum of Natural History* 171 (1981).

Hermann, Jack A. "The Mammals of the Stockton Plateau of Northeastern Terrell County, Texas." *Texas Journal of Science,* 30 September 1950.

Hubbs, Clark. "Fish Collections from Independence Creek and Pecos River." *Southwestern Naturalist,* 9 March 1991.

Larson, Greg. *Effects of Independence Creek Inflow on Pecos River Water Quality and Benthic M Facroinverterbrate Communities, Terrell and Crockett Counties, Texas.* Odessa: University of Texas of the Permian Basin, 1996.

Milstead, William W., John S. Mecham, and Haskell McClintock. "The Amphibians and Reptiles of the Stockton Plateau in Northern Terrell County, Texas." *Texas Journal of Science,* 30 December 1950.

Milstead, William W. "Relict Species of the Chihuahuan Desert." *Southwestern Naturalist,* 10 August 1960.

Rhodes, Kevin, and Clark Hubbs. *Recovery of Pecos River Fishes from a Red Tide Fish Kill.* Department of Zoology, University of Texas at Austin, 1989.

Scudday, James F. *Evaluation of Independence Creek, Terrell County, Texas as a Potential Natural Landmark.* Alpine, Tex.: Sul Ross State University, 1977.

Sneegas, Garold W. *Fishes of Texas Photos.* Lawrence, Kan.: Aquatic Kansas Images, 1999.

Thornton, Wilmot A. "Ecological Distribution of the Birds of the Stockton Plateau in Northern Terrell County, Texas." *Texas Journal of Science,* 30 September 1951.

Webb, Robert G. "North American Recent Soft-shelled Turtles." *Museum of Natural History* 13, no. 10 (16 February 1962).

Webster, Grady L. "Observations on the Vegetation and Summer Flora of the Stockton Plateau in Northeastern Terrell County, Texas." *Texas Journal of Science,* 30 June 1950.

INDEX

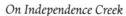

Index